SOCIAL EXCLUSION AND HOUSING:
Context and Challenges

Edited by ISOBEL ANDERSON and DUNCAN SIM

Chartered Institute of Housing
Policy and Practice Series
in collaboration with the
Housing Studies Association

The Chartered Institute of Housing
The Chartered Institute of Housing is the professional organisation for all people who work in housing. Its purpose is to take a strategic and leading role in encouraging and promoting the provision of good quality affordable housing for all. The Institute has more than 15,000 members working in local authorities, housing associations, the private sector and educational institutions.

Chartered Institute of Housing
Octavia House, Westwood Way
Coventry CV4 8JP
Telephone: 024 7685 1700
Fax: 024 7669 5110

The Housing Studies Association
The Housing Studies Association promotes the study of housing by bringing together housing researchers with others interested in housing research in the housing policy and practitioner communities. It acts as a voice for housing research by organising conferences and seminars, lobbying government and other agencies and providing services to members.

The CIH Housing Policy and Practice Series is published in collaboration with the Housing Studies Association and aims to provide important and valuable material and insights for housing managers, staff, students, trainers and policy makers. Books in the series are designed to promote debate, but the contents do not necessarily reflect the views of the CIH or the HSA. The Editorial Team for the series is: General Editors: Dr. Peter Williams, John Perry and Robina Goodlad, and Production Editor: Alan Dearling.

ISBN 1-900396-39-4

Social exclusion and housing: context and challenges
Edited by Isobel Anderson and Duncan Sim

Published by the Chartered Institute of Housing © 2000

Cover photographs supplied by Alan Dearling

Printed by Hobb the Printers, Totton

Contents

List of contributors   v

Acknowledgements   vii

Introduction

Chapter 1   Social exclusion and housing: an introduction   1
             Isobel Anderson and Duncan Sim

Chapter 2   Housing and social exclusion: the changing debate   6
             Isobel Anderson

Part 1: Inequalities and social exclusion

Chapter 3   Inequalities in income and wealth   22
             Karen Gardiner
Chapter 4   Employment inequalities and housing   42
             Janet Ford
Chapter 5   Hitting the target? Area disadvantage, social exclusion and the
             geography of misery in England   58
             Roger Burrows and David Rhodes

Part 2: Marginalisation in the housing system

Chapter 6   Social exclusion: the case of homelessness   81
             David Clapham and Angela Evans
Chapter 7   Housing inequalities and minority ethnic groups   93
             Duncan Sim
Chapter 8   Lone parenthood: two views and their consequences   108
             David Webster
Chapter 9   Housing and young single people   131
             Suzanne Fitzpatrick

Part 3: Housing intervention and social exclusion

Chapter 10   The impact of estate regeneration   147
             Rebecca Tunstall

Chapter 11   The changing role of housing associations   163
              Ian Cole
Chapter 12   Housing abandonment   177
              Stuart Lowe
Chapter 13   Developments in housing management   191
              Pauline Papps and Robert Smith

Conclusion: towards inclusion

Chapter 14   What constitutes a 'balanced' community?   207
              Ray Forrest
Chapter 15   Social exclusion and housing: conclusions and challenges   220
              Isobel Anderson

Bibliography   **230**

Index   **253**

List of contributors

Isobel Anderson is Lecturer in the Housing Policy and Practice Unit, Department of Applied Social Science, at the University of Stirling.

Roger Burrows is Co-Director of the Centre for Housing Policy at the University of York.

David Clapham is Professor at the Centre for Housing Management and Development, Department of City and Regional Planning, Cardiff University.

Ian Cole is Professor of Housing Studies at the Centre for Regional Economic and Social Research, at Sheffield Hallam University.

Angela Evans is Honorary Research Fellow at the Centre for Housing Management and Development, Department of City and Regional Planning, Cardiff University.

Suzanne Fitzpatrick is an ESRC Research Fellow in the Department of Urban Studies, University of Glasgow.

Janet Ford is Joseph Rowntree Professor of Housing Policy at the University of York.

Ray Forrest is Professor in the School of Policy Studies, University of Bristol.

Karen Gardiner is Research Fellow at the Centre for Analysis of Social Exclusion, at the London School of Economics.

Stuart Lowe is Senior Lecturer in the Department of Social Policy and Social Work at the University of York.

Pauline Papps is Research Associate at the Centre for Housing Management and Development, Department of City and Regional Planning, Cardiff University.

David Rhodes is Research Fellow in the Centre for Housing Policy at the University of York.

Duncan Sim is Senior Lecturer in the Housing Policy and Practice Unit, Department of Applied Social Science, at the University of Stirling.

Robert Smith is Lecturer in Housing at the Centre for Housing Management and Development, Department of City and Regional Planning, Cardiff University.

Rebecca Tunstall is Lecturer in Housing at the London School of Economics.

David Webster is Chief Housing Officer (Policy Review and Development) with Glasgow City Council. The views expressed here are not necessarily those of the Council.

Acknowledgements

The editors would like to extend their sincere thanks to all of the following: Peter Williams, for his initial support in developing the book proposal; all of the authors who contributed to the book; Robina Goodlad, Peter Williams, Alan Dearling, John Perry and staff at the Chartered Institute of Housing for comments on earlier drafts of the papers.

Thanks also to colleagues at the University of Stirling, particularly Sarah Pugh and Gina Griffiths, for administrative and secretarial support.

CHAPTER 1:
Social exclusion and housing: an introduction

Isobel Anderson and Duncan Sim

The origins and aims of this book

While the concept of social exclusion has been part of European discourse for many years, it only became established in British policy discussions during the 1990s. Following the election of the New Labour government in May 1997, social exclusion was placed firmly at the top of the social policy agenda, with housing issues, such as street homelessness and estate regeneration, a key focus for action. As the notion of social exclusion became more widely debated, the volume of related research and scholarly literature on the subject also grew significantly.

During the 1990s, a distinctive literature on housing and social exclusion began to emerge (e.g. Lee *et al* (1995) and Lee and Murie (1997)). A key focus within this emerging literature was the role of housing provision and management in the promotion of social inclusion and the building of cohesive communities. The body of research and literature grew rapidly, making it increasingly difficult for practitioners to keep up to date with primary sources. During 1998, the Chartered Institute of Housing produced two practice reports on housing and social exclusion (Anderson, 1998; CIH, 1998) and a good practice guide on housing and anti-poverty strategies (Brown and Passmore, 1998). However, there remained a need for a text which set out the context for the evolving debate on social exclusion and brought together relevant material for housing practice. This has become particularly relevant as the government's Social Exclusion Unit has started to produce its detailed work on housing-related issues. The Institute approached the Housing Policy and Practice Unit at Stirling University, and it was agreed that an edited collection would be commissioned to address this task. It is hoped that this book will assist readers by reviewing key developments, debates and research findings.

The main aim of the book is to inform housing practitioners and students of the key debates surrounding social exclusion/inclusion and their importance for housing policy and practice. This has been done in two ways. First, the book brings together ideas and information from recently completed research into inequality, marginalisation and intervention in relation to housing provision. Second, the contributors have also added new reflections on the impact of their research and its implications for practice. Together, the papers present the 'bigger picture' of how the housing system interacts with the processes which have come to be associated with exclusion. Although part of the CIH practice series, this book is not a good practice guide. Rather, it seeks to provide practitioners with an accessible overview of the social trends and policy debates which impact on practice. The book is primarily aimed at students of specialised housing courses and qualified practitioners, but will be of value to all readers with an interest in the key debates surrounding the relationship between the housing system and wider social change.

The initial working title for the book was *Housing and Social Exclusion*. Subsequently, at least two other publications of that title have been produced (Spicker, 1998; Spiers, 1999). The final title, *Social Exclusion and Housing: Context and Challenges*, emerged during the editing process as a reasonably accurate portrayal of the combined achievements of all of the contributors. The notions of contexts, critiques and challenges do not, however, relate directly to the three main sections of the book. Rather, they are themes that run throughout most of the chapters. Almost without exception, contributors have set their specific topic within the context of wider social processes; presented critiques of policy and practice which help understand the current situation; and set out challenges for the housing profession and for policy makers.

Housing research has always sought to locate practical housing issues within the wider social, political and economic context. Debates in housing research tend to follow contemporary discourse and policy directions and the current focus of that discourse is on exclusion and inclusion. Previous literature located housing issues within debates on inequality (Morris and Winn, 1990) and disadvantage (Clapham, Kemp and Smith, 1990). While this volume focuses on the changing discourse and the new emphasis on exclusion/inclusion, it does not lose sight of the value of those earlier debates. Many contributors emphasise inequality and disadvantage as fundamental concepts in developing an analysis of exclusion. While much of the policy debate has a highly contemporary focus, these contributions illustrate the merits of a long-term perspective in understanding contemporary circumstances.

Throughout the book, reference is made to the fact that social exclusion remains a contested concept. The editors did not prescribe any particular definition of social exclusion and contributors have set out their own operational definitions and links to the wider debate. For those 'dipping into' chapters, it should be noted that one author's definition and perspective will not necessarily be representative of the rest of the book. Similarly, authors have made their own connections to the social exclusion debates, though with a considerable degree of consistency.

The structure of this book

This book is divided into an introduction, three main sections and a conclusion. Following this introductory chapter, Isobel Anderson discusses the concept of social exclusion, tracing its evolution within social science and practical politics and setting the scene for an analysis of housing and social exclusion (Chapter 2). The three main sections of the book then look at broad patterns of inequality (Part 1, Chapters 3-5); marginalisation in the housing system (Part 2, Chapters 6-9); and intervention in the provision of housing (Part 3, Chapters 10-13). The concluding section (Part 4) reflects on where housing fits in moving towards inclusion, rather than exclusion.

Part 1 Inequalities and social exclusion

This section sets some of the broader context for the subsequent consideration of housing and social exclusion, focusing on inequalities in income and wealth, employment, and neighbourhood satisfaction. In Chapter 3, Karen Gardiner traces changing patterns in income and wealth in the UK over the last 30 years, analysing the factors associated with those changes. She introduces some key groups, which are particularly at risk of exclusion from adequate housing: homeless people, minority ethnic groups, lone parents, and young single people. Subsequent chapters also focus on these particular groups. The question of employment inequalities is addressed by Janet Ford in Chapter 4, which analyses the implications of labour market restructuring for housing provision and consumption. The final chapter in this section examines differentiation in terms of neighbourhood satisfaction (or dissatisfaction) and relates outcomes to different measures of deprivation (Burrows and Rhodes, Chapter 5).

Part 2 Marginalisation in the housing system

The chapters in this section illustrate how issues of social inequality have impacted on particular groups within society. Firstly, Chapter 6, by David Clapham and Angela Evans looks at the case of homelessness. The authors relate homelessness to the wider socio-economic issues raised in Part 1 of the book, and examine routes into homelessness and measures to reduce or prevent homelessness. In Chapter 7, Duncan Sim considers the housing experience of minority ethnic groups in Britain, tracing patterns of disadvantage and providing a critique of initiatives to redress the balance. The stigmatisation of lone parents in the housing system is considered in Chapter 8, in which David Webster contrasts two ideological interpretations of the lone parent household in relation to employment opportunities and housing outcomes. Finally in this section, Suzanne Fitzpatrick explores the opportunities and constraints facing young single people in setting up home, drawing together both the wider socio-economic constraints and the impact of the operation of the housing system (Chapter 9).

Part 3 Housing intervention and social exclusion

This section moves beyond the exclusion experienced by specific groups, to examine the ways in which communities or neighbourhoods have been marginalised. It has a distinct social housing focus, drawing upon recent research which has raised questions about the regeneration and management of social housing. The range of initiatives designed to regenerate council housing estates is the focus of Chapter 10, by Rebecca Tunstall. Drawing upon a long-term programme of research, the contributions of Estate Action funds, housing management initiatives, and tenant empowerment are assessed, as is the cumulative impact of the range of initiatives. The changing role of housing associations (or Registered Social Landlords) is then scrutinised by Ian Cole in Chapter 11. The limitations of policy initiatives for inner city regeneration are also addressed by Stuart Lowe in Chapter 12, which tackles the recently identified and increasingly controversial phenomenon of housing abandonment. The concluding chapter in this section reflects on the impact of exclusionary processes on the housing management task. In Chapter 13, Pauline Papps and Robert Smith examine the changing environment for housing managers and look at responses, particularly in relation to housing allocations and anti-social behaviour.

Part 4 Conclusion: towards inclusion

The book concludes with two contributions which reflect on the ways in which housing may contribute to social inclusion, rather than exclusion. First, Ray Forrest considers what might constitute a 'balanced' community (Chapter 14). Tracing the changing conceptions of community since the Second World War, Forrest raises some challenges with respect to 'heterogeneity versus homogeneity' and the idea of 'cohesion in adversity'. The discourse on social exclusion continued to evolve during the production of this book. In the final chapter (15), Isobel Anderson examines some of the most recent developments and identifies key challenges for the future.

In conclusion

While we have tried to select a range of papers that cover the key debates in social exclusion in housing, this volume cannot claim to be comprehensive either in terms of coverage or authorship. For example, there are no specific chapters on the problems of older people or those with disabilities. Similarly, the chapters have a mainly urban focus, though this is not to suggest that rural issues are less important. While we have examined changes in housing management, there are no specific chapters on 'anti-social behaviour' or community safety. It is acknowledged that debates in these latter areas were developing rapidly during the production of this book and, no doubt, others will take up the challenge of reviewing these important topics. We have tried to include a balance between the general (income, employment) and the particular (lone parents, abandonment). Beyond this, there was no particular rationale for selecting some issues rather than others, apart from the need to set some boundaries for a readable volume. The contributors have been drawn from academic and practice institutions across Britain. Consequently, some chapters refer specifically to the administrative frameworks for England, Scotland or Wales, while others take a Great Britain-wide perspective.

The book as a whole should be seen as a contribution to the debate, not the final word on social exclusion and housing. However, readers can draw on the broad policy and conceptual discussions in order to make links to other specific topics. Whatever the future holds, housing professionals are bound to be caught up in the delivery of policy initiatives associated with the social exclusion/inclusion agenda. Policy development and service delivery need to be founded on a firm understanding of both the detail of housing provision and the broader trends in welfare and society. It is hoped that the chapters in this book make a contribution to that process.

CHAPTER 2:
Housing and social exclusion: the changing debate

Isobel Anderson

Introduction: the age of exclusion?

In Britain, from the mid-1990s, debates on social policy increasingly embraced the concept of 'social exclusion' as well as the more traditional notions of poverty and inequality (Silver, 1994; Room, 1995a). Much of the debate revolved around the question of whether a significant group of people experienced sustained, multiple deprivation to the extent that they were, effectively, excluded from the 'mainstream' of society.

People's experience of housing and homelessness touches or interacts with virtually every dimension of social well-being, and the debates on social exclusion have become of fundamental importance to housing policy and practice. This chapter charts the changing debates on social exclusion, including the housing dimension, through the 1990s and up to the year 2000.

First, some of the key conceptual ideas associated with social exclusion are discussed. The evolution of the discourse on social exclusion is then traced with specific reference to key strands of thought: the 'New' Right; the 'European' influence; alternative 'empowerment' approaches; and the perspective of 'New Labour'. The chapter concludes by introducing the debates on housing and social exclusion and presenting some conclusions on operationalising the concept of social exclusion in relation to housing.

From poverty and inequality to social exclusion

The contemporary concept of social exclusion emerged from sociological and social policy debates on poverty, inequality and the role of the welfare state which are centuries old (see, for example, Alcock, 1997). While poverty can be taken as an indicator of the proportion of any population living below a given threshold, inequality provides a measure of the distribution of income and wealth across the entire population. Chapter 3 presents a detailed analysis of trends in income and inequality in relation to housing. The evolution of the concept of social exclusion can be traced from its origins in France in the 1970s, where exclusion came to refer:

… not only to the rise in long-term and recurrent unemployment, but also to the growing instability of social bonds: family instability, single member households, social isolation, and the decline of class solidarity based on unions, the labour market, and the working class neighbourhood and social networks (Silver, 1994, p533).

Contrasting interpretations of poverty, inequality and social exclusion are associated with differing political ideologies and social theories. For example, three welfare state 'regimes' influenced by prevailing ideologies were identified by Esping-Anderson (1990): the liberal welfare state, the conservative/ corporatist welfare state and the social democratic welfare state. The centrality of ideology and welfare provision to conceptions of social exclusion was also emphasised by Silver (1994), who viewed the discourse on social exclusion as a 'window', through which to view political cultures.

Arguing that social exclusion was a contested concept, with different meanings according to different ideologies, Silver (1994, p540) identified three distinct perspectives or 'paradigms' of social exclusion. The *solidarity* paradigm was based on French republicanism with integration arising from group solidarity, cultural mores and an economic model of flexible production. The *specialisation* paradigm was associated with economic liberalism, integration being dependent on specialisation and exchange in the market. The *monopoly* paradigm was based on social democracy. While powerful interests enjoyed a monopoly over scarce resources and social structures perpetuated inequality, integration was achieved through citizenship rights within an economic model linked to labour market segmentation. The monopoly paradigm was influenced by Marx and Weber, but Silver argued that strictly Marxist and neo-Marxist conceptions of capitalism could not constitute a paradigm of social exclusion as they denied the possibility of social integration within the capitalist system. Silver also acknowledged 'organic' models of social order based on functional, regional or primordial (e.g. ethnic, linguistic, and religious) groups. These organic perspectives were linked to authoritarianism and fascism, but also to Christian Democracy.

Silver argued that the three main conceptions of social exclusion should not be confused with institutional classifications such as welfare state regimes, as the latter were influenced by more than one paradigm over a long period of time (Silver, 1994). However, subsequent commentators have argued that Silver's typology could be linked to the debate on welfare regimes. For example, Cousins characterised France as an example of the solidarity paradigm, Germany as 'neo-organic', the UK as the specialisation paradigm and Sweden as following the monopoly model (Cousins, 1998).

It has been argued that much of the discourse on social exclusion within the European Union was borrowed from the French solidarity paradigm (Cousins, 1998, p140). However, others have linked the European discourse with the monopoly paradigm (Silver, 1994) and with the corporatist tradition (Room, 1995b). This lack of consensus highlights the limitations of 'models' of welfare regimes, as well as the dynamic, changing nature of national welfare states and cross-national social trends.

While the 'grand' debates on welfare state regimes and paradigms of exclusion provide a broad conceptual framework for the analysis of social issues, it is also important to consider local, as well as national, policy responses within Britain. Between 1979 and 1997, the prevailing ideology of successive Conservative governments was explicitly derived from New Right ideas associated with economic liberalism (Marsh and Rhodes, 1992), essentially, the specialisation paradigm. Economic and political strategies sought to 'roll back the frontiers of the welfare state' with poverty and inequality interpreted as outcomes of competition in a market-led economy. Neo-liberalism was less dominant in local government politics in Britain during the 1980s and early 1990s (Stoker, 1991), but there was virtually no reference to 'social exclusion' in British social policy debates until the mid-1990s.

Following the 1997 election, the New Labour government began to implement its ideology of a 'third way' between the neo-liberalism of the Conservative administrations and the traditional welfare collectivism of earlier Labour governments (the social democracy paradigm). Though there was no outright commitment to eradicating poverty or reducing inequality, the concepts of social exclusion, social inclusion and a cohesive society quickly became central to the new government's agenda for social policy and welfare reform.

Before social exclusion: the New Right and the 'underclass'

By the early 1990s, the notion of an identifiable, excluded 'class' of marginalised individuals, had become established within neo-liberal interpretations of poverty. Notably, essays by the American commentator Charles Murray were particularly influential upon debates as to whether an 'underclass' was emerging in Britain (Murray, 1990, 1994[1]). The origins of the term 'underclass' pre-dated Murray's work and the term has been used in different ways by different writers. For example, the work of Wilson (1987) on the racialised nature of inner city disadvantage in American cities adopted a structural perspective, while Murray focused on behavioural explanations and

---

1   Murray's first essay, *The emerging British underclass* was originally published in the *Sunday Times Magazine* and then by the Institute for Economic Affairs (IEA) in 1990. His second essay, *Underclass: the crisis deepens* was first published in the *Sunday Times Magazine* and then by the IEA in May 1994. Both of those essays, along with a series of commentaries, were reproduced in Lister (1996). In the discussion below, references to Murray's work are cited from Lister (1996) as Murray (1996a, 1996b and 1996c).

definitions. While in opposition, the Labour MP, Frank Field, also argued that some groups of poor people were so distinguished from others on a low income as to constitute an 'underclass' (Field, 1989, 1996a).

Charles Murray argued that poverty was directly related to the behaviour and decisions (agency) of individual poor people (Murray, 1996a, pp23-53). In particular, he referred to the deterioration of poor communities associated with drugs, crime, 'illegitimacy', homelessness, dropping out of school and the labour market, and casual violence. Murray focused particularly on motherhood outside of marriage, violent crime, and 'drop-out' from the labour force. In examining lone parenthood, Murray deliberately used the term 'illegitimacy', the notion of the married couple as the only appropriate model of parenthood being central to his ideas about families, communities and social roles.

Murray argued that the welfare state and the benefit system had led to the creation of a dependent 'underclass' by making lone parenthood and youth unemployment economically viable (Murray, 1996a, pp43-46). Murray was able to demonstrate that 'illegitimacy', and long-term unemployment were associated with social class, but failed to present any rigorous evidence about the *attitudes* of low income people towards work, family, and social values. Murray's main policy prescription was to curtail the scope of government intervention so that poor people's behaviour and decisions were more constrained by economic reality (Murray, 1996a, p50).

The notion of a socially excluded 'underclass', distinguished by attitudinal and behavioural characteristics, has been challenged by a substantial body of empirical research and analysis (e.g. Taylor-Gooby 1991; Smith, 1992; Gallie, 1994; Kempson, 1996). Murray's methods were criticised by Walker (1996) who cited established evidence that those on low incomes retained ordinary aspirations and values, despite their poverty (Rutter and Madge, 1976; Brown and Madge, 1982). Acknowledging the very serious problems of extreme poverty in Britain in the 1980s and 1990s, Alcock (1997) advocated the term 'social exclusion' as one which was much less pejorative than the term underclass':

> *Encapsulated in the term social exclusion is the problem of the interplay between the social and economic forces which are marginalising large groups of people who are more or less permanently outside of the labour force (including, but hardly exclusively, many lone parents) and the experience of this process by those who are the primary victims of it. It is a problem of class polarisation, of economic inactivity and disappearing opportunities, of demographic and cultural upheaval, and of the pressure to adapt social policy to meet the rapidly changing circumstances of people whose past expectations, and hopes, no longer meet their current needs* (Alcock, 1997, p148).

The views of Charles Murray represent one example of the neo-liberal interpretation of poverty and inequality. Despite the weakness of the empirical analysis in Murray's essays, economic and social policies under the then Conservative governments in Britain were broadly in line with his perspective. While the prevailing economic conditions during 1979-1997 caused the economic exclusion of a substantial minority of Britain's population, the analysis of the government focused on individual inadequacy and failed to acknowledge or address the resultant social issues.

The emergence of social exclusion: a European concept?

The concept of social exclusion has been utilised in policy debates at the European level, for a longer time than has been the case within the UK (Room, 1995a). By the early 1990s, the European Union's Observatory on social exclusion had defined the term with reference to multidimensional disadvantage, which was of substantial duration and which involved dissociation from the major social and occupational milieux of society (Room *et al*, 1992). The term social exclusion gradually became more frequently used within European Union bureaucracies in preference to poverty and with reference to policies to bring about greater social cohesion (Room, 1995b).

Social exclusion was understood to be closely associated with the labour market and the long-term, high levels of unemployment of the 1980s and early 1990s (Room *et al*, 1990; European Commission, 1994). European governments accepted that the long-term unemployed group would require practical assistance to reconnect with the jobs market, necessitating policies to tackle exclusion (Berghman, 1995, p16). The Maastricht Treaty and the objectives of the European Structural Funds both made reference to social exclusion and social cohesion (Council of the European Communities, 1992; Room, 1995b). The subsequent European White Papers on employment and social policy cited combating unemployment as the most important single element in combating social exclusion (European Commission, 1993; 1994).

There were also political reasons for the shift to discussion about social exclusion in that EU member states had reservations about acknowledging the existence of 'poverty' in their countries (Berghman, 1995). Moreover, Room cautioned that EU policies on labour market flexibility and reduced social support were in conflict with promoting secure employment and, along with public spending cuts required to meet conditions for monetary union, may actually increase social exclusion. Indeed, throughout its history, the European project has been associated with the free-market orientation of economic liberalism (McCormick, 1996). The prospect of European integration thus held threats of, as well as opportunities for combating, social exclusion (Room, 1995b).

A comprehensive and dynamic concept?

The question remains as to whether social exclusion is a useful concept, which can be distinguished from poverty, deprivation, disadvantage, etc. It has been argued that two key elements distinguish social exclusion from earlier concepts – the comprehensive and dynamic nature of both process and outcomes (Berghman, 1995). Social exclusion was argued to be *comprehensive* in that it embraced a range of social experiences, beyond work and income, including democratic participation, work, social welfare, family and community. Social exclusion was also *dynamic* in nature, in that, for individuals, poverty or disadvantage need not be a fixed, unchangeable state.

The comprehensive nature of social exclusion was outlined by Commins (1993) with reference to a breakdown of the major social systems that should guarantee full citizenship. In one of the few statements as to what might be understood by social *inclusion*, Commins stated:

> *Civic integration means being an equal citizen in a democratic system. Economic integration means having a job, having a valued economic function, being able to pay your way. Social integration means being able to avail oneself of the social services provided by the state. Interpersonal integration means having family and friends, neighbours and social networks to provide care and companionship and moral support when these are needed. All four systems are therefore, important. In a way, the four systems are complementary: when one or two are weak the others need to be strong. And the worst off are those for whom all systems have failed* (Commins, 1993, p4).

However, despite this comprehensive definition, exclusion from the labour force has tended to be seen as the key indicator of social exclusion. For example, there was much less debate about other policy areas such as housing or health in the collection of papers in Room (1995a). Further, Whelan and Whelan (1995) argued that simply combining various dimensions of disadvantage into the broad concept of social exclusion may not be fruitful in improving understanding of the underlying processes which created and sustained exclusion. An insistence on multidimensionality could obscure the distinctive influences of specific policies or processes. A differentiated understanding of individual policy areas, as well as of the combined effects was needed. By the mid-1990s, the analysis of the process of social exclusion remained underdeveloped while more progress had been made regarding its comprehensiveness (Berghman, 1995).

Social exclusion: some alternative perspectives

Alternative perspectives on social exclusion have recognised the 'agency' of individuals in a positive and constructive way (for example, Commission on

Social Justice, 1994; Jordan, 1996; Williams with Pillinger, 1996; Becker, 1997). In contrast to the individualistic 'victim-blaming' mode of neo-liberalism, and the structuralist nature of social democracy, the *empowerment* of those who have been excluded is emphasised as a constructive strategy for tackling exclusion.

In his book, *A theory of poverty and social exclusion*, Jordan (1996) argued that previous analyses had dealt mainly in the dynamic between markets and states, to the neglect of a more comprehensive view of how groups acted collectively, and how vulnerable individuals were excluded and marginalised. Jordan's theory was rooted in economic theory, particularly public choice theory. Essentially, public choice theorists argued that the collective action of groups (e.g. cartels or trade unions) restrained the free operation of markets by providing additional benefits ('job rents') for members, to the detriment of non-members. Jordan adapted the theoretical framework to investigate how the operation of groups or clubs, resulted in the marginalisation of those less able to compete.

Jordan analysed groups as *clubs*, which were distinguished by collective action, based on the mutual commitment of members over time. Welfare states were characterised as large clubs within which members also joined internal, overlapping clubs. At the other end of the spectrum lay 'informal' clubs, which often came into being as a form of resistance, by excluded individuals, against the collective action of powerful groups. Jordan argued that all groups were exclusive in some sense. The strongest groups in society had members who were like one another while social heterogeneity weakened collective action – most poor people were not in organisations for the poor.

An essential component of Jordan's thesis was that the poor, as rational actors, had opportunities for countering exclusion from formal clubs by semi-organised, informal collective actions of their own. Club theory allowed vulnerable people to appear as *actors* rather than simply as victims. Jordan argued that poor people could, and did, act rationally and strategically, by taking collective action through forming or joining informal clubs. The clearest example was where the rewards from low paid employment were so low that the optimal strategy for a poor individual was to claim public assistance and work informally at the same time. Informal clubs included such workers, as well as employers for whom the costs of formal employment were equally prohibitive.

Jordan characterised the state's response to exclusion as the politics of 'enforcement' through moves towards 'compulsory inclusion' (Jordan, 1996, p205). In contrast, Jordan argued that:

> ... *intelligent policy assessment eschews moral judgements and addresses economic realities* (Jordan, 1996, p242)

and further that:

Policy should not necessarily seek to 'integrate' the poor and excluded into mainstream employment, civic responsibility or suburban culture. Policy should instead study how poor people survive (including their illegal activities) and look at ways of legitimating, enhancing or supporting these activities, while minimising the social costs associated with them (Jordan, 1996, p243).

Jordan concluded that there was a need to address the fundamental causes of poverty and social exclusion through a *basic income* as the 'only feasible, inclusive institutional structure for balancing the market-oriented interests of the better off with the protection of the poor' (Jordan, 1996, p149). A basic, unconditional income, guaranteed to all citizens, would reduce institutionalised traps and barriers to labour market participation, and facilitate flexibility through the life course, while leaving individuals a degree of personal autonomy (Jordan, 1996).

An alternative perspective emphasises inequality as the key, structural dynamic in society, viewing social exclusion as a consequence of inequality (Williams with Pillinger, 1996). A degree of scepticism has been expressed with regard to terms such as integration, equality and citizenship which signify inclusion for all but result in exclusion for some (Williams, 1997). Questions have also been raised about the extent to which the shift from a focus on poverty to social exclusion recognised those who experienced poverty as creative agents in their own lives, rather than as the objects of policy. Neither the poverty, nor the social exclusion debates had resulted in a significant discourse of resistance in the manner of, for example, the disability movement (Williams, 1997).

Similarly, major enquiries into poverty and inequality such as those undertaken by the Commission on Social Justice (1994) and the Joseph Rowntree Foundation (1995) have been criticised for failing to give a voice to poor people (Becker, 1997). Although some shift in debate towards enabling poor people to speak out for themselves was identified during the 1990s, Becker questioned whether this had been effective, concluding that the voices of the poor still went largely unheard (Becker, 1997, p37). Becker argued that social policies, practices and structures acted as barriers to independence and security for citizens on low incomes. Further, welfare policy and practice had become part of the problem of, rather than the solution to, poverty and social exclusion (Becker, 1997).

Becker argued for an increased emphasis on the 'agency of the poor' rather than describing them as passive victims. Poor people were best able to articulate the barriers to a reasonable income and lifestyle and they needed to play a strategic role in formulating anti-poverty policies (Becker, 1997, pp163-164). Becker's approach had some similarities to that of Jordan (1996) in that he argued for a 'non-pauperising' minimum income, thereby ending long-standing debates about the adequacy of benefits and the culpability of the poor (Becker, 1997).

New Labour – new exclusion?

Following the election victory in 1997, the New Labour government in the United Kingdom rapidly adopted the language of social exclusion, triggering an escalation in references to social exclusion across policy areas and in the media. The government stated its own definition of social exclusion as:

> ... *a shorthand label for what can happen when individuals or areas suffer from a combination of linked problems such as unemployment, poor skills, low incomes, poor housing, high crime environment, bad health and family breakdown* (Social Exclusion Unit, 1998a).

Before considering New Labour's strategies for combating social exclusion, however, it is important to review the earlier influences upon, and development of, the party's economic and social ideology.

In the early 1990s, the then Leader of the opposition Labour Party, John Smith, set up the Commission on Social Justice, 'to develop a practical vision of economic and social reform' for Britain in the 21st century (Commission on Social Justice, 1994). While the policy recommendations of the Commission were never adopted as official policy of Tony Blair's 'New' Labour Party, the influence of the report upon subsequent debates, and ideological and policy directions, was not insignificant (for example, see Blair, 1996).

The introduction to the Borrie report set out the values of social justice as:

> ... *the equal worth of all citizens, their equal right to be able to meet their basic needs, the need to spread opportunities and life chances as widely as possible, and finally, the requirement that we reduce and where possible eliminate unjustified inequalities* (Commission on Social Justice, 1994, p1).

The report cited extensive evidence of increasing inequality, and acknowledged the economic implications of the globalisation of finance, technology and labour market changes, and demographic changes, particularly the changed role of women in society.

The Borrie Report also referred to the 'unwelcome' process of social exclusion, citing exclusion from work, transport, politics, education, housing, and leisure facilities as increasingly obvious features of British society (Commission on Social Justice, 1994, pp81-82). The Commission remained unconvinced by descriptions of the 'underclass', but recognised that there were people who were alienated and disaffected. Social viability would depend upon building a society based on *inclusion* in terms of an end to structural unemployment, a sustained attack on the accumulated disadvantages of deprived parts of the UK, and effective support for families of all kinds (Commission on Social Justice, 1994). The Commission argued for a future which combined the dynamics of a market economy with strong social institutions, families and communities. This was contrasted with the alternatives of 'Thatcherite' free-market deregulation or 'old

Labour' mechanistic redistribution, and eventually emerged as Tony Blair's 'third way' between neo-liberalism and social democracy.

In the run up to the 1997 election, the New Labour party campaigned on a small number of specific policy commitments, rather than a set of broad, ideological principles (Labour Party, 1997). The clear priority areas were 'Welfare to Work', education and health, with specific commitments on reducing youth unemployment, class sizes and hospital waiting-lists. With respect to housing policy, there would be support for both owner-occupation and the rented sectors through stability, flexibility and partnerships to meet needs. In implementing a welfare programme, there would be no increase in the basic or top rates of income tax and a New Labour government would seek to manage the economy so as to maintain stable economic growth and low inflation. Welfare spending would be funded through the benefits of steady economic growth (Labour Party, 1997).

Once in government, New Labour's 'flagship' 'Welfare to Work' initiative for young unemployed people was rapidly implemented (funded through a windfall tax on privatised utilities), and the 'New Deal' was gradually expanded to other groups who were marginalised in the labour market. For the first two years in office, the New Labour government adhered rigidly to the spending plans set by the previous Conservative administration. During this period, a comprehensive review of all government expenditure was undertaken, which resulted in some increased expenditure on welfare (including capital investment for social housing) during the final three years of the Parliament (*Times*, 1998).

New Labour's broad proposals for welfare reform were set out in a Green Paper published in 1998 (Department of Social Security, 1998b). Again, the approach was characterised as a 'third way' between neo-liberalism and social democracy, but the eight 'key principles' set out in the Green Paper were again pragmatic, rather than ideological. For example, a reformed welfare state would "encourage work", "encourage openness and honesty" and be "easy for people to use".

Besides the broad Prime Ministerial statement referring to the 'third way', there was little in the Green Paper which could identify New Labour as being specifically aligned with, say, the republican/solidarity paradigm which Silver (1994) characterised as the third way between neo-liberalism and democratic socialism. In many ways, New Labour's welfare reforms and the emphasis on 'reintegration through work' appeared to be influenced by European policy development as set out in Room (1995a). The increasing emphasis on community involvement in tackling social exclusion mirrored some of the ideas around empowering disadvantaged people in the policy process (e.g. Williams, 1997). However, family policy, as reflected in implementation of cuts in benefits to lone parents and the promotion of two-parent families in the Green Paper, *Supporting Families* (Home Office, 1998) remained reminiscent of previous Conservative policies and the ideas of Murray (1990,1994), discussed above.

New Labour's interpretation of social exclusion became more clearly articulated following the setting up of the Social Exclusion Unit (Dwelly, 1997; Lloyd,

1997; Mandelson, 1997). Announcing the creation of the unit, Peter Mandelson asserted that New Labour had to succeed in 'tackling the plight of the excluded' (Lloyd 1997, p14) and described the unit as 'the most important innovation we have made since coming to office' (Dwelly, 1997, p21). Reporting directly to the Prime Minister, the unit recruited staff from the civil service and non-government agencies, for an initial two-year period (Lloyd, 1997; Dwelly, 1997). Early reports indicated that the unit would target 1,300 of the country's 'worst' housing estates, as measured by crime levels (Dwelly, 1997, Lloyd, 1997). The focus would be on housing estates, if not on housing policy.

The Social Exclusion Unit was formally constituted and launched in December 1997. Writing in the *Independent*, the Prime Minister, Tony Blair, stated that social exclusion was about more than just financial deprivation. It was about the damage done by poor housing, ill health, poor education, and lack of decent transport, but above all, lack of work (*Independent*, 1997). As well as tackling current problems, the government intended to invest in order to prevent poverty and social exclusion happening. Further, problems would be resolved across departments and in ways that made life easier for clients. The key point about the Social Exclusion Unit was the recognition of the interactions between policy areas or 'joined up solutions for joined up problems'. In an interview for *Roof* magazine, Peter Mandelson was asked how the success of the Social Exclusion Unit would be measured. The reply suggested that a clear vision of 'social inclusion' had not yet been agreed:

> *Homelessness, levels of crime, persistent juvenile offending, exclusions from school and truancy. Those are the measures of social breakdown. When we start reversing these trends, then we will know we are on the right course* (Peter Mandelson, quoted in Blake, 1998).

As with most areas of government policy post-1997, from its inception, information on the role and work of the Social Exclusion Unit was regularly posted on the Internet (Social Exclusion Unit, 1998c). The first three priorities for the unit were the reduction of street homelessness, tackling truancy and developing a strategy for revitalising run down housing estates. A consultation exercise on tackling street homelessness was conducted in February 1998, with detailed proposals and a further consultation period announced later in the year (Social Exclusion Unit, 1998a). A new Rough Sleepers Unit was set up in April 1999, to take forward strategies on reducing street homelessness. The Social Exclusion Unit also reported on strategies for run down housing estates (Social Exclusion Unit, 1998a) with resources for implementation through the New Deal for Communities. By September 1999, the unit had also reported on truancy and school exclusions, teenage pregnancies, and 16-18 year olds.

A process of review of the role of the Social Exclusion Unit commenced in September 1999, although the current work programme was due to continue until at least the summer of 2000 (Social Exclusion Unit, 1999b). The end of 1999 and the early part of 2000 also sees further potentially valuable output becoming available as this volume went to press.

The SEU set up eighteen Policy Action Teams (PATs) each with a remit to examine one element of social exclusion. The PAT's sought to develop detailed recommendations in relation to their particular area and to contribute towards a wider National Strategy for Neighbourhood Renewal, due for publication later in 2000. The PATs most closely related to housing included those on housing management, unpopular housing, neighbourhood management and neighbourhood wardens. Their reports (as they emerge) can be found on the Cabinet Office website (www.cabinet-office.gov.uk).

Early in 1998, the Scottish Office also launched a Social Exclusion Network (initially confined to Scottish Office civil servants), and a broad ranging consultation paper, with the aim of developing comprehensive strategies to tackle social exclusion in Scotland (Scottish Office, 1998c). The Scottish network adopted a strong focus on area regeneration, rather than specific issues such as street homelessness or school truancy. Later in 1998, the network was expanded to include agencies outwith the Scottish Office and was renamed the Social *Inclusion* Network. Subsequent debate within the Scottish Office and the Scottish Executive (established in July 1999 following elections to the devolved Scottish Parliament) continued to emphasise inclusion, rather than exclusion. In March 1999, the Scottish Office announced the allocation of £48m to fund 23 multi-agency Social Inclusion Partnerships across Scotland, over a three year period (Scottish Office Development Department, 1999a). A detailed policy statement was also launched in the Spring of 1999, together with a strategy statement on how social inclusion would be promoted in Scotland (Scottish Office, 1999a; 1999b). From July 1999, however, the social inclusion brief became the remit of the new Scottish Executive and a further period of policy review ensued. Wendy Alexander MSP was appointed as Minister for Communities, with a brief which incorporated social inclusion, local government and housing (Scottish Office Development Department, 1999b).

New Labour's interpretation of social exclusion placed much more emphasis on the *comprehensive* nature of exclusion than on the *dynamic processes* which sustain inequality and exclusion. The policy focus was very much on joint working, as a solution to multidimensional problems, although there was discussion of the need for *preventative* action to tackle the root causes of social problems. As with other analyses, emphasis was placed on re-integration through moving from Welfare to Work. If 'integration' is simplistically equated with working/having a job, however, the other dimensions of multifaceted social exclusion, as well as the value of unpaid work, tend to remain neglected.

Housing and social exclusion

During a period when politicians and commentators on social issues were increasingly concerned about the 'breakdown of the fabric of society', it is perhaps surprising that weaknesses in housing policy and the housing system were not more central to the evolving debates on social exclusion and social integration. Following the 1997 election, however, the housing profession rapidly embraced the language of exclusion and inclusion (Anderson, 1998; Chartered Institute of Housing, 1998a).

Debates on housing and social exclusion need to be interpreted in the context of the evolution of housing policy in Britain. Space precludes a historical review of housing policy since 1979 but detailed accounts can be found in Birchall (1992), Kemp (1992), Malpass and Means (1993) and Williams (1997). In summary, during most of the 1980s and 1990s, housing policy was characterised by an emphasis on the expansion of home-ownership and reviving the privately rented sector at the expense of the contraction and residualisation of the council sector (Malpass and Murie, 1994). While housing association provision expanded for some of the period, trends of residualisation were also identified in that sector (Page, 1993; Lee et al, 1995). The broad trends of expansion of home-ownership and private renting concealed increasing differentiation and marginalisation of low income households within those tenures (Forrest, Murie and Williams, 1990; Lee and Murie, 1997).

For most of the 1980s and 1990s, demands upon the social housing sector from low income households remained consistently high. Levels of statutory and single homelessness increased significantly up to the early-mid 1990s and have since been sustained at a high level (Greve, 1991; Wilcox, 1996). Towards the end of the 1990s however, commentators increasingly focused on 'anti-social behaviour' on housing estates (Scott and Parkey, 1998) and 'lack of demand' for social housing in some parts of Britain (Lowe, 1998; Chapter 12, this volume).

Anderson (1997) argued that early debates on housing and social exclusion focused primarily on the changing role of council housing. For example, Malpass and Murie (1994, pp146-151) summarised the key trends up to the early 1990s. From 1980, much of the highest quality and most desirable council stock was transferred into owner-occupation through sales to sitting tenants. The 1980s and 1990s also saw sustained disinvestment in the building and repair of council housing and allocation of vacant dwellings to households in greatest need. Compared to the 1960s and 1970s, by the 1990s, the overall quality of council housing had declined substantially in terms of age, design, type, condition and desirability of properties. The characteristics of council tenants had also changed from 'the affluent, employed working-class family to a low income, benefit dependent group including disproportionate numbers of elderly persons and lone parent families' (Malpass and Murie, 1994, p147).

In line with the 'European' strand of thought outlined above, social exclusion was seen to result from multiple deprivation and a causal process in which different elements in exclusion reinforced one another (Malpass and Murie, 1994). The housing dimension to social exclusion was particularly evident in the increasing polarisation between the main tenures of renting and owning and in the spatial concentration of patterns of exclusion at regional and local levels. The term *residualisation* was used to describe the changes to council housing while the term *marginalisation* was applied to the experience of council tenants.

During the mid-1980s, government policy encouraged expansion of the housing association sector, particularly in the provision of new rented housing for low income groups. Although associations provided only around 3 per cent of the total housing stock by 1994, the sector continued to expand rapidly through new building and transfers of dwellings from the council sector. By that time, however, research evidence was accruing that the housing association sector was facing similar issues of residualisation and marginalisation as identified in council housing (Page, 1993).

It was broadly accepted by the mid-1990s, that the residual role of social housing had become that of a safety net for the poorest, most disadvantaged households in society. A number of studies in the mid-1990s investigated the management and community issues associated with the residualisation of social housing (e.g. Power and Tunstall, 1995; Cole *et al*, 1996) and the issues raised in these and subsequent research are explored in later chapters.

Among the first explicit considerations of housing and social exclusion were a review conducted by Lee *et al* (1995) and an empirical analysis of poverty and housing tenure by Lee and Murie (1997). Lee *et al* estimated that some 3-5 million people in Britain experienced social exclusion (Lee *et al*, 1995, p21). The widening divisions in income and expenditure were held to be directly attributable to changes in the economy and employment patterns, changes in welfare; and changes to the structures and needs of households. Although the problems facing the social housing sector were not all new, a number of new elements could be identified, including:

- *High unemployment and a changing labour market*
- *Concern about lawlessness on estates*
- *Homelessness and rough sleeping*
- *The implications of social divisions for the economy and geographical concentrations of social divisions, reinforced by housing policy*
(Lee *et al*, 1995, p1).

Lee *et al*'s study confirmed that the housing association sector was affected by trends towards social exclusion. Existing stock was being affected by incremental residualisation while new estates tended to have a narrow social mix reflecting the realities of tenure advantages in Britain as well as the operation of allocation policies (Lee *et al*, 1995, p28). The housing dimension to social exclusion was characterised as being *compound, persistent, concentrated and resistant to change* (Lee *et al*, 1995, p41).

Adopting a definition of social exclusion after Room (1995b), Lee *et al* accepted that a perspective based on the idea of social exclusion meant recognising the importance of the ways in which housing policy and the housing market interacted with other social systems. Consequently, breaking out of a residual role would involve fundamental action to affect the choices and alternatives of a wider range of people. The underlying problem was not simply a matter of housing management and the process of changing estates would require a long-term review of the financial measures, stock characteristics, services and facilities on estates, as well as wider measures to influence tenure choice (Lee *et al* 1995, p33).

The empirical analysis of housing and social exclusion conducted by Lee and Murie (1997) was also influenced by the approaches discussed in Room (1995b). Demonstrating the significant differentiation within tenures in Britain, the study showed that in some areas, concentrations of deprivation were found within the owner-occupied and privately rented sectors, as well as on council housing estates. Consequently, policies which exclusively targeted council housing may neglect excluded groups in other tenures (Lee and Murie, 1997).

It was argued, in Anderson (1997), that the emphasis on the residualisation of social housing, in debates about housing and social exclusion, neglected the experience of those who could not gain access to even this residualised tenure. For example, single homeless people were identified as a key group who were among the most marginalised in society, but largely excluded from social housing. Lee and Murie (1997, p6) argued that since most households registered as 'officially homeless' in Britain were eventually housed in the social rented sector, they experienced the process of social exclusion in much the same way as other marginalised tenants. However, this argument is much less applicable to non-priority homeless households (See Clapham and Evans, this volume). Pleace (1998) has also examined single homelessness as an outcome of the process of social exclusion. Criticising interpretations which focused on single/street homelessness as a 'unique and extreme problem', Pleace (1998) argued that homelessness needed to be seen within the wider picture of social and economic exclusion rather than as a discrete social problem.

By the end of the 1990s, concepts associated with social exclusion and inclusion were being widely debated in research and analysis on housing issues. Importantly, the social inclusion agenda offered the possibility of a higher profile for housing policy as part of the government's broader strategy to build cohesive communities.

Conclusion

From the above review of contemporary debates it can be concluded that social exclusion remains a contested concept, which is subject to ideological interpretation and eludes accurate quantification. The main areas where consensus could be identified were that social exclusion was more *comprehensive* than poverty (embracing all aspects of life, not just material resources) and that it was a dynamic concept, concerned with process as much as with outcome.

Divergence in views arose in the consideration of possible explanations of both the nature of, and the contributory processes to, social exclusion. For example, Levitas (1996) highlighted the problem that the 'European' conception of social exclusion obscured fundamental inequalities (e.g. relating to gender, class and race) which were inherent in capitalism. The conceptualisation of social exclusion within ideological frameworks (or paradigms) enabled Silver (1994) to explicitly acknowledge those limitations. Since definitional problems are endemic in social policy, commentators need to be clear about their own conception and definition of social exclusion within the context of broader debates. The recognition of varying interpretations of social exclusion is essential to a constructive debate which can challenge the prevailing ideology of the government of the day as the only legitimate approach to tackling social issues.

For this author, a working definition of social exclusion should emphasise *separateness from the life experiences common to the majority within society*, rather than some notion of being *outside of society* (see Anderson 1997, 1999). That is to say, those people who experience exclusion from various aspects of welfare remain very much a part of British society, and are in fact *a product of* that society. The better off and least well off groups co-exist in a form of *interdependency*, albeit with a highly differentiated experience of life. Social exclusion, then, is viewed as exclusion from aspects of well-being and social participation taken as 'usual' among the majority within society and the comprehensive and dynamic nature of social exclusion can be acknowledged.

An evident weakness in much of the discussion about social exclusion is the lack of detailed articulation of the concepts of *social inclusion, social integration* or *social cohesion*. The terms are widely used, most apparently to refer to the 'reverse' of social exclusion (multiple privilege?). However, there have been few rigorous attempts to provide a clear definition of these concepts. The question arises as to whether any society would ever expect to attain 'perfect' or 'total' social inclusion and how that outcome would be identified, defined or measured. Nevertheless, without a conception of social inclusion, it is difficult to see how 'policies to combat social exclusion' could be effective or how their impact could be evaluated.

Notwithstanding the above constraints, there are a number of ways in which housing policy and practice could contribute to tackling social exclusion. Social housing providers have been in the front-line of dealing with the social consequences of economic and social exclusion (Anderson, 1998; Chartered Institute of Housing, 1998a). Whelan and Whelan (1995) referred to civic, economic, social, and interpersonal integration as the basis for social inclusion. Decent, secure, habitable and affordable accommodation for all citizens, would provide a solid base for civic integration, and from which to engage in the labour market more effectively. Adequate housing could also facilitate effective take up of other welfare services and is fundamental to the nurturing of relationships with family and friends, and the building of social networks. The development of multi-agency responses to exclusion could herald a changing role for the housing profession, which may have much to contribute to the development of wider strategies for more cohesive communities.

CHAPTER 3:
Inequalities in income and wealth

Karen Gardiner

Introduction

Though this is a chapter on inequality in a book about social exclusion it is important to emphasize that the two concepts are distinct. Inequality in income is relatively straightforward to define, simply being some measure of the spread of incomes from the poorest members of society to the richest. Inequality rises when the gap between the well off and hard up gets bigger. In contrast, there is little evidence of an agreed definition of the term social exclusion. While it appears to encompass a general notion of being 'shut out from society', there is potential for confusion with related concepts such as poverty and multiple deprivation. Atkinson (1998) provides some assistance by identifying three key elements: relativity, agency and dynamics. Exclusion can only exist *relative* to the society in question – circumstances which result in exclusion from one society at one time may not do so in another time or in another society. Exclusion also depends on *agency*, the role individuals play in determining their own situation, since it matters whether people are excluded by choice or have been forced out. Further, exclusion is *dynamic* through the links with past and future events and circumstances: someone who experiences low income in one year, never having done so before and with the prospect of improving their circumstances in the near future is much less likely to be excluded than someone who is (and expects to remain) persistently poor.

The main analytical link between inequalities in income and social exclusion is in the realms of relative poverty and income mobility. Individuals experience relative poverty when their resources are below some share (definitions often use half) of the average. This is to capture the notion that they are thereby excluded from being able to consume many of the goods and services enjoyed by most of the population. Relative poverty is therefore a major determinant of social exclusion, but not the only one.

Analysis of income mobility provides information on how individuals' incomes fluctuate over time. In particular a picture emerges of the proportions of the poor for whom this is a one-off bad year and those where this is their usual standard of living, year in and year out. The dynamics of income relate to social exclusion in that those who are persistently poor are more likely to be 'shut out' than where low income in one year can be mitigated by savings and healthy prospects for the future.

Inequalities in income and wealth are therefore closely related to social exclusion. But the state of relative poverty, for example, does not *necessarily* imply exclusion (such as in the case of some students) and is not *sufficient* to explain exclusion – exclusion also relates to other forms of participation in society, including the labour market and friendship and family networks. Furthermore, some have argued that *areas* can be socially excluded, as well as individuals or groups of people[1].

The rest of this chapter will continue with the recent[2] estimates of the distributions of income and wealth in the United Kingdom (UK) as well as trends over time. More detail is provided on current evidence of relative poverty and income mobility. Explanations for the trends in inequality are sought by examining the major components of households' incomes and significant economic and social factors. Finally, with a view to illuminating the analysis later in the book on specific subgroups, there is an examination of incomes for different housing tenures, homeless people, minority ethnic groups, lone parents and young single people.

The income distribution

Income inequality

Before launching into the actual figures, it is helpful to describe briefly the underlying methodology used in calculating income distribution statistics. The measure of income most commonly used is 'equivalised disposable household income'. 'Household income' is calculated as the sum of each individual's income from earnings, self-employment, investments, cash benefits and private transfers (such as child maintenance). 'Disposable' means that income is net of direct taxes such as income tax and Community Charge, and 'equivalised' indicates that income has been adjusted using an equivalence scale to allow for differences in household size and composition. One simple example of equivalisation is to express figures on a *per capita* basis by dividing by the number of people in the household. However, most equivalence scales used in income distribution statistics assume that there are economies of scale (from sharing fixed costs such as heating) and that meeting the needs of a child requires a lower proportion of income than for an adult. Hence, equivalisation leads to a disposable household income measure which is expressed 'per equivalent adult' and is intended to represent the standard of living of each individual in the household on the assumption that income is shared out to equally meet the needs of all members in

---

1   See Jargowsky (1996).
2   All statistical data presented in this chapter is as up to date as was feasible at the time of writing/editing.

a household[3]. Since surveys of income data typically only collect information from the household population, certain groups such as those living in institutions and the street homeless are completely excluded from these analyses[4].

The national statistical series, *Households Below Average Income* (discussed below), uses the McClement's scale, which allows 0.61 for the first adult, 0.39 for the spouse and between 0.09 and 0.36 for children, depending on age. Taking the example of a couple, with one child aged 11 and disposable household income of £100 per week, they have 1.25 equivalent adults (0.61+0.39+0.25) on the basis of the McClement's scale. This means that their disposable household income per equivalent adult is £80 per week (£100 divided by 1.25). However, it should be noted that recent evidence undermines two assumptions in the McClement's scale (see Middleton et al, 1997). Firstly, they show that there is not such significant variation in costs of children by age and secondly, the costs of children are, at least in part, a fixed cost rather than a proportion of income.

The *Households Below Average Income*[5] (HBAI) series is the main official income distribution data set in the UK. The results are largely based on household income information from the *Family Expenditure Survey* (FES). The methodology follows that outlined above with an important addition – all results are presented both using 'income before housing costs' (BHC) which is equivalent to the definition above and 'income after housing costs' (AHC) where housing costs[6] are deducted from income. The major issues here relate to where variations in the costs of housing do not accurately reflect differences in quality, and where the individual has limited choice about their housing (which may be particularly true for those on low incomes). In this case, an AHC measure may more accurately reflect standards of living. Furthermore, it is important to be aware that Housing Benefit is included in the BHC income measure so that where Housing Benefit has increased over time to match rising rents this can give a potentially misleading picture for households receiving the benefit. For this reason, the AHC measure is often preferred for analysis of trends over time. However, since there is evidence that some of the increases in housing costs over the period do reflect improvements in housing quality[7], the true position probably lies somewhere between the two measures[8].

---

3   There is evidence to undermine this assumption which shows, in particular, that the
     distribution of resources within the household varies according to which individual
     controls the money (see Goode *et al*, 1998).
4   Evans (1995) provides analysis of a range of adjustments for the non-household
     population.
5   DSS (1997a).
6   The definition of housing costs includes rent, water charges, mortgage interest payments,
     structural insurance premiums, ground rent and service charges but excludes any estimate
     of the implicit value of home-ownership or subsidised (below market) rent. For a detailed
     discussion of the effects of adjusting for housing on income distribution statistics, see
     Gardiner *et al* (1995).
7   See DSS (1997a), p113 and Hills (1998a), p38.
8   For further discussion of this issue see DSS (1997a), p210.

Figure 3.1: AHC income by decile

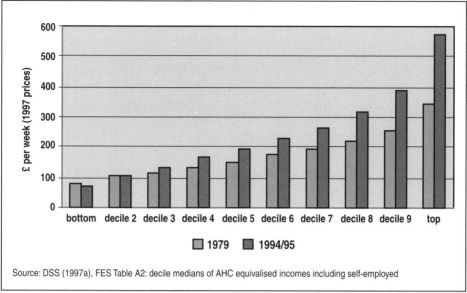

Source: DSS (1997a), FES Table A2: decile medians of AHC equivalised incomes including self-employed

Figure 3.1 presents income data after housing costs from HBAI for 1979 and 1994/95[9] expressed in 1997 prices. Individuals are ranked according to their income and then divided into ten equal sized groups called decile groups. Hence the poorest tenth of individuals in each year are in the bottom decile group and the richest are located in the top decile group. In 1979 the median equivalised income for the bottom decile group was £80 per week (in 1997 prices) whereas for the top decile group it was £340, over four times as big. By 1994/95 there had been a real *decline* in AHC weekly incomes for the bottom decile group to £73, whilst the top decile group were significantly better off at £570, nearly eight times the figure for the poorest tenth of individuals. This clearly shows that the spread of incomes widened. The equivalent results on a BHC measure of income suggest small real rises for the poorest (as opposed to a real drop), and rather less growth in inequality. The median weekly income for the bottom decile group rose from £96 to £105 between 1979 and 1994/95 and from £390 to £622 for those at the top. Using the ratio of the top to bottom decile medians as a measure of inequality, it increased from four to six over the period. In summary, in the context of average real incomes rises of about 40 per cent, the worst off experienced income growth between plus or minus 9 per cent and the richest enjoyed rises of around 60 per cent. As a result income inequality grew dramatically over the period.

---

9   All HBAI results denoted '1994/95' are based on combined data from the FES for the two financial years 1994/95 and 1995/96. This recent practice of combining two years of data is intended to improve the reliability of HBAI results. In the HBAI report most results are presented both including and excluding self-employed individuals. Unless otherwise stated, the results quoted in this paper include the self-employed.

Figure 3.2: Income inequality in the UK 1962-1996/97

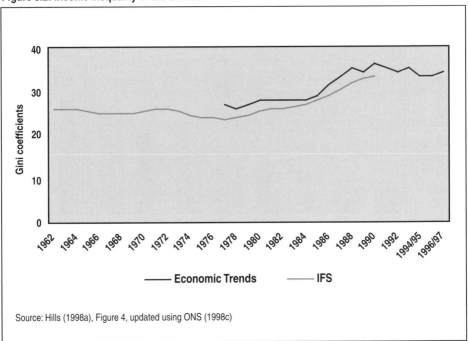

Source: Hills (1998a), Figure 4, updated using ONS (1998c)

The significant upsurge in income inequality is confirmed by other statistics presented in Figure 3.2. *Economic Trends*[10] annually produces an historical series of Gini coefficients, an inequality measure which is sensitive to changes in all parts of the distribution not just movements at the top and bottom. This measure ranges from 0 to 100, increasing as inequality rises. In 1977 the Gini was 27 for equivalised disposable income, peaked at 36 in 1990 and has been fairly constant in the mid-1990s with the more recent figure for 1996/97 at 34. Hence, there is some evidence that after 1990 inequality declined slightly although the downward trend does not appear to be continuing, with relative stability for the following three years. Since Gini coefficients have little intuitive meaning it is helpful to look at a longer-term picture provided by the Institute for Fiscal Studies (IFS). When the two sets of figures are compared, the level of the IFS Gini is lower (due to slight differences in definition[11]) but the trend is consistent with the *Economic Trends* results. The message here is that the increases in inequality up until the early 1990s were indeed substantial when compared with the relative stability in inequality between the early 1960s and the late 1970s.

---

10 ONS (1998c), Appendix 2, Table 2.
11 For the purposes of the analysis presented here, the IFS series is in fact preferable since it uses HBAI data (BHC income) and is therefore consistent with the other figures presented on income distribution and relative poverty.

So what does all this mean for those in the middle of the income distribution? Figure 3.1 showed that their real incomes had risen between 1979 and 1994/95. What is less clear from this chart is that because the gains for the top were so large there was a fall in the share of total household income going to households both at the bottom and in the middle of the distribution. On both BHC and AHC measures of income, all decile groups up to and including the eighth decile group had a lower share of income in 1994/95 than in 1979[12].

The story so far is that growth in inequality since the late 1970s has been due to large income gains at the top compared with small gains (or losses) at the bottom, and also less significant rises for the middle. Hence it is not just the gap between the rich and poor which has got bigger but also the gap between those on high and middle incomes.

Relative poverty

Returning to the link between inequality and social exclusion, what do these figures tell us about the numbers of people who are 'shut out of society'? As explained above, the most relevant indicator might be relative poverty. As its name suggests, *Households Below Average Income* is in fact primarily an analysis of households in relative poverty. Whilst there is no official UK government endorsement of the definitions of poverty used in HBAI and the language tends towards use of 'low income' rather than 'poor', such definitions have been widely used both in the UK and abroad[13]. In particular, half average income has been used in European Union official poverty reports[14].

There is no innate justification for choosing half of average income as a poverty line – it is arbitrary and is not intended to suggest that those with incomes just below this line are intrinsically different from those slightly above it. It does however provide a standard which can be applied across countries and over time. HBAI partly gets round the criticism that it is one arbitrary measure by presenting results for three poverty lines: 40 per cent, 50 per cent and 60 per cent of the average[15]. This provides a fuller picture of the UK's low income population whilst also implying that there is nothing special about one particular line[16].

---

12 Hills (1998a), Table 1.
13 See for example, Callan *et al* (1996) on Ireland, and Syntheses (1996) on France.
14 See European Commission (1989). Some subsequent poverty reports switched to a poverty line of half of average equivalised *expenditure* due to lack of availability of accurate income data for the relevant countries.
15 Furthermore, whilst most results use a relative measure (i.e. the figures for 1979 relate to average income in 1979 and those for 1994/95 relate to average income in 1994/95) there is some analysis using a fixed or absolute standard (i.e. the poverty line in all years relates to average income in 1979 with changes for inflation only). The figures reproduced in this paper all use the relative standard since this is the most relevant to social exclusion.
16 For an analysis of the sensitivity of poverty estimates to changes in definition, see Atkinson *et al* (1993).

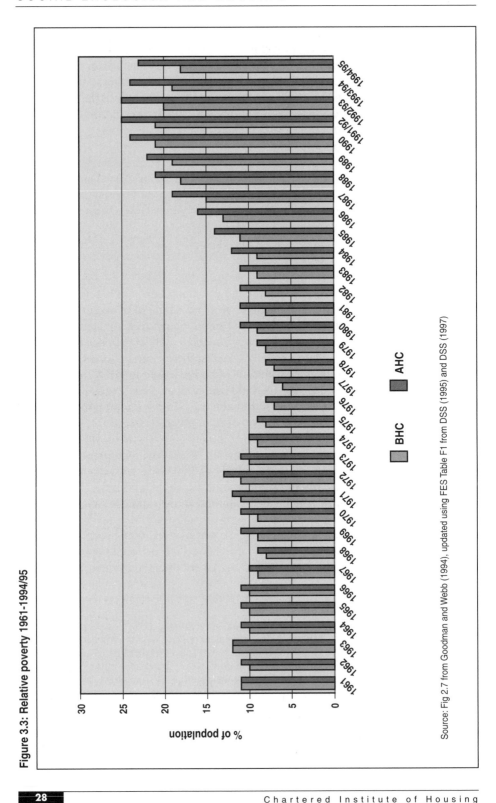

Figure 3.3: Relative poverty 1961-1994/95

% of population

BHC AHC

Source: Fig 2.7 from Goodman and Webb (1994), updated using FES Table F1 from DSS (1995) and DSS (1997)

Figure 3.3 shows the percentage of the population below 50 per cent of average income in each year from 1961 to 1994/95 for both BHC and AHC measures of income[17]. In the early 1960s, 10 to 12 per cent of the population had incomes below half the national average, falling to a low of 6 or 7 per cent in 1977. By the late 1980s levels of relative poverty were significantly higher than at any time in the two previous decades and reached a high in 1991/92 of 21 per cent on a BHC measure and 25 per cent on an AHC measure. Figures were only available up to 1994/95 but indicated a small reduction in relative poverty during the early 1990s, back down to the levels of the late 1980s. The latest available inequality figures for 1996/97 (see above) suggested that future HBAI reports may well show poverty levels having stabilised. One interesting feature of Figure 3.3 is that while it shows that there was little or no difference between the BHC and AHC results at the beginning of the period, by the early 1990s there was a differential of about five percentage points. Hence, the trend on an AHC basis implies a more dramatic growth in relative poverty than does BHC income. As discussed above, while both measures have their faults and merits, the true position probably lies between them.

Income mobility

Analysis of income inequality and its implications for social exclusion must take into account income mobility. Whilst the growing gap between rich and poor and the substantial rises in numbers in relative poverty point to a more divided society, these statistics *do not* necessarily mean that increasing numbers of *particular individuals* are poor year after year. All of the statistics presented so far have been based on cross-sectional data, which gives a 'snapshot' at one point in time. The implications for social exclusion of these observed trends very much depend on whether the poor tend to stay poor or whether someone who is in the bottom decile group in one year will have a good chance of being in the middle or top the following year. For answers to these questions we need to turn to longitudinal data and the analysis of income dynamics.

The UK's main source of longitudinal income data, where the same individuals are tracked over time, is the *British Household Panel Survey* (BHPS). Interviews have been carried out annually since 1991 and there are now six 'waves' of data available for analysis. Using the first four waves, Jarvis and Jenkins (1997) examined the income dynamics of the low income population. Starting with the individuals whose equivalent disposable incomes placed them in the bottom two decile groups in 1991, they followed their movements into and out of the bottom two decile groups in the three successive years. After the first wave, 39 per cent of this low income group had incomes which took them above this cut-off, leaving about three-fifths (12.3 per cent) of the original 20 per cent remaining in the bottom two decile groups. If the chances of 'escape' had stayed constant, by

---

17 Whilst the official HBAI series only starts in 1979, Goodman and Webb (1994) includes a consistent series back to 1961.

the end of the four waves it would mean a quarter (4.5 per cent) of the original 20 per cent would have been still stuck at the bottom. In fact, the figure was closer to a third (7 per cent) because the rate of escape from low income declines the longer one stays on low income. After two successive waves the chances of escaping the bottom two deciles falls from 39 per cent to 28 per cent and after three waves to 21 per cent. But this is not the end of the story – those who escape from low income are not 'home and dry'. Of the two-fifths (7.8 per cent) who leave in wave two only slightly more than a half (4.2 per cent) stay out, while the remainder (3.6 per cent) fall back into low income in either wave three or four.

Do these levels of mobility mean poverty is not a problem? Analysis presented in Hills (1998b) attempts to address this directly by defining five main types of income trajectory: flat, rising, falling, blips and other. The exact definition of each type depends on an individual's position in one of ten income groups[18], in each of the first four waves of the BHPS. Within each of the five trajectory types a 'poor' subgroup is also identified as those in the bottom two income groups. The first column of figures in Table 3.1 gives a breakdown of the percentage of individuals falling into each trajectory type; the second column shows how many of the low income observations (the bottom two groups) were experienced by each trajectory type.

Table 3.1: Analysis of four waves of the BHPS by trajectory type

Trajectory type		% of individuals	% of low income observations
Flat	Poor	9.2	43.0
	Non-poor	30.6	1.0
Rising	Poor	4.0	8.8
	Non-poor	6.4	–
Falling	Poor	3.3	8.5
	Non-poor	5.3	–
Blips	Out of poverty	3.7	13.3
	Into poverty	4.6	6.7
	Non-poor	15.2	
Other	Repeated poverty	4.4	11.2
	One-off poor	5.9	7.6
	Non-poor	7.6	–
Total		100	100

Source: Hills, 1998b

18 These income groups are similar to decile groups: in the first wave the groups are constructed the same as decile groups but in subsequent waves the income cut-offs are calculated by uprating for average income growth. Hence there are not necessarily 10 per cent of the population in each group after wave one and in particular, if inequality falls there would be less than 10 per cent in the top and bottom income groups.

It is worth considering each trajectory group in turn. First, there is the 'flat' category where income position varies little over the four waves (falls into at most two adjacent groups), with the 'poor flats' falling into one of the bottom two groups in at least two waves. 'Poor flats' suffer repeated if not persistent poverty and are therefore a high risk group for social exclusion and the figures bear this out. Whilst only 9 per cent of individuals are classed as 'poor flats', they experienced 43 per cent of observed poverty over the period.

Then there are the 'risers' whose income rises or stays the same in successive waves so that they end up at least two income groups above where they started. Mobility for this group means that they improve their position on the income 'ladder' over time, and even the 4 per cent of cases classified as 'poor risers' (started in one of the bottom two groups) clearly have good prospects for the future. Only 9 per cent of all poverty episodes are accounted for by 'poor risers'.

The 'fallers' have incomes which fall or stay the same over the four waves. The 3 per cent of individuals who are 'poor fallers' have seen their situation progressively deteriorate and so they may be of concern. They account for 9 per cent of poverty.

The 'blippers' do not experience a steady trend in income, they qualify as 'flat' except for one 'blip' year which may be higher or lower than their usual income level. Two poor blip groups are separated out: those who 'blip out of poverty' (poor in two of three flat years and non-poor in blip year) and those who 'blip into poverty' (poor only in blip year). Those who 'blip out of poverty' (4 per cent) have just one year out of the four when they manage to escape low income and hence are prone to substantial periods in poverty. They account for 13 per cent of all observed poverty. On the other hand, those who 'blip in' to low income (5 per cent) appear to have just one bad year (explaining 7 per cent of poverty), the detrimental impact of which will be possibly lessened by their more favourable income position in the other three waves.

Of the remaining 'others', 6 per cent are poor in one year (accounting for 8 per cent of poverty spells) and another 4 per cent suffer repeated poverty, making up 11 per cent of observed poverty.

To summarise, the trajectory type which might be considered most at risk of social exclusion are the 'poor flats'. These individuals account for 9 per cent of the population but as much as 43 per cent of the poverty. However, there are other groups who, while not being persistently poor, may suffer repeated poverty. The 'poor fallers', 'blips out of poverty' and 'repeatedly poor others' are also affected by low income. This group includes another 11 per cent of individuals and accounts for 23 per cent of observed poverty. Altogether, the persistently and repeatedly poor make up a fifth of the population, but, over the four waves, 76 per cent of all poverty is experienced by this group. This analysis therefore suggests that about three-quarters of observed poverty is of concern, with an associated risk of social exclusion.

10726

The wealth distribution

Though the wealth holdings of many individuals are unlikely to have much impact on their day-to-day standard of living they nevertheless are important. There are two main types of wealth: marketable wealth, which can be bought and sold, and non-marketable wealth in the form of accumulated pension rights. Marketable wealth facilitates the purchase of large assets such as property and cars and, moreover, can be turned into income in emergencies. It may therefore be important in avoiding debts and hardship. Furthermore, both forms of wealth are a key determinant of the standard of living for those who have reached retirement age, when the ability to earn and accumulate assets is likely to cease.

The most recent Inland Revenue figures on the distribution of holdings of marketable wealth show how such wealth is highly concentrated among a small minority of the adult population. In 1994, the most wealthy 10 per cent of adults held 51 per cent of marketable wealth, the top 1 per cent of the adult population owned 19 per cent (nearly a fifth of the total) and only 8 per cent of marketable wealth belonged to the least wealthy half of adults[19]. The Inland Revenue statistical series shows that the distribution of marketable wealth has been very constant over the last twenty years[20]. Earlier figures covering the period 1960 to 1981 are not strictly comparable with the Inland Revenue series but indicate that the distribution of marketable wealth was becoming more equally distributed until the late 1970s and confirm a stable trend thereafter[21].

Non-marketable wealth is relatively more important for low income people since everyone who earns enough to pay National Insurance contributions has state pension rights, even if they own no other assets. Figures for the total distribution of wealth, including non-marketable wealth, are only available from 1976. They show inequality of wealth growing, with the wealth holdings of the most wealthy 10 per cent of adults increasing from 34 per cent to 36 per cent but the share of the poorest 50 per cent declining from 22 per cent in 1976 to 17 per cent in 1994[22]. Changes in pension policy may be part of the explanation for this trend. After 1981, the uprating of the basic state pension was linked to inflation instead of earnings, thereby reducing its expected future value.

In summary, the distribution of marketable wealth became more equal during the 1960s and most of the 1970s, followed by a very stable period thereafter. However, when state and occupational pension rights are also included, a greater share of total wealth is held by less well off adults but this share has fallen since the mid-1970s.

---

19 See Inland Revenue (1997), Table 13.5.
20 See Stewart (1991), Table A.
21 See series 'AGH' in Hills (1998a), Figure 6.
22 See Inland Revenue (1997), Table 13.7 and Stewart (1991), Table J (historic series).

Major influences

The purpose of this section is to provide some understanding of the most important economic and social factors which have been driving the trends in income distribution. Three broad areas are considered: sources of gross income, effects of taxation and the distribution of work across households.

Sources of income

Examination of changes in individual components of income can help us understand the reasons for inequality trends. For all households the main sources of gross income (i.e. before the deduction of taxes) are earnings (63 per cent) and cash benefits (15 per cent). These income sources are also of interest because their relative importance varies dramatically across the income distribution. Cash benefits make up 69 per cent of gross income for the bottom decile group, but only 2 per cent for the top decile group, while earnings represent 17 per cent of gross income for the bottom income group compared to 65 per cent at the top[23]. Hence, any differential in the growth rates for cash benefits and earnings is, over time, likely to affect the gap between incomes of the rich and poor[24].

Between 1979 and 1995, average weekly earnings for those in work grew by 36 per cent in real terms (i.e. allowing for inflation). But, there were significant differences in increases over the range of the earnings distribution. For full-time males, those one quarter of the way up the distribution saw their earnings rise by 22 per cent but those three-quarters of the way up the distribution had double the increase, at 44 per cent. Hence, earnings inequality for men grew. The distribution of women's earnings also became more unequal. However, women caught up on men due to faster average growth: 40 per cent for those one quarter of the way up the distribution and 72 per cent for those three-quarters of the way up the distribution between April 1979 and April 1995 for full-timers[25].

There is a strong relationship between the pattern of earnings growth and the distribution of household incomes. Inequality of male earnings grew consistently between the late 1970s and about 1993. Figure 3.2 shows how inequality of equivalised disposable household income closely mirrors this path.

Hills (1998a) presents the changes in the value of particular cash benefits. Taking the examples of the basic pension and unemployment benefit (both for single people), it is apparent that while their real value has grown since 1979, there has been a significant decline in relation to average incomes[26]. This

---

23 Percentages of gross income are figures for 1996/97 from ONS (1998c), Appendix 1, Table 2A.
24 For an analysis of the impact of *non-cash* benefits on the income distribution, see Sefton (1997).
25 DSS (1997a), p48.
26 The value of benefits are tracked against personal disposable income per capita.

suggests that over this period those reliant on cash benefits would have seen their living standards falling behind the rest of the population. Furthermore, a higher proportion of the population are now receiving income-related benefits. The percentage of individuals living in recipient families went up from 17 per cent in 1979 to 24 per cent by 1994/95[27].

What was happening to earnings and cash benefits over this period is a significant chapter in the income inequality story. Earnings were growing quickly, but much more so for high earners than for those further down the wage ladder. At the same time, more people required benefits to reach a minimum standard of income and the value of these benefits increased at a much slower rate than earnings and other forms of income.

Effects of taxation

Having examined the influence of the main sources of gross income, the next step is to consider the effect of direct taxation, since direct taxes are deducted from gross income to arrive at disposable income.

The historical income distribution series in *Economic Trends* (ONS, 1998c) presents estimates of income inequality for various measures of household income. Comparing the distributions of gross and disposable incomes captures the impact of direct taxes on inequality. The figures point to a rather neutral effect of taxation on inequality during the period 1977 to 1991, but thereafter direct taxes appear to have a role in restraining inequality in household disposable incomes.

These findings may contradict expectations given the high profile tax cuts for the rich during the late 1980s. This apparent contradiction can be explained by distinguishing between two opposing forces at work. Firstly, in an economy where inequality is increasing (due to faster income growth for the rich than for others) and the tax system is static (with increases in allowances and tax bands for inflation only) then the effect of direct taxation is to restrain inequality. Because taxes are a higher proportion of income for the rich than for the poor, the growth in inequality of disposable income will be less than the growth in inequality of gross income. The second force is discretionary tax reforms which, in the UK in the 1980s, worked to make the system less redistributive from rich to poor. Effectively between the late 1970s and the early 1990s these two forces worked in opposite directions and resulted in direct taxation having a neutral impact on inequality. Subsequently, there is evidence that taxes became slightly more progressive. In particular, in 1993, the Community Charge was replaced by the Council Tax with the rebate for those on Income Support increased from 80 per cent to 100 per cent.

---

27   DSS (1997a), p47.

Distribution of work

The distribution of work is critical to understanding the distribution of household disposable income. It is not just a case of which *individuals* are in work (and receiving earnings) and which are unemployed (and dependent on benefits), but also the extent to which there are 'work rich' and 'work poor' *households*.

The unemployment rate has fluctuated significantly since the mid-1970s, but rose consistently between 1979 and 1985. This has been attributed some significance in explaining overall inequality in household incomes. However, during the late 1980s unemployment fell at a time when the distribution of household disposable incomes was still widening rapidly. While this may appear contradictory, part of the explanation lies with what was happening to the distribution of work amongst households at this time. Analysis in HBAI shows the extent of the growth in the number of households without any adults in work, increasing from around one in ten in 1979 to one in five by 1994/95. This phenomenon is true of all household types, but the case of couples with dependent children is particularly illuminating. Compared to the position in 1979, couples with dependent children in 1994/95 were twice as likely to be workless, but also had a higher chance that both adults would be working[28]. This points to the 'polarisation' of work. The growing number of work poor households have a particularly high risk of social exclusion, both because of low income and also due to lack of participation in the labour market.

Income position of certain groups

So far in the chapter, details have been presented for the entire household population on income distribution, relative poverty and income mobility. This section will focus on the income position of different tenure types and some specific groups, which are discussed further in later chapters.

Tenure type

In Figures 3.4a and 3.4b, each decile group of the BHC income distribution is divided to indicate the percentage in different tenure types in two years, 1979 and 1994/95. So, for example, taking the top decile group in 1994/95, 74 per cent are home-owners with a mortgage, 18 per cent own their homes outright, 7 per cent are private tenants and 1 per cent are in social housing (local authority and housing association).

The shift in the tenure pattern between 1979 and 1994/95 shows two striking features. First, is the decline in the proportion in social housing and corresponding increase in mortgagors for *every* decile group. This arises because

---

28   DSS (1997a), Table 3.2.

the share in social housing declined and the proportion of home-owners with mortgages rose. In the whole population, the proportion of social tenants fell from 42 per cent to 23 per cent and the proportion of mortgagors went up from 36 per cent to 50 per cent. Second, the contrast in tenure patterns at the top and the bottom of the income distribution was much more stark in 1994/95 than in 1979. In particular, social tenants became much more highly concentrated in the low income groups. Between 1979 and 1994/95, the percentage of social tenants in the bottom two income groups increased from 26 per cent to 40 per cent, while the share of social tenants in the top two decile groups fell from 13 to only 2 per cent by 1994/95. Hence, at the end of this fifteen-year period, fewer low income people were living in social housing, but more social tenants were on low incomes.

While this shift in tenure patterns might be considered the result of effective targeting of resources – social housing goes to those with the lowest incomes – there are potential negative features. The concentration of low income people in social housing implies concentrations of low income people 'on the ground'. Since low income is associated with other characteristics of social exclusion, such as unemployment, the result may be increasing concentrations of people at multiple risk of exclusion. Indeed, there is evidence of increased 'area polarisation' and increased 'concentrated poverty' over the 1980s[29].

Figure 3.4a: 1979 – Income deciles by housing tenure

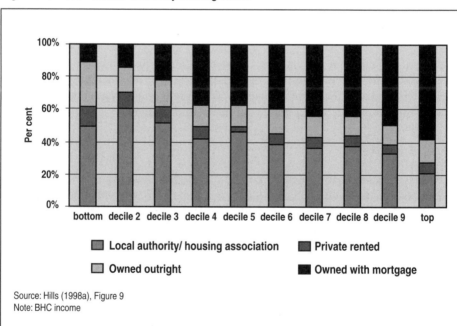

Source: Hills (1998a), Figure 9
Note: BHC income

---

29   See Hills (1995), p85.

Figure 3.4b: 1994/95 – Income deciles by housing tenure

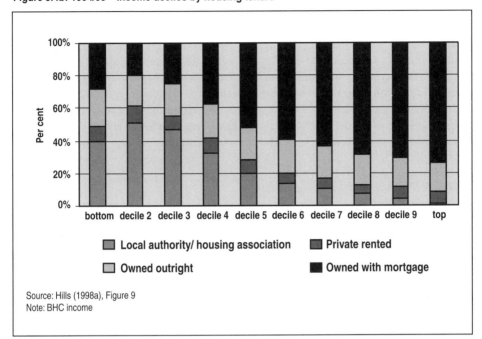

Source: Hills (1998a), Figure 9
Note: BHC income

Homeless people

What can be said about the income position of homeless people is extremely limited. As explained above, the surveys on which income distribution statistics are based only cover the 'household' population, and therefore completely omit those in institutions (such as those living in hostels and bed and breakfast) and the street homeless. However, it would seem safe to say that their incomes would typically be well below half the average. If this assumption is true, their inclusion would make levels of income inequality and poverty look worse (although the effect on trends would depend on how the size and incomes of this group have changed over time). For the non-household population as a whole, Evans (1995) calculated that their inclusion in income statistics for 1989 would mean a net increase in the population below half average BHC income from 17.4 per cent to between 17.8 and 17.9 per cent.

Minority ethnic groups

It has historically been difficult to build up an accurate picture of the income position of minority ethnic groups. This has been due to lack of appropriate questions in surveys and the relatively small numbers of individuals from different minority ethnic groups (reflecting the share in the whole population), so that separate income estimates would be unreliable.

Figure 3.5 presents results from the 1995/96 *Family Resources Survey* using a
BHC income measure broken down into quintiles (fifths of the income
distribution). Compared to the average, minority ethnic groups taken together
have relatively low incomes, making up 11 per cent of the bottom quintile,
compared to 6 per cent of the whole population. However, there is significant
variation between the different groups: about two-thirds of the Pakistani and
Bangladeshi population appear to have incomes in the lowest quintile, compared
to less than a third of blacks[30] and a quarter of Indians. The 'other' ethnic group,
including *inter alia* people of Chinese origin, appears to have the most
favourable income position, with 20 per cent falling into the top quintile.

Figure 3.5: Ethnic minorities by income quintile

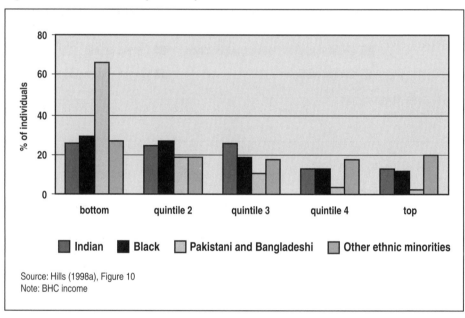

Source: Hills (1998a), Figure 10
Note: BHC income

Lone parents

Information on the incomes of lone parents is relatively plentiful, since the
HBAI standard 'family type' classification includes a lone parent category. In
1979, 4 per cent of individuals were in lone parent families, rising to 8 per cent
by 1994/95[31]. Real income growth over the period for this group is uncertain due
to small sample numbers, but is clearly well below the average for all
individuals. On a BHC measure of income, growth is in the range 7 to 28 per
cent (compared to 40 per cent for the whole population). Using AHC income,

30   Includes black Caribbean, black African and black other.
31   DSS (1997a), FES Table B1.

growth is calculated at between minus 5 per cent and positive 17 per cent (compared to 42 per cent overall)[32]. In 1994/95 the mean equivalised BHC income was £182 per week (in 1997 prices) for lone parent families, as opposed to £295 for all individuals, making lone parent families the poorest family type[33].

Despite the relatively low income growth for this group, their relative position has not necessarily declined. In 1979, 9 per cent of those in the bottom decile group were individuals from lone parent families, rising to 15 per cent by 1994/95, approximately double the proportions in the whole population in each year[34]. Hence, while individuals from lone parent families are highly over-represented at the bottom of the income distribution, this was no more true in 1994/95 than in 1979. However, there is some evidence that lone parent families have lost ground over time compared to the rest of population. In 1979, 16 per cent of those in lone parent families had incomes below half the national average (compared to 8 per cent of all individuals) going up to 39 per cent in 1994/95 (compared to the total figure of 18 per cent)[35]. So the proportion of people in lone parent families in poverty went from two times the total figure to 2.2 times, on a BHC measure of income. On an AHC measure of income, the same ratio went from 2.1 to 2.6. Hence, even taking account of the overall growth in poverty, there has been an increase in the proportion of lone parents and their children with incomes below half the average.

Young single people

Analyses of household income distribution have some potential shortcomings in the case of young single people living with their parents. Children are no longer considered to be part of their parents' family once they leave school (at sixteen or eighteen years of age). Whilst they will therefore be classed as a separate *family* unit, it is still assumed that income is shared between all the members of the *household*, where the definition of 'household' is based on sharing meals and the like. The efficacy of this assumption for grown-up children will depend upon the extent of their financial independence but in some cases may over-estimate the standard of living of a young adult who lives with their parents.

There are only very limited results in HBAI for young adults, based on the 1995/96 *Family Resources Survey*. These figures show the percentage of adults aged under twenty-five falling into each of the income quintile groups (fifths of the income distribution). Hence, if young adults were equally represented across the distribution it would be expected that 20 per cent would fall into each quintile group. The actual figures are quite close to this, although there are some differences depending on whether one takes a BHC or AHC income measure and

---

32 DSS (1997a), FES Table A4.
33 DSS (1997a), FES Table A5.
34 DSS (1997a), FES Table D1, BHC income measure.
35 DSS (1997a), FES Table F1, BHC income measure.

whether students are included or not. If students are excluded, young adults appear relatively well off with 44 per cent in the top two quintile groups and only 35 per cent in the bottom two quintile groups (on both BHC and AHC measures). When students are included, the group show a greater tendency towards low income, with 19 per cent in the bottom quintile group on a BHC income measure but 23 per cent based on AHC income[36]. As discussed above, the representativeness of these figures for the living standards of young people very much depends on how accurate it is to assume that those who live with their parents share in their income.

Conclusion

The purpose of this chapter has been to detail the extent of income inequality in the UK, along with related issues of wealth inequality, relative income poverty and income mobility. The figures presented have been framed within the historical trends going back some thirty years. They show that inequality was more or less stable during the 1960s, fell until the late 1970s, and then rose dramatically until 1990, since when there has been a slight decline. The proportion of the population in relative poverty, defined as having an income below half the national average demonstrates a similar trend. Relative poverty reached a low of 6 per cent in 1977, then more than tripled to peak at 21 per cent by 1991/92, followed by a slight fall back to 18 per cent in 1994/95, but still substantially higher than the levels of the 1960s and 1970s[37]. Analysis of income mobility in the UK shows that while, for some, low income represents only a rare spell of bad luck, about three-quarters of observed poverty is experienced by individuals who are persistently or repeatedly poor. It is these individuals who are most at risk of social exclusion.

Examining the main sources of household income casts some light on the forces behind these trends. High earners enjoyed large wage rises in the 1980s while low earners received more modest increases. Meanwhile, those without wages and reliant on means-tested benefits saw only small real increases in income, as the value of benefits grew much more slowly than other forms of income. Since the latter group are concentrated at the bottom of the distribution, the income distribution became more 'stretched out' as they rapidly lost ground to those in the middle and, especially, those at the top. For most of this time, taxation did little to rein in the growing gap between rich and poor. The growth in unemployment and the number of workless households only served to exacerbate this gap, by pushing up the numbers dependent on income-tested benefits.

Finally, a more detailed analysis of the incomes of particular groups that may be considered at risk of social exclusion suggested the following trends. Evidence

---

36   Figures from DSS (1997a), Table 2.8.
37   Based on BHC income (see Figure 3.3).

on income by tenure type showed that, at all levels of income, a smaller share of the population were in social housing by the mid-1990s compared to the late 1970s. Furthermore, current social tenants are significantly more likely to be on low incomes. Homeless people are excluded from income surveys, as are all people who do not live in 'private households' in the main tenures. Whilst one can speculate that incomes for this group are likely to be well below half the average, the lack of hard evidence makes it impossible to assess how their position has changed over time. Minority ethnic groups taken together have a greater risk of low income than the population as a whole. However, the variation between distinct ethnic populations is substantial, with two-thirds of Bangladeshis and Pakistanis in the bottom quintile group, compared with a quarter of the Indian population.

Lone parent families appear to be the least well off of all family types. Between the late 1970s and the mid-1990s they had the lowest income growth resulting in an average income in 1994/95 of only 60 per cent of the overall average. Taking account of the fact that over this period lone parents and their children doubled as a proportion of the population, the percentage of lone parent families at the very bottom of the distribution (bottom decile group) did not increase but a greater proportion fell into relative poverty.

Income information on young single people is limited, but the little there is suggests that, on the whole, their incomes are fairly evenly spread across the distribution. However, these results assume that young adults still living at home share in their parents' income, so the living standards of young adults may be overstated.

CHAPTER 4:
Employment inequalities and housing

Janet Ford

Introduction

Housing and employment are tightly interrelated. For example, the provision of stable, secure employment is a prerequisite of the success of British housing policy, with its emphasis on the expansion of owner-occupation where the form of financing is predominantly a loan repayable over a 20-25 year period. The implications of low wage employment for housing are also explicitly acknowledged in the provision of in-work housing benefits for households in the rented sector, as is the impact of unemployment. For homeless people, access to work is seen as a critical step in developing their ability to find and maintain permanent housing, and, for example, it is this connection that has been central to the development of the foyer movement (Anderson and Quilgars, 1995). In a proportion of cases, loss of work is implicated in the loss of the home as a result of rent or mortgage arrears (Burrows, 1998; Gray *et al*, 1994; Ford and Seavers, 1998). For many young people, the problematic relationship between the costs of housing and the income from employment is at least part of the explanation as to why increasing numbers of them are remaining longer in the parental home (Jones, 1995a; Ford *et al*, 1997), or are at greater risk of homelessness (Rugg, 1996).

In practice, these relationships are embedded in a wider context, significant aspects of which shape the detail of the housing-employment relationship at any one time and for different groups of people. These include: the nature of social security policy; macro economic and fiscal policy; and labour market change which is itself affected by national and global concerns and political ideologies. Thus, for example, the ability and willingness to take employment amongst currently unemployed people may be affected by the way the social security system treats housing costs on a return to work (Kempson *et al*, 1997). In a similar manner, the ideological promotion of owner-occupation (particularly post-1979 and in the context of a reduction in the capacity of alternative tenures), is argued to have influenced the growth of two-earner households and contributed to the developing polarity of work-rich and work-poor households by tenure (Hogarth *et al*, 1996). Thus the nature and implications of the housing/employment relationship has to be understood with reference to the impact of the wider context.

This chapter is primarily concerned with a discussion of the current pattern of employment and some of the implications of recent employment trends for housing and households. The first section reviews the evidence on employment trends and identifies their relationship to tenure composition. The second section explores some of the ways in which these trends have implications for the policy objective of encouraging people to move from 'Welfare to Work' by examining the issue of work disincentives.

Employment trends

The current labour market context

Following a decline in the overall number of jobs in the early 1990s, employment has started to grow again and in 1997 stood at over 26 million. Table 4.1 shows something of the changing balance between the main forms of employment between 1981 and 1996.

Table 4.1: % Composition of employment. 1981, 1991, 1996

	1981	1991	1996
Full-time employees	71.8	64.2	62.7
Part-time employees	19.0	22.7	24.5
Self-employed	9.2	13.1	12.8
	100.0	100.0	100.0

Source: Lindley and Wilson, 1998

Table 4.1 refers to all individuals in employment. In 1996, the majority of people in work were full-time employees. The next largest group were those with part-time employment. Almost 13 per cent of those in employment were self-employed in 1996.

The important changes in the distribution of employment opportunities that are documented in Table 4.1 have come about in a number of different ways. Some of the changes reflect the fact that there have been two major recessions (the early 1980s and late 1980s/early 1990s). In particular, manufacturing industries that employed large numbers of full-time, male workers have reduced their workforces considerably. Some changes reflect longer-term structural shifts in the way employment is organised, brought about by a series of important developments, such as the spread of, and continuing innovation in information technology; global economic relationships; and deregulation of the labour market designed to enhance the competitiveness of British industry – issues that need not be explored here because again they are widely discussed elsewhere

(Beatson, 1995). However, some key consequences are that manufacturing jobs have fallen substantially and service jobs have grown; full-time work has fallen steadily since 1981 and part-time employment has grown. Even compared to 1991 there are already approaching a further million part-time jobs. Male employment has fallen and female employment has risen; self-employment has grown since 1981, and although it fell in the early 1990s it is growing again now, particularly part-time self-employment. While not shown in Table 4.1, temporary employment is also now growing and accounts for more than seven per cent of employment (Purcell, 1998). In short, it is forms of 'non-standard' or 'flexible' employment that have increased and it is also these forms of employment that are predicted to grow further into the next century (Dex and McCullogh, 1997).

Alongside the changing pattern of full-time/part-time employment, there are also developments in the form and use of employment contracts. There is evidence of an increase in the number of jobs where employees take responsibility for their own pension and insurance provision. Further, there are developments such as jobs that specify 'zero' hours work or, alternatively, 'annualised' hours, where employees do not know from one day to the next whether and what hours of work they will be offered, although in the case of annualised hours the total over the year is known. In various ways, these changes which aim to increase the flexibility and competitiveness of employers, transfer responsibilities and uncertainties from employers to employees. Thus there are inequalities in employment in relation to the terms and conditions that are offered. These developments are often summarised by the use of terms such as 'good' jobs and 'bad' jobs, or jobs in the 'primary' sector and jobs in the 'secondary' sector.

One other important aspect of the changing pattern of employment is a reduction in average employment durations and so a trend to a higher rate of job turnover. The average duration amongst the types of jobs that are growing is shorter than that found amongst full-time permanent jobs. Thus, in 1995, full-time self-employment had an average duration of three years, roughly half that of full-time permanent employment. Part-time self-employment and temporary employment averaged about 10 months. Equally, it is important to keep in mind that the majority of jobs remain full-time and permanent, many part-time jobs are permanent and there has been only a small reduction in the average duration of these forms of employment (Gregg and Wadsworth, 1995). While currently a minority of all labour market opportunities (see Table 4.2 below), nevertheless more flexible forms of employment are growing and, to the extent this trend continues, year on year the overall structure of labour market opportunities is changing. Further evidence for this shift comes from a consideration of the nature of vacancies in the labour market. For much of the 1990s, temporary and fixed term vacancies have predominated, although in 1997, this trend appeared to reverse with a higher proportion of vacancies being for permanent work.

Changes in the level of unemployment have also been pronounced since 1981, rising and falling before rising again in the late 1980s and early 1990s with the cycle of recession and recovery. Since the early 1990s officially recorded unemployment has fallen rapidly and in early 1998 stood at 6.4 per cent. Part of this fall is due to the economic recovery in the mid-1990s, but part is also a result of a substantial growth in economically inactive non-claimants (Green, 1998; Beatty *et al*, 1997); a stricter benefit regime, not least the introduction of the Job Seekers' Allowance, and a series of changes in the measurement of unemployment. However, the rate of decline of claimant based unemployment has been slowing (*Labour Market Trends*, 1988) and unemployment may be starting to edge upwards once again. There is also a socio-economic gradient with respect to unemployment. While unemployment remains concentrated amongst those in manual occupations, one feature of employment in the late 1980s and 1990s is that those in professional, managerial and other white-collar occupations are also at risk as seen in the recession of the early 1990s. Structural change has also contributed to a rise in unemployment, for example when organisations relocate their production (or suppliers) abroad because of cheaper labour costs (and so greater competitiveness and enhanced profits), or when technological change and/or overproduction result in wholesale redundancies as seen in the recent announcement of the closure of a number of microchip manufacturers in the UK.

Table 4.1 provides a snapshot of employment amongst individuals at a particular point in time. It cannot indicate the *incidence* of forms of employment; that is the number of people who over a period of time have had these different kinds of positions. However, studies that have looked at this issue have concluded, for example, that considerably in excess of 13 per cent of people have had a spell of self-employment because the rate of entry to and exit from self-employment has been increasing since 1980 (Eardley and Corden, 1996). Similarly, studies of the incidence of unemployment indicate that over any given period of time a higher percentage of people will have been unemployed than are suggested by the numbers claiming (or reporting unemployment) at any one date. For example, responses to the *British Social Attitudes Survey* indicate that 20 per cent of all respondents (individuals, as is the claimant count of the unemployed) have experienced one or more spells of unemployment at some time over the period 1991-1995 (Spencer, 1996). A recent omnibus survey of individuals showed that of those currently in employment (or self-employed for less than five years) 30 per cent had had one spell of unemployment in the last five years. Twelve per cent had been unemployed between two and four times over the same period and 1 per cent had had at least five spells of unemployment (Cebulla *et al*, 1998). There was also a considerable socio-economic gradient with more than half of manual workers reporting one or more spells of unemployment compared to a third of professional workers (the lowest incidence of any socio-economic group). Thus, the incidence of unemployment is higher than suggested by point-in-time figures and while manual workers are most at risk, the risk to professional workers is not insubstantial.

So, full-time permanent employment remains the norm but the distribution of forms of employment is changing. What are often referred to as 'riskier' forms of employment are growing and more people are likely to have been involved in a risk situation than the figures in Table 4.1 and the claimant figures on unemployment indicate.

The final issue in this section concerns the current relationship between forms of employment, unemployment and re-employment. Poorer jobs such as temporary or casual jobs have often been portrayed as entry or re-entry jobs, taken for example by young people, women returners or those leaving unemployment as a way of gaining a foothold in the labour market, but with the expectation of better employment in due course. However, as the balance of jobs moves slowly towards a higher proportion of 'flexible' opportunities, there is some evidence that this is less likely to be the case for unemployed people. Evidence from a recent study of more than 850 people, unemployed between late 1990 and 1992 who were then tracked until late 1995, showed that:

> ... *three in four of the jobs which unemployed people got were temporary, part-time, self-employed or at a substantially lower skill level than previously...[and that]...people were subsequently more likely to stick to the kind of job they initially entered, or else fall back into unemployment, than to move to a different and better job. This was particularly true of part-time employment* (White and Forth, 1998).

Thus, the changing pattern of employment, the growing risk of unemployment, and the likelihood of re-employment in particular types of jobs has the potential to trap a growing number of people in employment that is relatively poorly protected, likely to be poorly paid and relatively short-term. Those in permanent full-time employment are not immune from unemployment and low wages, but these risks are still *relatively* more limited, and the terms and conditions of employment *relatively* more advantageous.

Low wage employment

The average wage of all those in employment has risen year on year for many years. The average, however, masks some important trends in the distribution of income from employment, not least a growing polarity and in particular, the growth of low paid employment. Definitions of low pay vary. It might be defined as wages below the £3.60 National Minimum Wage, but another definition is that adopted by the Council of Europe which sets a 'decency' threshold, at two-thirds of male manual earnings. In 1996, the threshold was £239.16 per week. Defined in this way, there was an increase of over one million low paid jobs in Britain between 1982 and 1996 (Low Pay Unit, personal communication). In total, counting full and part-time jobs, over 10 million are low paid, approaching a third of all current employment. Table 4.2 shows the growth of low pay between 1982 and 1996 for men and women in full-time employment.

Table 4.2: Low pay in the UK: 1982-1996

	1982 millions	1988	1991	1992	1993	1994	1996
Women	2.75	2.91	2.92	2.8	2.72	2.71	2.73
Men	1.83	2.77	2.81	2.97	2.73	2.76	2.88
All	4.58	5.68	5.72	5.77	5.45	5.47	5.61

Source: Derived from the *New Earnings Survey* by the Low Pay Unit

Note: Earnings are for all workers on adult rates, excluding overtime

Low pay has traditionally been concentrated amongst women and in the service sector. Table 4.2 indicates that the proportion of men amongst low paid workers has increased. The distribution of low pay by tenure is considered in the section below along with some of the implications of this development for the relationship between housing and employment.

Employment status and tenure

Employment opportunities are not evenly distributed throughout society. Given the concerns of this chapter, this section considers the pattern of employment opportunities by tenure. Table 4.3 shows the distribution of forms of employment by tenure in 1997 amongst the economically active. Unlike the previous tables, Table 4.3 indicates the employment status of heads of households, rather than that of all individuals. When considering employment by tenure this makes more sense because it is households that are housed, although where appropriate, it is also interesting to consider household employment patterns (Dex and McCullogh, 1997; Pleace *et al*, 1998).

Table 4.3: Employment status of heads of households in, or seeking employment, by tenure Winter 1997/98

	Mortgagor Head of Household %	Renter Head of Household %	All[1] Head of Household %
Full-time permanent employee	76	51	67
Part-time permanent employee	3	12	6
Full-time self-employed	14	11	14
Part-time self-employed	1	5	2
Full-time temporary employee	3	2	3
Part-time temporary employee	1	1	1
Trainee or unpaid family worker	–	–	1
Unemployed	2	18	6

Source: *Labour Force Survey,* Winter (Dec 1997–Feb 1998)

1 In addition to mortgagors and renters this figure includes outright owners, shared owners, those living rent free and squatting

Table 4.3 indicates considerable employment inequality by tenure. Considering those who are economically active, while more than three-quarters of mortgagor heads of households are in permanent employment, more than one in five has a form of flexible employment with a further 2 per cent unemployed. A higher percentage of renters are in flexible employment (31 per cent), but a much higher percentage of them are unemployed and a much lower percentage are in permanent employment. Putting together forms of flexible employment and unemployment, these account for just under a quarter of mortgagor heads of household while just under half of renters' heads are in this position. Around 2.5 million mortgagor households are headed by someone not in permanent full-time employment; approximately 3.5 million households in the rented sectors are in a similar position.

There are also some differences in the distribution of the newer, flexible forms of employment between the two tenure groups. Compared to renters, a higher proportion of heads of home-buying households are in full-time self-employment, but a smaller proportion are part-time self-employed. Four per cent of mortgagor heads of household are in temporary employment; a slightly higher figure than for renters. Not surprisingly, given the entry criteria for home-ownership, and the traditional white-collar nature of owner-occupation, mortgagors are also more likely to be in permanent full-time work than renters and less likely to be unemployed, although as seen above there is a social class gradient to unemployment and professional heads of mortgagor households are only half as likely to be unemployed as manual worker heads of household.

Concentrating employment disadvantage

The relatively low percentage of renters currently in full-time employment and the high percentage unemployed has not always been the case. Table 4.4 indicates the changing distribution of employment by tenure from 1981 to 1996/97.

Given the earlier discussion on the changing balance of full and part-time employment, it is not too surprising to see that the percentage of households headed by someone in full-time employment has fallen in every tenure since 1981. The percentage of owner-occupier households unemployed in any year has varied slightly, but remained low. By contrast, the proportions of unemployed households in all rental tenures in each year has grown. All these proportions are, however, affected by other characteristics of households in the tenures, particularly the age distribution and so the number of retired households.

Statistics on total make-up of households also make it difficult to identify the extent to which, and how, the characteristics of those entering each tenure are changing year by year. To explore this, it is necessary to look at the employment characteristics of recently housed households. Table 4.5 shows these data.

Table 4.4: Employment status of household heads by tenure (%)

Year	Tenure	In employment:		All Employed	Unemployed	Retired	Other Inactive	Total
		Full-time	Part-time					
1981	Outright owners	37	4	42	3	44	12	100
	Home buyers	92	1	93	3	2	2	100
	Council renting	43	4	47	9	28	15	100
	Housing association	42	4	46	6	34	13	100
	Unfurnished private	51	4	56	4	30	11	100
	Furnished private	65	1	66	9	5	20	100
	All tenures	58	3	62	5	24	10	100
1991	Outright owners	26	6	32	3	58	7	100
	Home buyers	86	3	89	4	4	4	100
	Council renting	25	5	30	11	40	19	100
	Housing association	29	5	34	9	42	15	100
	Unfurnished private	54	5	59	6	28	8	100
	Furnished private	56	5	61	12	4	23	100
	All tenures	54	4	59	6	27	9	100
1995/96	Outright owners	24	7	30	2	62	7	100
	Home buyers	84	4	88	3	4	5	100
	Council renting	22	6	28	12	38	22	100
	Housing association	23	6	29	12	38	22	100
	Unfurnished private	50	7	56	9	20	14	100
	Furnished private	49	4	54	14	4	29	100
	All tenures	52	5	57	5	27	10	100
1996/97	Outright owners	24	6	30	2	62	6	100
	Home buyers	84	4	88	2	5	5	100
	Council renting	23	6	29	10	37	24	100
	Housing association	27	8	34	12	31	23	100
	Unfurnished private	53	7	60	8	19	14	100
	Furnished private	57	6	63	12	3	22	100
	All tenures	52	5	58	5	27	10	100

Sources: Housing trailers to the 1981 and 1991 *Labour Force Surveys, Survey of English Housing* 1995/96 and 1996/97.

Table 4.5: Employment status of recently moving households by tenure 1984-1996/7 (%)

Year	Tenure	In employment: Full-time	Part-time	All Employed	Unemployed	Retired	Other Inactive	Total
1984	Outright owner	31	5	36	9	31	19	100
	Buying with mortgage	94	1	95	3	–	2	100
	Council	29	5	33	24	17	26	100
	Housing association	40	12	52	16	12	10	100
	Private, unfurnished	74	4	77	11	3	11	100
	Private, furnished	52	4	56	16	1	28	100
	All tenures	64	3	67	11	7	14	100
1991	Outright owner	37	5	42	6	42	8	100
	Buying with mortgage	93	2	94	3	1	2	100
	Council	28	3	31	22	20	27	100
	Housing association	30	6	35	13	28	24	100
	Private, unfurnished	75	4	79	9	2	9	100
	Private, furnished	55	4	59	11	1	28	100
	All tenures	64	3	67	10	8	15	100
1995/96	Outright owner	32	8	40	2	49	9	100
	Buying with mortgage	92	3	95	2	2	2	100
	Council	26	6	32	22	15	32	100
	Housing association	21	6	27	19	20	34	100
	Private, unfurnished	58	7	65	15	2	17	100
	Private, furnished	50	4	54	12	1	33	100
	All tenures	58	5	63	11	8	18	100
1996/97	Outright owner	27	12	39	4	43	14	100
	Buying with mortgage	92	3	95	2	1	3	100
	Council	26	8	34	15	15	13	100
	Housing association	27	8	34	21	12	11	100
	Private, unfurnished	61	5	66	13	3	5	100
	Private, furnished	56	7	64	10	0	4	100
	All tenures	58	6	64	10	8	6	100

Source Housing trailers to the 1984 and 1991 *Labour Force Surveys, Survey of English Housing* 1995/96 and 1996/97

Table 4.5 indicates that, between 1984 and 1996/97, there was a decrease in the proportion of households entering the social housing sector (local authority or housing association) whose heads were employed either full or part-time. The drop is particularly marked for housing association tenants where, in 1984, 52 per cent of entrants were households with an employed head but only 34 per cent in 1996/7. The proportion of households with employed heads entering the private rented sector also fell, but more so in the unfurnished than the furnished sector. This relatively long-standing pattern, however, reversed in 1996/7 with a slight increase in the proportion of employed heads entering Registered Social Landlord (RSL) property and the furnished PRS sector. Over the period 1984-1996/7, however, there was no change in the proportion of employed entrants to the local authority sector which was a consistent 34 per cent, or amongst mortgagors where the figure was 95 per cent.

With respect to unemployment, the proportion of mortgagor households entering as unemployed has always been low and has fallen since the early 1990s. A higher percentage of unemployed households enter local authority property each year, but between 1984 and 1996/7, the percentage fell from 24 to 15 per cent. For housing associations, however, the increase was from 16 to 21 per cent according to the *Survey of English Housing* and even higher according to the CORE data on new lettings (Pleace *et al*, 1998). 1996/7 was the first year in which the proportion of unemployed entrants to RSLs exceeded the proportion of unemployed entrants to local authority property.

Taken together, the information in Table 4.5 points to growing concentrations of households headed by someone who was unemployed in the rented sectors and particularly in housing association property. It is these trends that contribute to the perception of social housing as a residualised sector, a term initially directed at just local authority housing but increasingly directed towards RSLs. If instead of considering just unemployed entrants, all households where the head is workless are considered (i.e. unemployed, retired or economically inactive), then in 1996/7, this was 6 per cent of mortgagors, 43 per cent of local authority entrants, 44 per cent of housing association entrants and 21 and 14 per cent of private rental entrants. Again, the potential concentration of disadvantage is clear.

One indicator of the extent of employment inequality is income from work. While there are low paid individuals and households in all tenure groups, there is also a clear pattern by tenure with lower than average pay a particular feature of social housing tenants. For example, in 1996/7, the average net weekly household income of working households in RSL property (principally housing associations) was £189 (below the 'decency' threshold noted above). Amongst households with one part-time worker it was £136 and £286 for households with two full-time workers (Pleace *et al*, 1998). Estimates of the average net income amongst all in-work mortgagor households indicate a figure roughly double that available to full-time, dual earner RSL households. These inequalities are not surprising given the recent history and role of social housing, and would probably have been less but for the open market expansion of owner-occupation on the one hand and the impact of low cost home-ownership schemes on the other which are used overwhelmingly by higher income households. Further, as will be discussed later, the higher proportion of unemployed households, plus the lower average incomes from work found in the social housing sector, have important implications for individuals, households and communities.

The changing pattern of labour market opportunities described above is one important influence on employment profiles by tenure, particularly, for example, generating some *similar* trends *across* tenure groups such as the (albeit unequal) increase in the incidence of part-time working or temporary employment across all tenures. However, many other factors interact with labour market change to play a critical role in shaping and maintaining some *differences* in the employment composition of tenures, for example the growing concentration of unemployed heads of households in social housing and particularly the RSL sector.

Accounting for these differences in the employment inequalities by tenure is a highly complex matter and the full range of influences and issues cannot be discussed in detail here. However, contributory factors are likely to include: the operation of the private housing market and the barriers to entry that operate there, of which unemployment is a major barrier; the impact of policies such as Right-to-Buy and other low cost home-ownership initiatives that are most likely to be taken up by in-work tenants (Forrest and Murie, 1988; Dunmore *et al*, 1997; Pleace *et al*, 1998); the extent of housing need and the nature of allocation policies (Maclennan and Kay, 1994; Ford *et al*, 1998); the relative costs of different forms of renting and of buying which are themselves variable geographically; the impact of rent setting policy and the level of rents in different tenures, and the availability and nature of state assistance with housing costs for those in different tenures. Thus, on top of differential exposure to unemployment, individuals in different tenures may find it more or less feasible to accept re-employment and retain new work. They may also find employment more or less difficult to come by. These issues are taken up in more detail below, primarily through a discussion of work disincentives.

Taking work? The impact of housing

Commitment to work

There has been a lively debate around the issue of whether or not unemployed people are committed to finding work. The arguments polarise around two main perspectives. One argues that unemployed people have a tendency to become socialised to non-work and to benefit dependency. Sometimes these ideas are put forward in terms of the development of an 'underclass' (Murray, 1990), although this is a highly contested concept. Supporters of this perspective, however, would argue that the development of spatial concentrations of unemployed people (by area or estate) is likely to support such a development. The second view argues that the commitment to work remains high amongst unemployed people, but structures and processes preclude their access to employment. These might include changes in industrial structures that remove employment from particular areas or from some occupational groups; attitudinal and discriminatory processes for example, if employers were opposed to recruiting unemployed people, but also processes and structures that create work disincentives such as might be associated with a lack of affordable child care provision.

Clearly, the idea of a culture of benefit dependency cannot be discounted completely, and it will always be possible to identify individuals and households who give this argument some credence. Notwithstanding this, the bulk of the studies examining attitudes and values with respect to work and employment strongly suggest that unemployed individuals and households remain committed to and keen to work (Gallie, 1994; Jordan, 1996). Thus, in policy terms, the emphasis has to be on understanding the obstacles to unemployed people finding employment and acting to minimise their effects.

Employment is central to many of the current government's policies designed to address both economic and social issues. Encouraging people from 'Welfare to Work' is perceived as critical, and the importance of this transition has been set out in relation to combating individual social exclusion as well as the exclusion of disadvantaged groups. Through the various forms of the 'New Deal', employment initiatives have an important role alongside both social interventions and infrastructure improvements in the regeneration of estates, areas and communities. However, as shown below, the existence of jobs alone is insufficient to be certain that work will be taken up. Amongst other things, housing costs have to be considered, not least because they form a substantial part of any household's budget.

Paying for housing; a work disincentive

Current policy provides for assistance with housing costs to both renters and mortgagors under certain clearly defined circumstances, although the provisions are not identical across the tenures. Irrespective of tenure, all unemployed households receive assistance with housing costs: social housing tenants in full; private rented sector tenants over the age of 25 in full with a reduced rate for the under 25s, but only mortgagors who are claiming Job Seekers' Allowance (JSA) receive help. For these people, mortgage interest can be paid in full, subject to a number of qualifying conditions which have been progressively tightened since 1989. Once in employment, only tenants are eligible for means-tested assistance with housing costs. Mortgagors receive no help whatsoever.

There is also a long-standing view that the system of housing benefits operates in such a way as to present individuals and households with disincentives to work.

These are due to the current relationship between wages, benefits and housing costs (Wilcox, 1994; Ford *et al*, 1996; Kempson *et al*, 1997), and they take the form of both an unemployment trap and a poverty trap. The former is where it may be disadvantageous for households to take up paid employment because their income would be little or no better in work than on benefit. This occurs for a range of reasons including the steep withdrawal of tenants' Housing Benefit (the taper), currently 65p for every additional pound earned above a threshold. For mortgagors, (where no help with housing costs accrues to those in work) the issue is one of being able to find a job with a wage that at least matches the combined amount of Income Support (or JSA) and the mortgage payment. Typically, this is likely to be a relatively well paid job. The poverty trap relates to the reluctance of those already in work to increase their hours of work and so earnings, again because of the steep withdrawal of benefits that results in their having to work substantially more hours in order to be 'better off' (Wilcox, 1994). The poverty trap applies primarily to tenants as in many instances the whole of any additional income earned by mortgagors is retained (except in some instances where there is a claim for Family Credit).

While the disincentive effects are clear in principle and the source of many discussions and proposals as to how they can be minimised, a key issue in this area concerns how individuals respond in practice to such situations – their behavioural response to work disincentives. The prevalent model for considering these relationships assumes first, that households make rational calculations about the ways in which any change faced will result in their being better or worse off and second, that households act in order to maximise income (Blundell, 1994). Only if they are financially 'better off' will they take a job or increase their hours of work. This perspective, however, has been questioned by a number of writers (McLaughlin, 1992; Millar, 1994; Ford *et al*, 1996).

In a small qualitative study of 40 tenant and mortgagor households where someone was either unemployed and seeking work or had recently taken employment, Ford *et al* (1996) identified three main patterns of decision making as indicated by the respondents themselves. These were where job seekers:

- made a 'better off' calculation and acted in accordance with the outcome;
- made a 'better off' calculation but then overrode it in terms of their subsequent actions, with non-economic variables informing their behaviour;
- did not make a 'better off' calculation at all. The decision to take employment or remain on benefit was informed by non-economic factors.

The first group was the largest, providing some support for the economistic perspective that underpins current policy. But while this group tried to make rational decisions, few had enough knowledge or understanding of the interactions between income, housing costs and benefits to make detailed or accurate calculations. The most frequent misapprehension found amongst tenants, was the belief that once in work they would assume responsibility for the full rent. Inevitably, this deepened the unemployment trap for these people by raising what they thought had to be their reservation wage. The second group, who formed around a quarter of respondents, undertook 'better off' calculations (sometimes accurately and sometimes not) but then overrode the calculations. Typically they worked for less than they had been receiving while unemployed. The third group, made up of non-calculators, were often in this position because their income was 'irrelevant' in terms of benefit calculations; for example, where any contribution from partners of working mortgagor heads of household added *in full* to the household income and did not affect the partner's income.

The research also showed that decision making was frequently influenced by non-economic factors or only indirectly financial variables such as very positive attitudes to work, the concern for high quality child care, negative attitudes towards the bureaucratic nature of the social security system and in some cases a dislike of claiming whilst in work. The range of pertinent influences and the ultimate decisions made were also variable by household structure.

Whilst there is only a limited amount of empirical work on the behavioural response to work disincentives, other studies offer some general support for the direction of the conclusions noted above. For example, there is more quantitative evidence of mortgagors working, yet being 'worse off' than on benefits. In the mid-1990s there were approximately 600,000 mortgagor households in work but with incomes below that available through Income Support (Wilcox, 1994). Several other studies have noted that while the provision of child care will encourage some to take employment, others parents express a preference for providing their own child care rather than taking employment irrespective of the costs or the income available. However, while some studies have highlighted the role that non-financial matters play in the type of employment taken, particularly by women, others have given equal prominence to the extent to which households may require all members to maximise their earnings.

Labour market trends and work disincentives

Several aspects of current labour market developments are likely to worsen the impact of the disincentives outlined above either because they result in more households being drawn into the benefit orbit or more being retained on benefit for longer periods of time. For example, the growth of low paid employment noted above has increased the number of tenant households at risk of work disincentives by increasing the number of in-work, low income households able to claim benefits. The percentage of new housing association tenants each year who are in work and in receipt of at least some Housing Benefit has increased from 27 per cent in 1989/90 to 48 per cent in 1996/7. (Although not the focus of this chapter, it needs to be noted that rising rents have similar effect.) Low income employment may also contribute to mortgagors remaining unemployed and in receipt of Income Support for Mortgage Interest (ISMI) because the wage offered for many jobs, if taken, would not meet their housing and living costs. Amongst those mortgagors who opt to work for less than their 'true' reservation wage, the growth of low wage work increases the likelihood of in-work mortgage arrears (Ford, 1989; 1998).

Disincentive effects may also be created as a result of a poorly structured interaction between administrative rules relating to the receipt of benefits and a labour market characterised by a growth of shorter duration jobs, casualised jobs and an increase in unemployment and job mobility. Thus, a benefit such as Housing Benefit that requires tenants to notify to the Housing Benefit office all changes of circumstance, and requires the re-calculation of benefit entitlement on a change by change basis, is poorly adapted to developments such as casual work, zero hours contracts or short-term contract work. Potential recipients of in-work benefits may then respond either by forgoing any entitlement to in-work assistance with housing costs or by being unwilling to take such employment. In the first case, in-work poverty and rent arrears may be the outcome, while in the second the social and economic poverty and isolation of unemployment are potential consequences.

Unemployment and access to employment

The discussion above has assumed that the availability of jobs and employment is not an issue. In practice it often is, but again this is on a variable basis, both between regions and areas and within them. But where there are jobs, given the evidence already presented that, for example, unemployed households cluster in social housing, and other studies which indicate clustering by areas (Green and Owen, 1997) and on estates (Power and Tunstall, 1995; Social Exclusion Unit, 1998b), it is interesting to consider whether employers' attitudes, preferences and beliefs about 'places' or 'areas' come into play in allocating work.

There is a large body of evidence that indicates employer discrimination by social characteristics, including unemployment itself. But here the issue is whether concentrations of unemployed households – or unemployment places – convey negative messages to local employers, about the attitudes, reliability, suitability and acceptability of people living in those places. This might then minimise the likelihood that people from areas of high unemployment will gain employment. This process is often referred to as 'addressism'. To the extent that this occurs, and alongside the current profile of entrants to social housing, the existing inequalities with respect to employment by tenure will continue to grow.

This too is a substantial issue that has not yet received the attention it warrants. With respect to the 1990s, only anecdotal and/or indirect evidence exists. Wrench *et al* (1996), for example, reported that young Bangladeshi people perceived 'addressism' to be at work, and other surveys of job seekers, have reported similar views (Fieldhouse, 1996). But direct evidence of 'addressism' will be necessary to remove the possibility that such respondents are, in fact, reporting rationalisations for their rejection from jobs determined on other grounds. Interestingly, there is also an emerging discussion that unemployed people too restrict their job search, believing that employers discriminate against people from 'their area'.

Finally, there is rather more evidence that concentrations of unemployed households are disadvantaged in searching for employment because an increasing proportion of vacancies are notified informally through existing workers (Ford *et al*, 1987; Bottomley *et al*, 1997). Being connected to these people through informal social networks is therefore essential, but less and less likely where areas are characterised by unemployed people. This is more likely to be the case in some social housing areas than amongst areas of home-ownership and lends support to the argument that potentially mixed tenure areas carry significant social, employment and economic advantages.

Conclusion

The above discussion has primarily been concerned to set out briefly the recent and ongoing nature of labour market change and to discuss some of its relationships to housing and particularly tenure. It has raised as many questions about the way in which housing and employment relate as it has answered. It has, however, indicated that many employment inequalities are systematically distributed by tenure and that housing costs and the different ways of paying for housing are one important component in individuals' and households' ability to take and sustain employment. The chapter has not been concerned explicitly with the policy implications of the developing relationships and outcomes of labour market change for housing, but they are important, not just to government but also to housing managers, to those seeking to regenerate areas and address social exclusion and to those seeking employment. The implications relate, for example, to the nature of structures and processes that need to be in place if both home-owners and tenants are to make and sustain the move from Welfare to Work, and to the form of allocation and letting policies in social housing that will encourage the development of more areas in which those seeking work do not become isolated or their contact limited only to other unemployed people. There are also implications for administrative as well as substantive reforms of the benefit system. Further, there is evidence that detailed and systematic research is needed into the role of place in employers' recruitment and selection policies and practices.

CHAPTER 5:
Hitting the target? Area disadvantage, social exclusion and the geography of misery in England

Roger Burrows and David Rhodes

Introduction

The emphasis given to the concept of social exclusion in contemporary social policy debates has led to renewed interest in the mechanisms by which disadvantaged areas are identified. It is already apparent that the targeting of socio-economic resources towards particular places will be a central feature of future policy responses to poverty and its consequences. However, as has been well rehearsed, the identification of disadvantaged areas is not always a simple matter. The perception one gains of the geography of poverty is highly sensitive to the measurement tools used. As has recently been noted (Dorling, 1996; Lee *et al*, 1995; Philo, 1995), contemporary policy makers and social researchers in Britain are now confronted with a confusing plethora of such measures. In addition to 'official' scales of deprivation such as the *Index of Local Conditions* (DoE, 1995; Robson *et al*, 1995) we have others vying for our attention such as the *Jarman Index* (Jarman, 1983), the *Townsend Index* (Townsend, 1987; Townsend *et al*, 1988) and the *Breadline Britain Index* (Gordon and Forrest, 1995; Gordon and Pantazis, 1997; Mack and Lansley, 1985; Lee and Murie, 1997).

Although the *construction* of these various measures can be a matter of much technical complexity, the *choice* of which measure to use is anything but academic. The use of one measure of area disadvantage over another in the targeting of social spending can, on occasion, lead to very different outcomes in that the rank order of deprivation scores varies significantly between indices (Lee *et al*, 1995 pp39-56). Following Dorling (1996), we are strongly of the view that to be of any use to those working on issues of social exclusion, the existing work on indices of area deprivation must be supplemented with new data. In particular, we need to know if the areas identified as being disadvantaged by existing indices are the same areas which would be identified as such by the people who live in them. In essence, this chapter asks whether the map of neighbourhood squalor generated by the use of existing indices is the same as that which results if one pays close and systematic attention to what residents are saying about their local environments?

But how could this be done? Inspired by Dorling (1996), this chapter demonstrates that it is possible to use national level data in order to identify what types of people express high levels of dissatisfaction with their localities and then use this information, in conjunction with the census, in order to identify what Dorling terms 'areas of misery'. (Fuller details of this analysis can be found in Burrows and Rhodes 1998).

Patterns of area dissatisfaction amongst residents in England

The *Survey of English Housing* (SEH) (the details of which can be found in Green *et al* (1996)) contains a number of questions about the perceptions that people have of their neighbourhoods. These questions were asked of heads of households (HoH) or, if they were not available, their partners (if any). If either the HoH or their partner was not available for interview the questions were not asked. The term 'householder' is used to refer to the respondents who provided answers to these questions.

The *SEH*, following on from the earlier *Housing Attitudes Survey* (Hedges and Clemens, 1994), contains a large number of questions which are relevant to any analysis of residents' perceptions of their neighbourhoods (Green *et al*, 1996, Chapter 3). In the analysis which follows we have selected 17 different questions all of which relate to some aspect or other of a very general conceptualisation of area dissatisfaction. The full set of questions, with the key dimensions of potential sources of dissatisfaction italicised, are shown in Figure 5.1.

Figure 5.1: Questions concerned with area dissatisfaction in the Survey of English Housing 1994/95

- How *satisfied generally* are you with this area as a place to live?
- Generally speaking, how *secure* do you feel when you are inside your home?
- On the whole, would you describe the people who live in this area as *friendly*, or not?
- Is *vandalism and hooliganism* a problem in your area?
- Is *graffiti* a problem in your area?
- Is *crime* a problem in your area?
- Are *dogs* a problem in your area?
- Is *litter and rubbish* in the streets a problem in your area?
- Are *neighbours* a problem in your area?
- Is *racial harassment* a problem in your area?
- Is *noise* a problem in your area?
- How good or bad do you think your area is for *schools*?
- How good or bad do you think your area is for *public transport*?
- How good or bad do you think your area is for *street lighting*?
- How good or bad do you think your area is for *rubbish collection*?
- How good or bad do you think your area is for *leisure facilities*?
- How good or bad is the *general appearance* of your area?

Table 5.1 shows that the most widespread source of high levels of area dissatisfaction relate to the issue of crime. Over one-fifth of respondents perceived crime to be a major problem in their area. Other major sources of area dissatisfaction which impact on over 10 per cent of households were: problems with dogs; poor leisure facilities; high levels of vandalism; and litter and rubbish in the streets. Over 5 per cent of households reported high levels of dissatisfaction with public transport; graffiti, noise, and poor street lighting. Just under 5 per cent of households were generally highly dissatisfied with their neighbourhoods. Over 2 per of households reported widespread problems with the general appearance of the area, the behaviour of neighbours, and poor local schools. Over 1 per cent of households reported severe problems associated with: poor rubbish collection; feelings of insecurity when inside their homes; unfriendliness in their neighbourhood; and racial harassment.

Table 5.1: Rank order of sources of area dissatisfaction

Problem/Issue	Rank order	Percentage who perceive as a major problem or issue
Crime	1	21.6
Dogs	2	16.3
Leisure facilities	3	15.3
Vandalism and hooliganism	4	14.0
Litter and rubbish	5	12.9
Public transport	6	8.6
Graffiti	= 7	6.1
Noise	= 7	6.1
Street lighting	= 7	6.1
Generally unsatisfied	10	4.9
General appearance	11	4.0
Neighbours	12	3.9
Schools	13	2.4
Rubbish collection	14	1.9
Security	15	1.3
Unfriendliness	= 16	1.1
Racial harassment	= 16	1.1

It would clearly be helpful to have some sort of summary measure able to encapsulate all the various dimensions of neighbourhood dissatisfaction within one index. There are a number of different ways of constructing such an index, all of which have advantages and disadvantages, and we have experimented with a number of different procedures. We are fortunate that our data appear to be resistant to different scaling and index construction procedures, in the sense that the conclusions that one reaches about which households are, and which households are not, highly dissatisfied with their areas remain remarkably stable, independently of which procedure is adopted. For this reason we have decided to adopt a simple counting procedure in order to construct a scale of area dissatisfaction. We have taken our 17 questions and counted the number of times each householder has rated a problem as very serious. This results in a simple scale running from a low of '0' (no problems or issues in the area considered to be very serious) to a possible high of '17' (all problems or issues in the area considered to be very serious). The frequency distribution of responses which results is shown in Table 5.2.

Table 5.2: Number of problems or issues identified as being very serious by householder

Number of problems or issues relating to the area identified as serious	Number of households (000s)	Percentage	Cumulative percentage
0	8473	44.0	44.0
1	4859	25.2	69.3
2	2690	14.0	83.2
3	1353	7.0	90.3
4	765	4.0	94.3
5	492	2.6	96.8
6	297	1.5	98.4
7	133	0.7	99.0
8	70	0.4	99.4
9	59	0.3	99.7
10	28	0.1	99.9
11	18	0.1	100.0
12	6	0.0	100.0
13	2	0.0	100.0
14	2	0.0	100.0
Total	19246	100.0	

Forty four per cent of householders reported no problems or issues which they considered to be very serious relating to their areas. Just over 25 per cent reported one problem that they considered to be very serious. Another 14 per cent identified two problems and 7 per cent identified three problems. This means that just over 90 per cent of households identified 3 or fewer problems or issues that they considered to be serious in their neighbourhoods and just under 10 per cent of households identified four or more serious problems or issues with their area. In the spirit of keeping the operationalisation of area dissatisfaction as clear and as simple as possible we consider the 10 per cent of households who perceive that they have four or more serious problems or issues with their area as being unambiguously dissatisfied with their areas.

Using this simple measure of area dissatisfaction we are able to see which demographic and socio-economic characteristics of households are most strongly associated with high levels of area dissatisfaction. Table 5.3 shows the percentage of households with differing characteristics who perceive that they face four or more serious problems or issues in their area. The broad patterns may be summarised as follows:

- households living in urban areas are more likely to be dissatisfied than households living in rural or semi-rural areas;
- households living in the northern regions of England and also in London are more likely to be dissatisfied than households living in the rest of England;
- households living in flats are more likely to be dissatisfied than households living in houses. Of householders living in houses, those living in terraces are more dissatisfied than those in semi-detached accommodation who in turn are more likely to be dissatisfied than those living in detached accommodation;
- in relation to tenure, those living in social housing are the most likely to be dissatisfied, followed by those living in the private rented sector (PRS). Amongst owner-occupiers, those with a mortgage are more likely to be dissatisfied than outright owners;
- patterns of high levels of area dissatisfaction also possess a very clear social class gradient. Using the standard classification of the Registrar General, households in social class I are the least likely to be dissatisfied and those in social class V are the most likely to be dissatisfied with their areas;
- there is also a strong association with current economic status. Those who are retired or employed full-time are the least likely to be dissatisfied whilst those who are economically inactive or unemployed are the most likely to be dissatisfied;
- patterns of dissatisfaction are also strongly related to age. Younger householders are significantly more likely to be dissatisfied than older ones;
- patterns of area dissatisfaction are also associated with ethnicity. Those who identify themselves as Pakistani or Bangladeshi are more likely than those who identify themselves as white, black or Indian to be dissatisfied with their areas;
- finally, there is clear variation across household type. In particular lone parents are significantly more likely than other household types to be dissatisfied, and the highest of all the different groups examined.

Table 5.3: Proportion of different types of household who express high levels of area dissatisfaction

Socio-demographic characteristics		Proportion scoring 4 or more	Number of households (000s)
All		9.7	19198
Region	London	14.0	2699
	South East	5.9	2898
	South West	5.8	1995
	Eastern	5.3	2309
	East Midlands	7.9	1540
	West Midlands	10.4	2017
	Yorks & Humber	10.8	2038
	North East	18.1	980
	North West	12.9	2764
Urban/rural	Rural	6.6	996
	Semi-rural	6.1	2320
	Urban	10.4	15930
Type of accommodation	Detached house	4.1	3904
	Semi detached house	7.8	6114
	Terraced house	12.4	5453
	Flat etc	15.0	3727
Tenure	Outright owner	6.2	4626
	Mortgagor	7.1	8280
	PRS	10.4	4407
	Social housing	18.0	1932
Social class of HoH	I	4.5	1351
	II	7.1	5048
	IIIN	10.1	2780
	IIIM	10.9	5295
	IV	12.5	2800
	V	14.0	1063
	Other	10.3	909
Age of HoH	16-44	11.4	8235
	45-64	10.2	6053
	65+	6.3	4958
Current economic status of HoH	Employed full-time	8.3	9964
	Employed part-time	12.0	887
	Unemployed	20.8	1189
	Retired	6.1	5226
	Other inactive	18.6	1967
Ethnicity of HoH	White	9.7	18319
	Black	9.5	329
	Indian	9.3	242
	Pakistani/Bangladeshi	13.0	136
	Other	10.4	216
Household structure	Couple, no dep. children	8.5	7002
	Couple, with dep. children	9.1	4694
	Lone parent	22.2	1101
	Large adult household	8.8	1183
	Single male	11.1	2241
	Single female	8.3	3024

Disentangling the socio-demographics of area dissatisfaction

In order to disentangle which combination of variables gives us the greatest purchase on explaining variations in high levels of area dissatisfaction, we use a method known as segmentation modelling. This is a statistical technique that is useful in any situation in which the overall goal is to divide a population into segments that differ with respect to some designated criteria – in this case whether a householder is highly dissatisfied with their area or not. The technique divides a population into two or more groups based on categories of the 'best' predictor of a dependent variable. It then splits each of these groups into smaller subgroups based on other predictor variables. This splitting process continues until no more statistically significant predictor variables can be found. The technique displays the final subgroups, or segments, in the form of a conceptually tidy and analytically useful tree diagram.

The analysis carried out on our SEH data on patterns of area dissatisfaction is shown in Figure 5.2. The analysis begins with the total sample at the top of the diagram. As we have already seen, overall some 9.7 per cent of householders are classified as being dissatisfied with their area on our measure. The procedure first considers which of the variables under consideration is the most strongly correlated with variations in the proportions of those who are dissatisfied. This turns out to be housing tenure. As there is no significant variation in area dissatisfaction amongst those who are outright owners and those who are mortgagors these two categories are collapsed leaving just three categories. The next line of the diagram thus shows that the 9.7 per cent of the total population who were dissatisfied can be split into three main subgroups. Amongst outright owners and mortgagors 6.8 per cent were dissatisfied, amongst those living in the PRS 10.4 per cent were dissatisfied, and amongst those living in social housing 18.0 per cent were dissatisfied. The procedure considers which of the remaining variables best predicts significant differences in area dissatisfaction within each of these different housing tenure subgroups.

Home-owners

Amongst outright owners and mortgagors, the variable which best differentiates variations in area satisfaction is the type of accommodation in which the household lives. Owners living in detached houses were the least likely to be dissatisfied with their neighbourhoods; in total just 3.8 per cent were dissatisfied. However, the analysis shows that this proportion varies significantly across social class. Amongst those in non-manual occupations the proportion is just 3.2 per cent whilst amongst those in manual occupations it is significantly higher at 5.8 per cent. No other variables significantly differentiate these proportions.

Figure 5.2: CHAID analysis of predictors of area dissatisfaction, first split by housing tenure

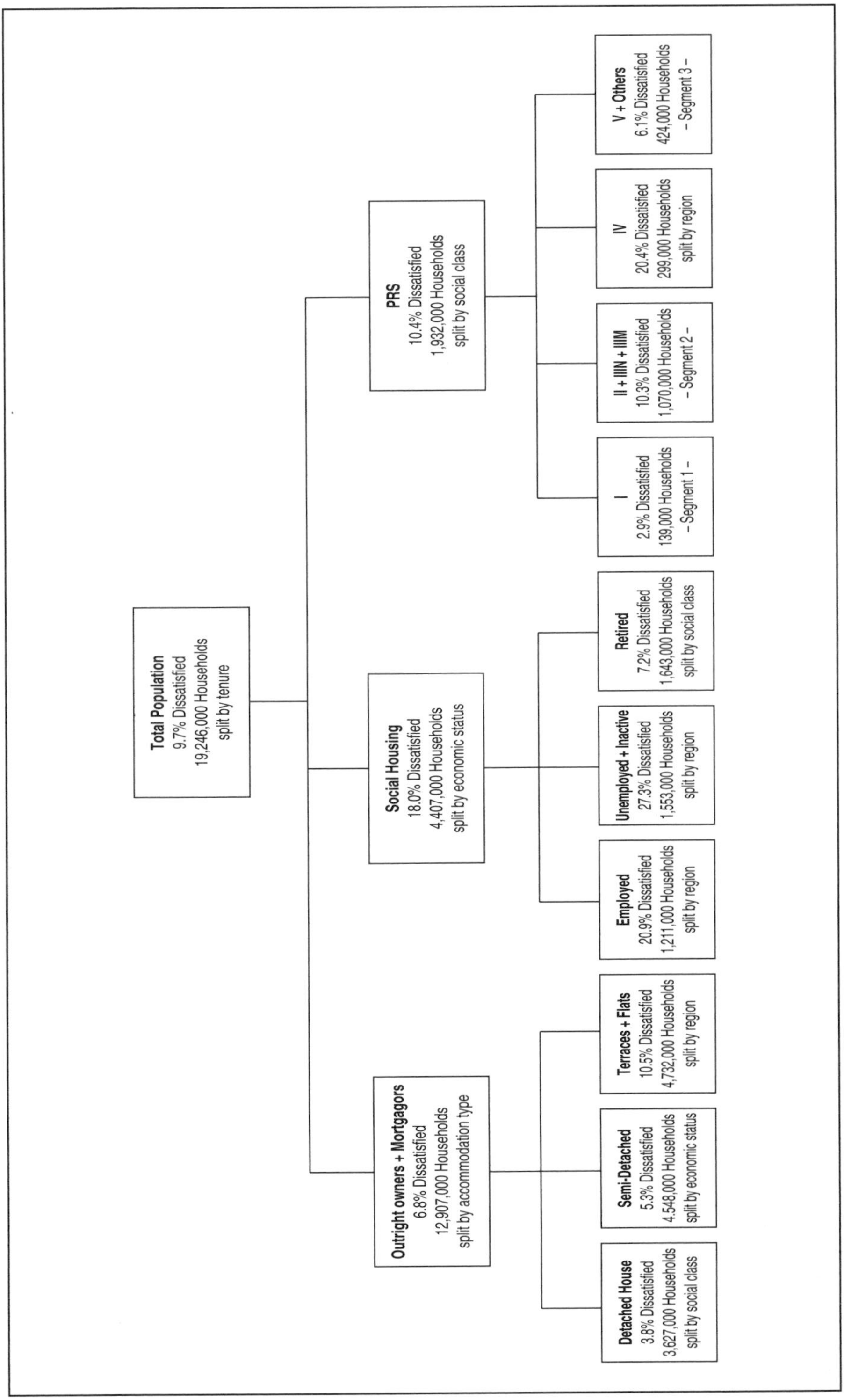

Total Population
9.7% Dissatisfied
19,246,000 Households
split by tenure

Outright owners + Mortgagors
6.8% Dissatisfied
12,907,000 Households
split by accommodation type

Social Housing
18.0% Dissatisfied
4,407,000 Households
split by economic status

PRS
10.4% Dissatisfied
1,932,000 Households
split by social class

Detached House
3.8% Dissatisfied
3,627,000 Households
split by social class

Semi-Detached
5.3% Dissatisfied
4,548,000 Households
split by economic status

Terraces + Flats
10.5% Dissatisfied
4,732,000 Households
split by region

Employed
20.9% Dissatisfied
1,211,000 Households
split by region

Unemployed + Inactive
27.3% Dissatisfied
1,553,000 Households
split by region

Retired
7.2% Dissatisfied
1,643,000 Households
split by social class

I
2.9% Dissatisfied
139,000 Households
– Segment 1 –

II + IIIN + IIIM
10.3% Dissatisfied
1,070,000 Households
– Segment 2 –

IV
20.4% Dissatisfied
299,000 Households
split by region

V + Others
6.1% Dissatisfied
424,000 Households
– Segment 3 –

Figure 5.2 continued: CHAID analysis of predictors of area dissatisfaction amongst those living in the private rented sector: class split by region

PRS
10.4% Dissatisfied
1,932,000 Households
split by social class

I
2.9% Dissatisfied
139,000 Households
– Segment 1 –

II + IIIN + IIIM
10.3% Dissatisfied
1,070,000 Households
– Segment 2 –

IV
20.4% Dissatisfied
299,000 Households
split by region

V + Others
6.1% Dissatisfied
424,000 Households
– Segment 3 –

London + Yorks & Humber + NE + NW
34.8% Dissatisfied
118,000 Households
– Segment 17 –

Rest of England
11.0% Dissatisfied
181,000 Households
– Segment 18 –

Figure 5.2 continued: CHAID analysis of predictors of area dissatisfaction amongst outright owners and mortgagors; detached houses split by social class; semi-detached houses split by economic status; and terraced houses and flats split by region

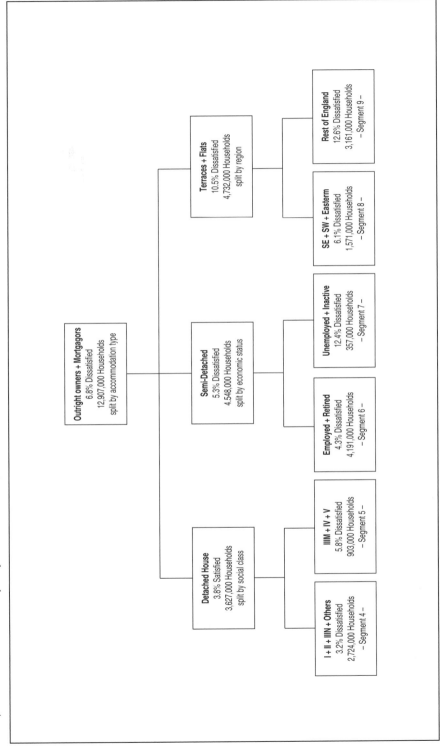

Outright owners + Mortgagors
6.8% Dissatisfied
12,907,000 Households
split by accommodation type

Detached House
3.8% Satisfied
3,627,000 Households
split by social class

Semi-Detached
5.3% Dissatisfied
4,548,000 Households
split by economic status

Terraces + Flats
10.5% Dissatisfied
4,732,000 Households
split by region

I + II + IIIN + Others
3.2% Dissatisfied
2,724,000 Households
– Segment 4 –

IIIM + IV + V
5.8% Dissatisfied
903,000 Households
– Segment 5 –

Employed + Retired
4.3% Dissatisfied
4,191,000 Households
– Segment 6 –

Unemployed + Inactive
12.4% Dissatisfied
357,000 Households
– Segment 7 –

SE + SW + Eastern
6.1% Dissatisfied
1,571,000 Households
– Segment 8 –

Rest of England
12.6% Dissatisfied
3,161,000 Households
– Segment 9 –

Figure 5.2 continued: CHAID analysis of predictors of area dissatisfaction amongst those living in social housing: employed split by region; unemployed and inactive split by region; and retired split by social class

Social Housing
18.0% Dissatisfied
4,407,000 Households
split by economic status

Employed
20.9% Dissatisfied
1,211,000 Households
split by region

Unemployed + Inactive
27.3% Dissatisfied
1,553,000 Households
split by region

Retired
7.2% Dissatisfied
1,643,000 Households
split by social class

SE+SW+Eastern+E.Midlands
14.0% Dissatisfied
494,000 Households
– Segment 10 –

Rest of England
25.6% Dissatisfied
717,000 Households
– Segment 11 –

NE
42.4% Dissatisfied
142,000 Households
– Segment 12 –

London+Yorks+Humber+NW
29.6% Dissatisfied
839,000 Households
– Segment 13 –

Rest of England
20.0% Dissatisfied
572,000 Households
– Segment 14 –

I + Others
0.0% Dissatisfied
133,000 Households
– Segment 15 –

All other social classes
7.9% Dissatisfied
1,510,000 Households
– Segment 16 –

Amongst households living in semi-detached houses, 5.3 per cent were dissatisfied with their neighbourhoods. However, the analysis shows that this proportion varies significantly not across social classes, as was the case above, but by current economic status. Amongst those currently employed (full-time or part-time) or retired the level of area dissatisfaction runs at just 4.3 per cent. However, amongst those currently unemployed or otherwise economically inactive the proportion is almost three times greater than this at 12.4 per cent. No other variables significantly differentiate these proportions.

Amongst households living in terraced houses or in flats there were no significant differences in levels of area dissatisfaction, with 10.5 per cent being dissatisfied with their neighbourhood. However, the analysis shows that this proportion differs significantly across the regions of England. In the south of England outside of Greater London the proportion of householders who were outright owners or mortgagors living in terraces or flats dissatisfied with their areas is just 6.1 per cent. However, in the rest of England the figure for householders with the same combination of attributes is over double this at 12.6 per cent.

Thus, the analysis reveals that although those in the owner-occupied sector were likely to be the least dissatisfied with their neighbourhoods overall, this masks very wide patterns of variation within the tenure. Within this tenure those from non-manual social classes living in detached houses were, not surprisingly perhaps, the households which were the least likely to express high levels of dissatisfaction with their locality. Outright owners and mortgagors living in terraced houses or flats in London or outside of the South East, the South West and the Eastern regions, were the most likely to express dissatisfaction. This pattern illustrates the extent to which owner-occupation has become a tenure which is increasingly socially differentiated (Ford and Burrows, 1999).

Private rented sector

Amongst those living in the PRS the variable which gives the greatest purchase on variations in area dissatisfaction within the tenure is social class. The PRS is known to be a highly differentiated tenure (Bevan and Sanderling, 1996; Bovaird *et al*, 1985; Carey, 1995; Crook and Kemp, 1996) with huge disparities in both rent levels (Rhodes and Kemp, 1997) and in the quality of accommodation – ranging from the luxurious down to the pitifully inadequate. We might expect this variation in the sector to be reflected in some quite stark variations in levels of area dissatisfaction amongst PRS tenants, and this proves to be the case. Amongst those living in the PRS and located in social class I, levels of dissatisfaction were very low at just 2.9 per cent. It is likely that these households live, for the most part, in high rent, high quality accommodation in pleasant neighbourhoods. No other variables significantly differentiate these proportions.

Households in the PRS located in social classes II, IIIN and IIIM show much higher levels of area dissatisfaction. Amongst this subgroup 10.3 per cent express high levels of dissatisfaction with their neighbourhood. No other variables significantly differentiate between these subgroups. Households in the PRS located in social class IV were even more likely to be dissatisfied with their neighbourhoods. Amongst this subgroup 20.4 per cent express high levels of dissatisfaction – a proportion almost twice as great as amongst those in social classes II, IIIN and IIIM. Further, this level of dissatisfaction can be shown to vary greatly across different regions of England. In London, Yorkshire and Humberside, the North East and the North West the proportion expressing high levels of dissatisfaction is over one third whilst in the rest of England the proportion is less than half of this at 11.0 per cent. No other variables significantly differentiate between these subgroups. Amongst households in the PRS located in social class V or who could not be classified within the class schema used here, the proportion expressing high levels of dissatisfaction with their area was lower at 6.1 per cent.

Those in the PRS were, in general, more likely (10.4 per cent) to be dissatisfied with their neighbourhoods than were those living in the owner-occupied sector (6.8 per cent). Further, as we shall see below, they were also less likely to be dissatisfied with their neighbourhoods than households living in social housing (18.0 per cent). However, these findings mask very wide patterns of variation within the tenure. Some subgroups in the PRS express levels of dissatisfaction lower than those found anywhere in the owner occupied sector, whilst other subgroups express levels of dissatisfaction as high as those found amongst those living in social housing.

Social housing

Amongst those living in social housing, the variable which gives the greatest purchase on variations in area dissatisfaction is current economic status. Amongst employed (full-time and part-time) householders, levels of area dissatisfaction run at 20.9 per cent. However, this proportion varies significantly across the regions of the country. In the South East, the South West, the Eastern region and the East Midlands the proportion is significantly lower at 14.0 per cent than it is for the rest of the country. Outside of these regions, levels of area dissatisfaction amongst those living in social housing who were employed is over one quarter.

Levels of area dissatisfaction amongst householders living in social housing where the head of household is either unemployed or economically inactive under retirement age were significantly greater than for those households where the head is employed. Overall 27.3 per cent express high levels of area dissatisfaction. This already high proportion is also revealed to vary significantly across the regions of England. In the North East the figure is the highest for any of the subgroups identified in the analysis. Amongst households living in social housing where the head is either unemployed or economically inactive under retirement age, over 42 per cent express high levels of dissatisfaction with their neighbourhoods. Levels of dissatisfaction were also higher than they were nationally for such households living in London, Yorkshire and Humberside and the North West. Amongst this subgroup just under 30 per cent express high levels of dissatisfaction with their areas. In the other regions of England exactly one-fifth of households in this subgroup express high levels of dissatisfaction with their areas.

Levels of area dissatisfaction amongst households living in social housing where the head of household has retired were significantly lower than for other groups in the tenure. In general just 7.2 per cent of such households express high levels of dissatisfaction. This figure is also significantly associated with differences in the social class backgrounds of such household heads. For the great majority of the subgroup, levels of area dissatisfaction run at 7.9 per cent. However, for a very small subgroup of retired households headed by someone who could not be classified using the social class schema or from a social class I background, levels of area dissatisfaction were so low that they were practically non-existent. Close examination of this group reveals that it is predominantly made up of single women aged over 65 who have lived in the local authority sector for many years and who were either widowed or have never married. In general this group tends to possess positive views about the quality of both their accommodation and their neighbourhoods.

Table 5.4 shows the final 18 segments which result from the analysis, whereby there were no further statistically significant differences in levels of area dissatisfaction to be found. The 18 categories have been ranked according to the level of estimated householder dissatisfaction with their neighbourhood.

The geography of misery

We have applied the probabilities of area dissatisfaction for each of our 18 segments to population data at ward level from the 1991 census (obtained via a specially commissioned table supplied to us by the Office for National Statistics (ONS)). For each ward in England we have examined how many households in each of our 18 segments reside in the ward. This enabled us to estimate the mean level of area dissatisfaction in the ward as a whole. A full listing of our estimates of levels of area dissatisfaction for all of the wards in England is precluded because of considerations of space. However, readers who require a full listing can obtain one by downloading an SPSS portable file from the Centre for Housing Policy web site at the University of York (<<http://www.york.ac.uk/inst/chp/misery.htm>>).

Table 5.4: Rank order of area dissatisfaction subgroups

Rank	Characteristics of subgroup					% Dissatisfied with area	% of all households in England	Number of households in England (000s)
	Housing tenure	Regions	Economic status of HoH	Social class of HoH	Accommodation			
1	Social housing	NE	Unemployed or inactive	Any	Any	42.4	0.74	142
2	PRS	London + YH + NE + NW	Any	IV	Any	34.8	0.61	118
3	Social housing	London + YH + NW	Unemployed or inactive	Any	Any	29.6	4.36	839
4	Social housing	London + WM + YH + NE + NW	Employed	Any	Any	25.6	3.73	717
5	Social housing	SW + SE + E + EM + WM	Unemployed or inactive	Any	Any	20.0	2.97	572
6	Social housing	SW + SE + E + EM	Employed	Any	Any	14.0	2.57	494
7	Owner-occupiers	London + WM+ EM + YH + NW + NE	Any	Any	Terraced house or flat	12.6	16.42	3161
8	Owner-occupiers	Any	Unemployed or inactive	Any	Semi-detached house	12.4	1.85	357
9	PRS	SW + SE + E + EM + WM	Any	IV	Any	11.0	0.94	181
10	PRS	Any	Any	II + IIIN + IIIM	Any	10.3	5.56	1070
11	Social housing	Any	Retired	II + IIIN + IIIM + IV +V	Any	7.9	7.85	1510
=12	PRS	Any	Any	V + Others	Any	6.1	2.20	424
=12	Owner-occupiers	SW + SE + E	Any	Any	Terraced house or flat	6.1	8.16	1571
14	Owner-occupiers	Any	Any	IIIM + IV + V	Detached house	5.8	4.69	903
15	Owner-occupiers	Any	Employed + retired	Any	Semi-detached	4.3	21.78	4191
16	Owner-occupiers	Any	Any	I + II + IIIN + Others	Detached house	3.2	14.15	2724
17	PRS	Any	Any	I	Any	2.9	0.73	139
18	Social housing	Any	Retired	Others + I	Any	0.0	0.69	133

Perhaps the most insightful way of describing the distribution of high levels of area dissatisfaction at the ward level is by making use of an ONS system of area classification. This clusters wards together into a set of exhaustive and mutually exclusive categories differentiated in terms of *groups* and *clusters* of different types of ward. Table 5.5 shows the estimated levels of area dissatisfaction for each group and cluster. The highest levels of area dissatisfaction are estimated to occur in Inner City Estates – those in London in particular – Liddle in Southwark and Evelyn in Lewisham are prime examples. Next, come Deprived Industrial Areas, especially those marked by heavy industry – Pallister and Thorntree in Middlesbrough are examples. Third, come wards characterised as Deprived City Areas – those in inner London in particular. Fourth, come Industrial Areas, those involved in primary production in particular. Fifth, come Lower Status Owner-Occupied wards – those dominated by Miners' Terraces in particular. Sixth, come wards dominated by Metropolitan Professionals – especially those with large numbers of young single people.

Ward level estimates can of course be aggregated to produce district level estimates. Table 5.6 shows the rank ordering of local authority area districts beginning with those with the highest proportion of householders who we estimate will be dissatisfied with their areas. This listing of districts can be interpreted in a number of ways. It shows marked concentrations of high levels of area dissatisfaction in both inner London and the North East with slightly lower intensities of dissatisfaction in the urban North West and some urban areas of Yorkshire and Humberside.

Perhaps the easiest way to 'frame' this distribution of high levels of area dissatisfaction at a district level is by again utilising the ONS classification, this time of local authorities, into different *families*, *groups* and *clusters* (Wallace and Denham, 1996). Table 5.7 has used this classification in order to calculate estimat-ed mean levels of area dissatisfaction for each subgroup of local authorities.

Table 5.7 shows that Inner London has the highest proportion of dissatisfied householders – almost 15 per cent. The family of districts which have the second highest levels of area dissatisfaction are those associated with mining and industry. Within this family the group of districts associated with ports and industry have higher levels of area dissatisfaction than do districts within the family associated with the coalfields. The cluster of districts within the ports and industry group marked by high concentrations of social housing, display levels of area dissatisfaction matched only by London Inner City Boroughs – districts such as Sunderland and Middlesbrough. Not surprisingly, amongst coal mining areas, those districts where the mines have now closed display significantly higher levels of area dissatisfaction than do those districts where the mines are still in operation.

Table 5.5: Estimated mean levels of the proportion of HoHs who are dissatisfied with their areas by the ONS classification of wards – groups and clusters

Groups		Groups %	
	Clusters		Clusters %
1	**Inner City Estates**	**17.96**	
	London public housing		18.09
	High-rise housing		17.38
2	**Deprived Industrial Areas**	**15.57**	
	Heavy industry		17.04
	Ethnic groups in industry		13.68
3	**Deprived City Areas**	**14.55**	
	Inner London		15.59
	Low amenity housing		14.79
	Cosmopolitan London		13.90
4	**Industrial Areas**	**12.07**	
	Better off manufacturing		11.54
	Growth points		11.70
	Traditional manufacturing		10.87
	Primary production		13.48
5	**Lower Status Owner-occupation**	**10.58**	
	Declining resorts		9.51
	Industrial towns		9.91
	Textile towns terraces		10.71
	Margins of deprivation		11.57
	Miners terraces		13.65
6	**Metropolitan Professional**	**10.16**	
	Urban achievers		9.73
	Young singles		11.17
7	**Middling Britain**	**8.90**	
	Small towns		8.36
	West Midlands manufacturing		8.49
	Expanding towns		9.19
	Mixed economies		9.26
8	**Suburbia**	**7.63**	
	Leafier suburbs		7.05
	Classic commuters		8.35
9	**Mature Populations**	**6.84**	
	Coastal very elderly		5.61
	Remoter retirement areas		6.65
	Better off retired		7.06
	Retirement areas		8.12
10	**Rural Fringe**	**6.80**	
	Edge of town		6.67
	Industrial margins		6.68
	Town and country		7.09
11	**Rural Areas**	**6.72**	
	Agricultural heartland		6.68
	Accessible countryside		6.64
	Remoter coast and country		7.06
12	**Transient Populations**	**6.56**	
	Transient populations		6.56
13	**Established Owner-occupied**	**5.96**	
	Green belt		5.74
	Outer suburbs		6.12
14	**Prosperous Areas**	**5.68**	
	Concentrations of affluence		5.07
	Established prosperity		5.68
	Affluent villages		5.95

Table 5.6: Rank ordering by levels of area dissatisfaction of 'districts'

Rank	District	%	Rank	District	%	Rank	District	%
1	Tower Hamlets	17.54	62	Pendle	11.06	123	South Lakeland	8.92
2	Islington	17.14	63	Croydon	11.06	124	Harlow	8.86
3	Hackney	17.09	64	St. Helens	11.04	125	Cleethorpes	8.85
4	Southwark	16.87	65	Wakefield	11.03	126	Northampton	8.77
5	Easington	16.52	66	Barrow in Furness	11.02	127	Nuneaton & Bedworth	8.76
6	Sunderland	15.99	67	Preston	10.95	128	Dudley	8.76
7	Lambeth	15.96	68	Teesdale	10.89	129	Warwick	8.71
8	South Tyneside	15.57	69	Hyndburn	10.86	130	East Yorkshire	8.69
9	Newham	15.27	70	Leeds	10.81	131	East Staffordshire	8.65
10	Middlesbrough	14.95	71	Rotherham	10.76	132	Isles of Scilly	8.64
11	Newcastle upon Tyne	14.83	72	Richmond upon Thames	10.71	133	Boothferry	8.60
12	Wear Valley	14.81	73	Coventry	10.69	134	Newcastle under Lyme	8.54
13	Lewisham	14.76	74	Bolton	10.66	135	Stockport	8.51
14	Camden	14.74	75	Bradford	10.66	136	North Warwickshire	8.47
15	Gateshead	14.53	76	Sandwell	10.64	137	Hambleton	8.45
16	Hammersmith & Fulham	14.49	77	Birmingham	10.55	138	High Peak	8.40
17	Barking & Dagenham	14.38	78	Calderdale	10.50	139	Ribble Valley	8.37
18	Greenwich	14.37	79	Rossendale	10.48	140	Norwich	8.36
19	Haringey	14.35	80	Sutton	10.45	141	Harrogate	8.33
20	Sedgefield	14.30	81	Tynedale	10.44	142	Fylde	8.33
21	Derwentside	14.16	82	Doncaster	10.40	143	Macclesfield	8.32
22	Hartlepool	14.09	83	Wigan	10.36	144	Rugby	8.32
23	Kensington & Chelsea	14.00	84	Barnet	10.26	145	Bolsover	8.32
24	Manchester	13.99	85	Carlisle	10.22	146	Cannock Chase	8.26
25	Wansbeck	13.91	86	Hillingdon	10.22	147	Derby	8.20
26	Knowsley	13.86	87	Blackpool	10.19	148	Holderness	8.19
27	Kingston upon Hull	13.85	88	Kirklees	10.05	149	Wychavon	8.13
28	Westminster,City of	13.76	89	Scarborough	10.00	150	Wellingborough	8.11
29	Liverpool	13.47	90	Hereford	9.98	151	Stevenage	8.08
30	Wandsworth	13.46	91	Castle Morpeth	9.94	152	Oswestry	8.06
31	North Tyneside	13.33	92	West Lancashire	9.93	153	Solihull	8.04
32	Blyth Valley	13.31	93	Walsall	9.92	154	Beverley	8.03
33	City Of London	13.30	94	Wolverhampton	9.91	155	Selby	8.02
34	Waltham Forest	13.01	95	Havering	9.87	156	Chesterfield	8.00
35	Chester-le-Street	12.87	96	Ellesmere Port & Neston	9.85	157	Ryedale	7.98
36	Berwick upon Tweed	12.70	97	Wirral	9.81	158	Mansfield	7.94
37	Langbaurgh-on-Tees	12.69	98	Bexley	9.78	159	Glanford	7.93
38	Brent	12.59	99	Leicester	9.74	160	Ashfield	7.93
39	Durham	12.52	100	Stoke on Trent	9.73	161	Wyre	7.93
40	Ealing	12.43	101	Redditch	9.70	162	Wyre Forest	7.92
41	Halton	12.42	102	Warrington	9.68	163	Shrewsbury & Atcha	7.90
42	Salford	12.32	103	Corby	9.67	164	Bromsgrove	7.76
43	Stockton on Tees	12.27	104	Kingston upon Thames	9.67	165	Stratford on Avon	7.74
44	Hounslow	12.23	105	Nottingham	9.63	166	Kettering	7.73
45	Merton	12.14	106	Bury	9.58	167	South Ribble	7.71
46	Blackburn	11.97	107	Bromley	9.54	168	Stafford	7.68
47	Alnwick	11.93	108	Sefton	9.48	169	Cambridge	7.66
48	Enfield	11.93	109	Richmondshire	9.47	170	Oxford	7.62
49	Rochdale	11.57	110	Eden	9.43	171	Bassetlaw	7.57
50	Darlington	11.48	111	Harrow	9.39	172	Crawley	7.57
51	Copeland	11.37	112	Trafford	9.37	173	Bristol	7.57
52	Oldham	11.34	113	The Wrekin	9.29	174	Southampton	7.55
53	York	11.22	114	Tamworth	9.24	175	Bridgnorth	7.55
54	Burnley	11.21	115	Chester	9.23	176	South Shropshire	7.54
55	Great Grimsby	11.19	116	Crewe & Nantwich	9.23	177	Plymouth	7.48
56	Sheffield	11.16	117	Lincoln	9.22	178	East Northamptonshire	7.47
57	Tameside	11.16	118	Lancaster	9.16	179	North Shropshire	7.46
58	Barnsley	11.15	119	Worcester	9.16	180	Malvern Hills	7.42
59	Redbridge	11.14	120	Vale Royal	9.11	181	Amber Valley	7.38
60	Scunthorpe	11.13	121	Craven	9.01	182	Leominster	7.38
61	Allerdale	11.07	122	Chorley	8.95	183	North East Derbyshire	7.38

Table 5.6: Rank ordering by levels of area dissatisfaction of 'districts' – contd.

Rank	District	%	Rank	District	%	Rank	District	%
184	Thurrock	7.36	245	Eastbourne	6.57	306	Purbeck	6.09
185	North West	7.34	246	Salisbury	6.55	307	North Devon	6.08
186	Leicestershire	7.34	247	Melton	6.52	308	South Oxfordshire	6.08
187	Lichfield	7.33	248	South Northamptonshire	6.52	309	East Cambridgeshire	6.08
188	Ipswich	7.32	249	Taunton Deane	6.51	310	Stroud	6.07
189	Boston	7.31	250	Hertsmere	6.50	311	Kingswood	6.07
190	Portsmouth	7.28	251	Thanet	6.49	312	Guildford	6.05
191	Slough	7.23	252	South Holland	6.46	313	Forest of Dean	6.05
192	Erewash	7.23	253	Gillingham	6.45	314	Canterbury	6.04
193	Newark & Sherwood	7.19	254	Southend on Sea	6.44	315	Suffolk Coastal	6.04
194	Welwyn Hatfield	7.19	255	Cotswold	6.44	316	South Hams	6.03
195	Congleton	7.18	256	Cherwell	6.44	317	Runnymede	6.03
196	South Kesteven	7.16	257	Tunbridge Wells	6.43	318	Woking	6.03
197	Peterborough	7.15	258	Broxbourne	6.42	319	Windsor & Maidenhead	6.00
198	Basildon	7.15	259	Tonbridge & Malling	6.41	320	Worthing	5.99
199	Brighton	7.11	260	South Bedfordshire	6.41	321	Wycombe	5.98
200	South Staffordshire	7.11	261	North Bedfordshire	6.40	322	Northavon	5.97
201	Bath	7.06	262	Harborough	6.38	323	Vale of White Horse	5.96
202	Milton Keynes	7.06	263	Mid Devon	6.37	324	Reigate & Banstead	5.96
203	Watford	7.05	264	North Kesteven	6.37	325	Uttlesford	5.96
204	West Lindsey	7.03	265	Mendip	6.36	326	Chelmsford	5.96
205	Daventry	7.02	266	Maidstone	6.32	327	Teignbridge	5.95
206	Derbyshire Dales	7.01	267	Shepway	6.31	328	Tewkesbury	5.94
207	Reading	7.01	268	Test Valley	6.31	329	Horsham	5.93
208	South Derbyshire	6.99	269	King's Lynn & West	6.30	330	Blaby	5.93
209	Exeter	6.99	270	Norfolk	6.30	331	Wansdyke	5.91
210	Luton	6.98	271	Epping Forest	6.30	332	Mid Suffolk	5.90
211	Staffordshire Moorlands	6.97	272	Aylesbury Vale	6.28	333	South Cambridgeshire	5.87
212	Charnwood	6.91	273	Colchester	6.28	334	Brentwood	5.87
213	Dacorum	6.90	274	South Somerset	6.28	335	South Wight	5.86
214	South Herefordshire	6.89	275	North Wiltshire	6.26	336	East Devon	5.86
215	Gosport	6.88	276	Three Rivers	6.26	337	Lewes	5.86
216	Bracknell Forest	6.88	277	Restormel	6.25	338	Poole	5.86
217	Rutland	6.85	278	Chichester	6.24	339	East Hampshire	5.84
218	North Hertfordshire	6.85	279	North Cornwall	6.23	340	Waverley	5.83
219	Kennet	6.81	280	East Hertfordshire	6.22	341	Eastleigh	5.82
220	Havant	6.79	281	West Dorset	6.20	342	Woodspring	5.81
221	Gravesham	6.78	282	Waveney	6.20	343	West Devon	5.80
222	Gedling	6.78	283	Adur	6.20	344	Tandridge	5.77
223	Broxtowe	6.77	284	St.Albans	6.20	345	Elmbridge	5.77
224	Hastings	6.75	285	Sedgemoor	6.19	346	Mid Sussex	5.76
225	Dartford	6.75	286	Mid Bedfordshire	6.18	347	Maldon	5.76
226	Gloucester	6.74	287	Medina	6.18	348	Mole Valley	5.75
227	Great Yarmouth	6.71	288	Sevenoaks	6.17	349	South Bucks	5.71
228	Thamesdown	6.71	289	Torbay	6.17	350	Arun	5.67
229	Rochester upon Medway	6.70	290	Caradon	6.16	351	South Norfolk	5.67
230	East Lindsey	6.70	291	Bournemouth	6.16	352	Tendring	5.66
231	Rushmoor	6.67	292	North Norfolk	6.16	353	Chiltern	5.65
232	St.Edmundsbury	6.66	293	Fenland	6.14	354	Epsom & Ewell	5.62
233	Penwith	6.66	294	Huntingdonshire	6.13	355	Rother	5.59
234	Swale	6.66	295	Babergh	6.13	356	New Forest	5.57
235	Weymouth & Portland	6.65	296	Torridge	6.13	357	Rochford	5.57
236	Hove	6.62	297	Rushcliffe	6.13	358	Fareham	5.56
237	Ashford	6.61	298	Winchester	6.13	359	Broadland	5.53
238	Forest Heath	6.61	299	Newbury	6.12	360	Hart	5.47
239	Basingstoke & Dean	6.61	300	Breckland	6.11	361	Castle Point	5.46
240	Cheltenham	6.60	301	Spelthorne	6.11	362	Wealden	5.46
241	Braintree	6.58	302	North Dorset	6.10	363	Christchurch	5.45
242	Hinckley & Bosworth	6.58	303	Kerrier	6.10	364	Surrey Heath	5.41
243	Oadby & Wigston	6.57	304	West Somerset	6.10	365	Wokingham	5.24
244	Dover	6.57	305	West Wiltshire	6.10	366	East Dorset	5.16

Table 5.7: Estimated mean levels of the proportion of HoHs who are dissatisfied with their areas by the ONS classification of local authorities - families, groups and clusters

Families
  Groups
    Clusters
	Families %
	  Groups %
	    Clusters %		

Inner London	**14.73**		
Inner London		14.73	
Cosmopolitan outer boroughs			*13.59*
Central London			*13.96*
Inner city boroughs			*16.76*
Newham and Tower Hamlets			*16.40*
Mining and industrial areas	**12.16**		
Ports and industry		13.54	
Areas with inner city characteristics			*14.12*
Coastal industry			*13.96*
Concentrations of social housing			*16.76*
Coalfields		11.33	
Mining and industry, England			*10.29*
Former mining areas, Durham		14.63	
Urban centres	**9.17**		
Mixed economies		7.56	
Established service centres			*7.16*
New and expanding towns			*7.60*
Manufacturing		10.32	
Pennine towns			*10.69*
Areas with large ethnic minorities			*10.04*
Maturer area	**7.86**		
Services and education		9.37	
University towns			*7.16*
Suburbs			*10.77*
Resort and retirement		6.68	
Traditional seaside towns			*7.03*
Smaller seaside towns			*5.68*
Rural areas	**7.40**		
Coast and country		7.08	
Remoter England			*7.28*
Heritage coast			*6.54*
Accessible amenity			*7.12*
Mixed urban and rural		8.46	
Towns in country			*6.71*
Industrial margins			*8.21*
Prospering areas	**6.17**		
Growth areas		6.94	
Satellite towns			*7.62*
Growth corridors			*6.19*
Areas with transient populations			*10.04*
Metropolitan overspill			*7.25*
Market towns			*6.87*
Most prosperous		6.08	
Concentrations of prosperity			*5.44*
Established high status			*7.16*

The third highest family of districts are those associated with large Urban Centres. However this family differs across its two groups of districts. Those in manufacturing areas display significantly higher levels of dissatisfaction than do those in mixed economies and within this the Pennine Towns cluster displays similar levels of area dissatisfaction to the districts of mining and industrial cluster in the Mining and Industrial Areas family.

The final three families of districts – Maturer Areas, Rural Areas and Prospering Areas – display overall significantly lower levels of area dissatisfaction. However, within these families there are some clusters of districts which possess mean levels of area dissatisfaction which are similar to those found in clusters contained within the top three families. In particular districts located within maturer areas within the services and education group and the suburbs cluster – areas such as Croydon for example – show levels of area dissatisfaction running at almost 11 per cent. Even some clusters of districts within the prospering areas family and the growth areas group show levels of area dissatisfaction into double figures. Areas with transient populations – such as Cherwell for example – are estimated to have mean levels of area dissatisfaction at about 10 per cent.

The analytic status of the geography of misery

This geography of misery is of course entirely synthetic. By this we mean that the probabilities of area dissatisfaction estimated for each ward in England are not based upon data collected from real people in those wards. Rather, the estimate is based on national level patterns of area dissatisfaction, and the data on population characteristics in each ward are used to estimate what the level of dissatisfaction would be *if* the national level figures operate uniformly. This method of estimation means that no allowance has been made for cultural factors. We have been forced to assume that differences in attitude are primarily a function of economic forces. In reality of course this is a dangerous assumption to make. We know from contemporary cultural studies (Featherstone, 1995), and from the new cultural geography (Urry, 1995; Watson and Gibson, 1995; Westwood and Williams, 1997), that the cultural sphere has always possessed a powerful efficacy in the determination of individual attitudes and beliefs, and also in the formation and 'feel' of places.

Our geography of misery is then best thought of as (what sociologists would call) an 'ideal typical' construct. Our estimates are for the pattern of area dissatisfaction which would pertain if spatial variations in attitude were simply a function of demographic and socio-economic variations over space, and if any cultural differences over and above those related to demographic and socio-economic variations did not exist. The accuracy (or otherwise) of our estimates are, however, something which can be explored empirically.

The geography of misery and the geography of area disadvantage: a comparison

We are now in a position to be able to take our estimates of levels of area dissatisfaction at ward level and compare them with some of the more common scales of area disadvantage. An exhaustive description, critique and comparison of a wide range of scales has already been undertaken by Lee *et al* (1995). Here we limit ourselves to a consideration of just a subset of the scales considered by Lee and his colleagues: the DoE 1991 *Index of Local Conditions*; the *Townsend Index*; and the *Breadline Britain Index*. We have limited ourselves to a systematic comparison with these three scales as they represent perhaps the three most commonly utilised measures in both the policy and the social research literature.

Our conclusions are that it is the *Breadline Britain Index which is most strongly associated with our measure of area dissatisfaction* and the DoE Local Conditions Index which is the least strongly associated with our measure. Variations in the *DoE Index* can – at best – account for only about 54 per cent of the ward based variation in levels of area dissatisfaction. The strength of the association is stronger if one uses the *Townsend Index* – it is possible to account for 68 per cent of the variation using this measure. However, it is the *Breadline Britain Index* which is most clearly associated with variations in levels of area dissatisfaction – it is possible to 'explain' over 70 per cent of the variation in ward level differences in area dissatisfaction by regressing on the *Breadline Britain Index*. It follows that *if one is interested in identifying areas where there are likely to be high levels of area dissatisfaction amongst residents then, of the available indices, it is the Breadline Britain measure which does the best job and the DoE Local Conditions measure which is the least adequate for this purpose.*

Concluding comment

The concept of neighbourhood dissatisfaction which has been the focus of our work is, of course, a problematic construct, not least because it will always be a function of both objective realities and sometimes highly variable subjective evaluations of these realities. However, we are not overly concerned about this mixing of objective and subjective spheres because, as Wilkinson (1996) has recently demonstrated, our health and well-being is as strongly influenced by our perceptions of material phenomena as by the material phenomena itself. For instance, *feelings* of insecurity and/or *fear* of crime can be just as damaging to us as their actuality.

Nevertheless, even if our measure of neighbourhood dissatisfaction is a complex amalgam of objective and subjective elements we have shown that it is profoundly and starkly socially and spatially patterned. It has a decipherable epidemiology (relating to a range of socio-economic and demographic variables) and, correspondingly, we suggest that it has a clear geography. What though are the substantive implications of an analysis of housing and social exclusion?

First, it is clear that householders experiencing the deprivations associated with high levels of dissatisfaction with their neighbourhoods are not only located within the social rented sector – problematic neighbourhoods are also experienced by home-owners and households living in the PRS. Consequently any area regeneration targeting of the 'worst estates' will miss a significant proportion of households living in what they perceive to be squalid neighbourhoods – on this point our analysis strongly concurs with the conclusions of Lee and Murie (1997). In particular, the 118,000 households living in the PRS in London, Yorkshire and Humberside, the North East and the North West headed by someone from a social class IV background (ranked at number 2 in Table 5.4) are a group who demand urgent investigation. We estimate that almost 35 per cent of these households will be highly dissatisfied with their neighbourhoods – a proportion significantly higher than that found amongst the great majority of households living in the social rented sector. Also worth noting are the high proportion of home-owners towards the 'bottom end' of the owner market who express high levels of dissatisfaction with their neighbourhoods (ranked at positions 7 and 8 in Table 5.4). Owner-occupiers living in terraced houses or flats in all areas of England except the South East, the South West and East Anglia (some 3.161 million households), and owner-occupiers living in semi-detached houses with a HoH who is unemployed or inactive (some 357,000 households) are estimated to possess levels of neighbourhood dissatisfaction of above 12 per cent – significantly higher than the national average of about 10 per cent.

Second, our analysis suggests that the geography of misery in England most clearly corresponds to the map of poverty generated by the *Breadline Britain Index* and is most weakly associated with the perception of the spatial distribution of poverty one gains when using the *DoE Index of Local Conditions*. The policy implications of this are clear. If one were to be guided by our geography of misery, rather by any of the existing indices of area disadvantage (but especially the *DoE Index of Local Conditions*), when targeting social resources, then some areas (in the North East of England in particular) would fare much better than is currently the case.

CHAPTER 6:
Social exclusion: the case of homelessness

David Clapham and Angela Evans

The sight of a rough sleeper bedding down for a night in a shop doorway or on a park bench is one of the most potent symbols of social exclusion in Britain today. Tony Blair, in a foreword to the Social Exclusion Unit's report on Rough Sleeping, July 1998, Social Exclusion Unit (1998a).

Introduction

To say homelessness causes social exclusion is a little like saying that poverty creates disadvantage. The relationship is such an obvious one that it seems to render analysis unnecessary. With rough sleeping, in particular, the evidence of lives lived on the margins is there for all to see – no bed, let alone home comforts, no family support, exclusion from mainstream services and a life of considerable physical adversity.

There is extensive research evidence highlighting the range and extent of disadvantage experienced by homeless people more generally, not just those living on the streets, but those without a settled home of their own. For example, it is more difficult for homeless people to find and keep a job and to get qualifications and training. They frequently feel socially isolated and their physical and mental health is often adversely affected. Those on the street face even greater dangers – they are vulnerable to drug and alcohol abuse and crime and run a high risk of serious illness and premature death. The acute problems experienced by rough sleepers is one of the main reasons why rough sleeping was selected as an early priority for the government's Social Exclusion Unit set up in December 1997. The unit's report on rough sleeping, published in July 1998, outlines a package of preventative and responsive measures which aim to reduce the number of people sleeping rough by two-thirds by 2002 (Social Exclusion Unit, 1998a).

Although there is clearly a strong relationship between homelessness and the range of disadvantages we associate with social exclusion, the connections can be complex. Most importantly, homelessness does not just create social exclusion, it is also a consequence of it. Homelessness can blight almost anybody's life, but it is far more likely to happen if a person is already socially and economically disadvantaged. The demographics of homelessness are also the demographics of poverty. For example, unemployed people, lone parents, and those from black and minority ethnic populations are significantly over-represented amongst homeless people. Of course, not everyone who is poor becomes homeless – the problem arises when someone on a low income also lacks a family home or support and is unable to secure other accommodation, either because they lack priority for social housing[1] or have inadequate purchasing power in the private sectors. A cocktail of circumstances is then often involved, but poverty is the common denominator.

In this chapter we examine, first, the different ways in which various socio-economic disadvantages give rise to homelessness and, second, the ways in which the experience of being homeless intensifies the social exclusion of those involved. The Chapter concludes by outlining how an understanding of these different interrelationships is essential if responses to the problem of homelessness are to be effective and sustainable.

Routes into homelessness

Homelessness has many different explanations and manifestations. The very different circumstance of homeless people, and their often hidden situations, makes it difficult to construct a panoramic and dynamic view of the problem. Our knowledge is based largely on snapshots of specific groups in specific circumstances – for example, rough sleepers, those living in hostels or bed and breakfast hotels and people approaching advice agencies. In spite of these different perspectives, the findings of these studies are remarkably consistent. People who become homeless are significantly more likely than average to be socially and economically disadvantaged. Homelessness is not a problem that strikes the population at random. Disadvantaged groups such as lone parents, black and minority ethnic people, care-leavers and those leaving prison are particularly vulnerable, although their routes into and ways through homelessness may vary. The evidence that exists on the over-representation of these groups amongst homeless people is outlined briefly below.

Black and minority ethnic groups

A number of studies have clearly shown that black and minority ethnic people are significantly over-represented amongst homeless groups. Despite making up only 6 per cent of the national population, studies have shown that black and

---

1   The legislation governing homelessness and access to housing across the UK is not explored in depth in this chapter, but has been widely debated in earlier publications, notably Burrows, Pleace and Quilgars (1997) and Hutson and Clapham (1999). Readers who are not familiar with the homelessness and housing allocations procedures contained in the Housing (Scotland) Act 1987 and the Housing Act 1996 (for England and Wales) should consult these, and other relevant sources.

minority ethnic people make up between a tenth and a quarter of homeless people. The proportion varies with the samples studied. For example, the proportion of rough sleepers from minority ethnic groups is typically low at around 5 per cent or less, but disproportionately high numbers live in temporary accommodation such as hostels and bed and breakfast hotels and apply to statutory and voluntary agencies for help:

- 12 per cent of Shelter's clients in 1997/98 were black or from a minority ethnic group (Shelter, 1998);
- A Centrepoint survey of young people who approached homeless agencies in England and Northern Ireland during 1994/95 found that over two-fifths of those who applied were from black or minority ethnic groups, while in London the proportion was much higher at 54 per cent (Centrepoint, 1996);
- 19 per cent of single homeless people living in hostels and bed and breakfast accommodation in ten local authority areas in England were black or from a minority ethnic group (Department of the Environment, 1993b);
- A quarter of homeless applicants to nine local authorities in 1992/93 were black (16 per cent), Asian (4 per cent) or from another minority ethnic group (5 per cent). In London the proportion from minorities rose to over half (52 per cent) (Department of the Environment, 1996).

Lone parents

Lone parents are similarly over-represented amongst homeless people. The fact that they are usually eligible for rehousing under the homelessness legislation means that they are more likely to show up in official statistics. Whilst lone parents with dependent children represent just 7 per cent of the general population[2], surveys of homeless applicants have found much higher proportions:

- 40 per cent of homeless households who had been placed in temporary accommodation by local authorities in England in 1988 were lone parents and a further 2 per cent were single women who were pregnant (Department of the Environment, 1989a);
- Over a quarter (27 per cent) of all homeless applicants to nine local authorities in 1992/93 were lone parents while a further 5 per cent were single and pregnant (Department of the Environment, 1996).

Young people leaving care

Young people leaving care are particularly vulnerable to homelessness. Surveys have found that between a fifth and a half of young homeless people have been in

---

2   Office for National Statistics (1997) *Living in Britain: Results from the 1996 General Household Survey*, London: HMSO.

care and that care-leavers are particularly over-represented amongst those
sleeping rough or living in temporary accommodation:

- The Social Exclusion Unit's report on rough sleeping estimates that
  between a quarter and a third of rough sleepers have been looked after
  by local authorities as children (Social Exclusion Unit, 1998a);
- A survey of young homeless people in London found that a half had
  run away from a previous care arrangement, with a third having done
  so on more than nine occasions (Craig et al, 1993).

Given that only 1 per cent of all children and young people under the age of 18
have been in care, it is clearly the case that care-leavers are much more likely
to become homeless than other young people.

Ex-prisoners

Ex-prisoners often experience serious problems obtaining both housing and
employment. Many are unable to sustain tenancies while they are in prison,
while for others homelessness is the consequence of relationship breakdown.

- A quarter of single homeless people in temporary accommodation,
  and almost half of people sleeping rough, had been in prison or a
  remand centre (Anderson, Kemp and Quilgars, 1993);
- A national survey of prisoners found that 40 per cent expected to be
  released to no fixed abode (Home Office, 1992)[3];
- A small-scale study of 61 ex-prisoners undertaken in 1995 found that
  38 (62 per cent) lost their accommodation when they came out of
  prison (Carlisle, 1996).

Economic disadvantage

Although it would be wrong to suggest that these groups have a pathological
tendency towards homelessness, there is little doubt that they share a range of
social and economic disadvantages, which exposes them more to the dangers
of homelessness. For example, they are more likely to be living in poor
housing conditions. While minority ethnic households have a generally high
level of home-ownership, the quality of their accommodation is often poor.
Around 30 per cent of Pakistani and 47 per cent of Bangladeshi families live in
overcrowded conditions compared with just 2 per cent of white families. These
groups also lack the resources to be able to buy their way out of their housing
difficulties. Unemployment rates are typically high and incomes low.
Similarly, one third of lone parents live in 'absolute poverty' (defined as £175
per household per week), compared with 20 per cent of the population as a

---

3   Reported in Carlisle, J. (1996), The Housing Needs of Ex-prisoners, Centre for Housing
     Policy, University of York.

whole[4]. The unemployment and poverty rates for black people are also above average. For example, unemployment rates for black and other minority ethnic groups have been roughly twice that of white people since 1984 (CPAG, 1996). Young people leaving care are similarly disadvantaged, around half are unemployed compared with 15 per cent of young people more generally (Broad, 1993).

Social disadvantage

Family support often provides a buffer against adversity. By providing support in the form, for example, of accommodation, child care and financial help, families can insulate their members against the worst effects of living on a low income. When this type of family support is missing, and a person's housing options are limited by a low income, homelessness becomes a very real possibility.

People are most vulnerable to homelessness at certain life cycle stages when family support and ties are under pressure. One of the most significant junctures is when young people leave home, and this is reflected in the fact that family conflict is the most important, immediate cause of homelessness amongst young people. A number of studies show that it accounts for the majority of cases of homelessness amongst young people. For example, research covering 7,500 homeless young people in seven different locations across the country found that 86 per cent had been forced to leave home rather than chose to leave (Centrepoint, 1996). This was in marked contrast to a survey undertaken by the charity in 1987 which found that 'pull' factors such as moving to find work or needing to be independent were far more prominent, and were mentioned by a half of young people, compared with just 14 per cent in 1996 (Centrepoint, 1996). Similarly, a more recent Family Policy Studies study of young homeless people found that two-thirds had lived in disrupted households. Other studies have shown the importance of family support to a smooth transition to independence. When support is not available during this difficult time, homelessness is much more likely to occur (Jones, 1995a).

Another critical life cycle juncture is relationship breakdown. A study by the Department of the Environment found that relationship breakdown is a significant cause of housing difficulty, including homelessness (DOE, 1993b). A separate study attempted to quantify the additional demand for housing created by relationship breakdown, and concluded that for every 100 divorces there was a demand for 53 new homes (Walker *et al*, 1991). The fact that debts often accumulated during the period leading up to a separation meant that one partner retaining the property was not always a feasible option (Walker *et al*, 1991).

---

4   Absolute and Overall Poverty in Britain, Bristol: School for Policy Studies, University of Bristol (1997).

Not only are the groups described above disadvantaged economically, but some also lack the family support that can help to reduce the risks of becoming homeless. Many care-leavers, for example, not only lack family support but they are also expected to make the transition to independence at a much younger age than other young people. Around two-thirds have left care by their eighteenth birthday, whereas the average age of leaving home for other young people is around 22 years (Ermisch et al, 1995). Leaving care is a once-only event with no opportunity to return should a young person experience difficulties. Young people who have left the parental home, on the other hand, usually return home at least once before making the final break (Jones, 1995a).

Research into the housing problems of ex-prisoners has also found that a lack of support from either family or a partner is a major contributory factor to homelessness (Carlisle, 1996). Family rifts often occur as a consequence of an ex-prisoner's criminal activities and associated problems such as drug or drink dependency. Indeed, a lack of family support is not always the consequence of callousness. Mental health and drug and alcohol dependency problems, in particular, can place a considerable strain on families and in many cases relationships suffer and the person with the problem becomes homeless. This is a relatively common pattern for people sleeping rough. Between one third and one half of rough sleepers suffer from mental health problems and the great majority (88 per cent) of these were ill before they became homeless (Craig et al, 1993). A large proportion of rough sleepers have a serious alcohol or drug problem. It is estimated that 50 per cent have an alcohol problem and some 20 per cent misuse drugs, and in many cases the problem predates homelessness and co-exists with some other problem such as mental illness. About one third of rough sleepers in central London have multiple problems and needs[5].

In summary, homelessness is the consequence of a cocktail of social and economic disadvantages and as such affects some groups, such as lone parents and black and ethnic minority people, more than others. Without family support or a statutory right to social housing, a homeless or potentially homeless person's only option is to look for accommodation in the private sector. Research has shown, however, that with few resources this is often a fruitless task (see, for example, Anderson, Kemp and Quilgars, 1993). We shall see, below, how the experience of being homeless compounds the disadvantages already experienced by people who become homeless.

The reality of homelessness

Just as the causes of homelessness vary considerably according to individual circumstances, so does the experience of homelessness itself. Of course homelessness can mean many things from sleeping rough to being in unsatisfactory accommodation, and it can be a short lived experience or exist for

---

5   Homeless Network: official monitoring statistics

a considerable period of time. The differences are illustrated by two examples of particular homelessness experiences found during research into homelessness amongst young people in Glasgow (see Fitzpatrick and Clapham, 1999).

In the first example young people had a transitory existence, in and out of the family home, sleeping at the houses of friends and sleeping rough normally for only a night or two at a time when other arrangements fell down. They had friends in their local area and had a strong attachment to it. When they slept rough it was usually very close to home and they would not take advantage of services or support outside that area, for example in the city centre. Some young people would find themselves in local hostels or supported scatter flats although not all could sustain this position for long.

The young people usually had long-term problems, which were at the root of family conflict. They had regularly truanted from school and had drink or drug problems, and often were involved in minor criminal activity from an early age. Although these problems had led to their leaving or being thrown out of home, they often maintained some contact from their family and received support and some practical help such as a hot meal or bath.

In the second example young people were in a very unstable situation, with periods of rough sleeping in the city centre interspersed with stays in hostels, drug rehabilitation units or prisons. They sometimes moved around from city to city and had few friends apart from those with whom they slept rough. They had few, if any, links with their immediate family although they often had some contact with a member of the wider family. They had a long history of disruption, insecurity and trauma and many had suffered physical abuse as children and had spent time in residential care.

In these two examples the young people moved through a number of different situations, all of which could be categorised as homelessness. The physical circumstances could be very different, but in all of these the young people lacked a home. 'Home' itself has many dimensions. As Watson and Austerberry argued:

> *The word home conjures up such images as personal warmth, comfort, stability and security, it carries meaning beyond the simple notion of a shelter* (Watson and Austerberry, 1986).

Therefore, almost by definition someone who is homeless is experiencing social exclusion in the sense that they are lacking the personal identity and the link into social networks which are part of mainstream society.

This concern with the social and emotional aspects of homelessness is important, given the increase in the number of empty council and housing association houses in many areas of Britain. Even in areas of acute housing shortage, such as in London, people are not accepting available shelter because they consider that the social environment is so poor that they are unable to make a home there. It also has to be said that sometimes when shelter is available people are unable to make a home because of the problems they may face, whether practical, emotional or social. When homeless young people are asked what they think of a home they stress physical safety and the security of the accommodation. They also stress privacy and 'being surrounded by your own things' and having 'somewhere decent'. Many of these aspects of home are clearly not present for a person sleeping rough, but they may also not be available for those in bed and breakfast accommodation or in hostels.

The absence of home may be one factor in the poor health of many homeless people. Single homeless people are more likely to suffer a wide range of health problems than the general population (Bines, 1997). They were three times as likely to suffer chronic chest or breathing problems and over a thousand times more likely to suffer from depression, anxiety or nerves. The prevalence of all the health problems was higher for those sleeping rough than among those in hostels or bed and breakfast accommodation. The difficulty in interpreting such findings is in disentangling the cause and effect. Does poor health cause homelessness, or is it a consequence of it? Undoubtedly it is a mixture of both:

> *Many of the health problems that were particularly prevalent among single homeless people, such as chest, skin and musculoskeletal problems, were those that could conceivably be caused or made worse by sleeping rough* (Bines, 1997, p146).

There is a particularly high incidence of mental health problems among single homeless people, but it is unclear why this is the case. Homelessness itself is undoubtedly stressful and is sometimes triggered by a stressful event such as relationship breakdown, but many single homeless people have a long psychiatric history and a high proportion of single homeless people with mental health problems also report heavy drinking (Bines, 1997).

Pleace and Quilgars (1997) argue that homelessness is just one of many risk factors and that any relatively deprived group of the population is exposed to similar and often identical risks to health. Homelessness represents an increased risk to health, but like other risk factors it will not necessarily cause health problems in the individuals and families who experience it. They argue that, with the exception of rough sleeping, which brings special dangers associated with exposure to assault and the weather, homelessness does not consistently constitute a unique risk to health. Whatever the reasons for their poor health, it is generally accepted that the access of homeless people to health care services is poor. The key to the receipt of these services is registration with a GP, but registration rates of homeless people are poor. Pleace and Quilgars (1997) argue that there are many barriers to registration for homeless people, including financial disincentives for GPs to take on mobile people and prejudice, as well as a lack of skills necessary for accessing the system. As Bines (1997) concludes, many homeless people are trapped in a revolving door of homelessness, crime and mental illness.

Routes out of homelessness

We have stressed the dynamic and complex nature of homelessness. Homeless people suffer a range of disadvantages and can change their situation often, moving from one temporary solution to another. It has sometimes been thought that there is a spiral of homelessness with people descending inexorably into a worse situation. It is certainly true that the longer a person is homeless the less likely they are to be able to sustain the resources and support structures which can enable them to avoid, for example, rough sleeping. However, there is no general rule and rough sleeping can occur at different times depending on the particular circumstances. Some people remain in a homelessness situation for a long period of time and may not ever escape from it, whereas others may extricate themselves with or without the support of outside help. The key question for public policy is how to react in a flexible way, to intervene in an appropriate way and at an appropriate time to help the homeless person overcome their social exclusion.

Underpinning strategies of intervention are social constructions of the causes and meaning of homelessness. These can be crudely split into those which focus on the young person and their family, and those which focus on the structural causes of homelessness and the welfare policy deficiencies which result in young people not being able to secure housing and aspects of welfare. Undoubtedly, most focus in political debate has been on the former issues and current policy is based round a view that young people should be at home if they cannot afford to support themselves. Previous Conservative governments have considered any help to young people as undermining the family and have sought to delay leaving home by making young people financially dependent on their parents.

Examples of the impact of this kind of thinking are the unavailability of social security benefits for those under 18, and the restriction of Housing Benefit for single people under 25 to the rent of a room in the private sector rather than self-contained accommodation. There is an assumption that young people do not deserve their own accommodation and should share with others. Therefore the predominant policy response to homelessness is the provision of hostel places which do not offer the elements of home identified earlier. Hostel places and other forms of help often come with strings attached and are regarded with suspicion by some homeless people. Managers of this provision are caught in a difficult position of finding a balance between giving people freedom and independence and exerting control. If independence is overemphasised too strongly there can be problems of drugs, drink and violent and disruptive behaviour within hostels, which is off-putting to some of those in need of the facilities. For example, research in Glasgow revealed that a number of homeless young people would not use the hostels because of the fear of violence and drugs (Fitzpatrick, 1997). On the other hand some hostels are considered to undermine, rather than promote, independence because of the strict control imposed over residents which may establish order, but which may alienate some people (Fitzpatrick, 1997).

Hutson (1999) shows that homeless people have different views on the experience of staying in hostels. Some people have found them very threatening places. Pleace (1995) concludes that residents and some staff regarded hostels as unsafe environments in which harassment and bullying occurred. Randall and Brown (1996) found that 40 per cent of rough sleepers would not accept a hostel bed if it were available because of concerns about safety and the behaviour of other residents. Behavioural problems mean that exclusions from hostels are not uncommon.

However, older people who have stayed in hostels for a long period of time tend to be much more satisfied with them and the way they are run. For example Garside *et al* (1990) found that 88 per cent overall of residents were satisfied with the way hostels were run, although there were complaints about noise, petty pilfering and violence. The difference in perceptions may be explained by the institutionalisation of long-standing residents. For example, in a study of people living in hostels in Cardiff, Dix (1995) found that a minority of residents, who were all men over the age of 40, did not want to move out. Staff attributed this to a lack of confidence and a desire to stay with what they knew. The problems of hostel living are reflected in all forms of shared living. There seems to be a mismatch here between the views of service providers and professionals who are in favour of shared living and many homeless people themselves who point to the dangers inherent in putting vulnerable people together who do not know one another (see Hutson, 1999).

There has been a move towards the provision of more self-contained accommodation for homeless people which seems to meet their expressed need for their own space in which they can be independent and away from trouble or danger. However, there are still problems here. Because many of the vacancies in mainstream public sector housing are in unpopular areas, some homeless people have found themselves in areas where they do not feel safe. Some single homeless people have suffered from serious disagreements with neighbours who complained about their lifestyle (Pleace, 1995). In addition many mainstream tenancies have broken down and it is argued that many homeless people need support to maintain a tenancy.

The issue of support is an interesting one and it has come to dominate the response to homelessness because of its link to accommodation in many forms of provision. For example, the current fashion for young homeless people is the foyer where hostel-type accommodation is linked to help with employment and other problems (Quilgars and Anderson, 1997). However, it has been argued that there is a lot of confusion and misunderstanding about the nature of support, so that it is often provided inappropriately (Franklin, 1999). Support can be divided into six categories:

1. Support involved in finding appropriate accommodation.
2. Functional skills (development of the ability to function in a neighbourhood by accessing public and private facilities).

3. Financial skills in terms of maximising income and managing on a budget.
4. Household skills such as shopping, cooking and laundry.
5. Personal skills such as maintaining a healthy and integrated lifestyle and the ability to access training and employment opportunities.
6. Self actualisation in which the focus is on the maintenance of a sense of identity and self worth.

(Franklin, 1999)

The focus on support in the provision of services to homeless people may be seen as an essential part of enabling them to deal with their problems which are often wide ranging and involve far more than just the provision of shelter. However, support may also be seen as merely reflecting the need for professionals to establish an important role (Hutson, 1999). It could also be viewed as a form of social control, making the provision of shelter dependent on conforming to social norms of behaviour. The emphasis in foyers is in reinforcing the work ethic through the link to training and employment initiatives and those who are not prepared to take advantage of these (for whatever reason) are then denied accommodation in the foyer[6]. Individual supported accommodation projects may vary in the emphasis they place on supporting independence as against social control.

In a recent survey of single homeless people, Hutson and Jones (1997) found that 71 per cent said that they did not need support if they were given tenancies. Those that did say they needed support mostly needed help with benefits and budgeting and only 8 per cent said they needed more intensive support such as help with cooking and shopping.

Problems seem to arise where the support is not tailored to the individual needs of the homeless person and where it is too rigidly tied to accommodation so that those not needing the support are either given it inappropriately or denied shelter. The examples of the young people given earlier show that homelessness is a process in which circumstances may vary considerably in a short period of time and so flexibility is vital. This can best be achieved with open access to mainstream housing and flexible floating support which can be based on the needs and wishes of the homeless person and can be reassessed as these needs change. Finally, the problems that lead to homelessness are often, for many homeless people, deeply rooted:

> *The young people's problems, including homelessness, can be seen in the majority of cases, as a continuation of disruption and problems commencing long before they came into contact with agencies ... The lesson is that if children and young people are unsettled early in life, the style of life is likely to continue the same in adolescence* (Stockley *et al*, 1993, p2).

---

6   Assistance may be provided with finding alternative accommodation.

Services such as the Rough Sleepers' Initiative are focused on dealing with homelessness when it occurs and this is clearly needed. However, the key to the prevention of homelessness is clearly in tackling the wide ranging problems which many people suffer in order to prevent personal and family breakdown which is often the precursor of homelessness. Therefore, the key to tackling homelessness is tackling social exclusion.

Conclusion

A huge volume of research continues to be conducted into the many dimensions of homelessness and it has not been possible to cover every aspect in this chapter. Rather we have focused on key examples which illustrate many of the significant issues and trends. We have argued that homelessness is a complex phenomenon, which cannot simply be ascribed to a shortage of housing or to personal inadequacy. The causes of homelessness are wide ranging and often have their roots in social exclusion. Homelessness is both a potent symbol of social exclusion and a symptom of it.

Although the predominant image of homelessness is the rough sleeper, the nature of homelessness varies considerably with many homeless people moving, often rapidly, backwards and forwards between situations. Sometimes sleeping rough, sometimes staying with friends or in temporary accommodation, the precise circumstances of homeless people vary depending often on the degree and type of support they receive from family and friends.

Services for homeless people are increasingly realising the multifaceted nature of their needs, and attempt to provide both accommodation and support. Present provision seems to be skewed too much towards the provision of temporary shared accommodation, although this is changing as the problems of lack of security and safety inherent in this kind of solution become apparent. The move towards more self-contained accommodation is commonly combined with the imposition of often inappropriate support arrangements. The present system of intervention is rigid, frequently providing uniform levels of support whether they are needed or wanted, and sometimes excluding people from accommodation because they are not assessed as needing the support.

In theory, the concept of social exclusion focuses the attention on empowering people to take charge of their own lives and to enjoy the same rights and lifestyle as others. In reality, too much of current provision seems to sustain dependence and exclusion through its treatment of homeless people as passive recipients of services. Rather, homeless people should be supported to make their own decisions in a framework within which they can choose the type of accommodation and support which best meets their needs and wishes.

CHAPTER 7:
Housing inequalities and minority ethnic groups

Duncan Sim

Introduction

People from black and minority ethnic communities have long experience of
social exclusion in relation to housing. Access to good quality housing has often
been quite varied with some households failing to obtain accommodation which
fully meets their needs. Many houses are too small and many are simply in the
wrong place, distant from family, friends, places of worship and community and
support networks. There has also been widespread experience of harassment
which has resulted in a reluctance on the part of minority households to accept
accommodation in certain areas of our towns and cities. Experience – or simply
fear – of harassment has led to the tendency of high concentrations of black and
minority ethnic families living in relatively few neighbourhoods, often in older
inner city housing.

This chapter focuses on the experiences of minority groups. It examines the
different forms which exclusion can take, in relation to access to housing, access
to finance and the conditions in which some minority households are forced to
live. It considers the background to this exclusion, focusing on the failings of
allocation systems, the experience of harassment, and homelessness. Finally, it
looks at ways in which exclusion might be and is being tackled, including
different approaches to lettings, the establishment of black and minority ethnic
housing associations and the use of Housing Plus in housing renewal.

Forms of exclusion

There is probably fairly general agreement as to the main areas of exclusion
affecting minority ethnic groups. First, it is recognised that, across most minority
groups, the numbers in the social rented sector are small compared to the
population as a whole. While choice may play a part in explaining this pattern, it
is likely that constraints of access and location are at least partly responsible.
Secondly, the average household size of many minority ethnic households is
larger than within the white population and too large to be comfortably housed
within much of the housing stock available. This mismatch between household

and dwelling sizes creates difficulties of overcrowding and acts as a powerful deterrent against minority families seeking accommodation in the social rented sector. Thirdly, the condition of much of the housing occupied by minority ethnic households is generally poor and this is particularly so in the private sector, where minority home-ownership cannot necessarily be equated with prosperity. Finally, for those who seek to buy their own home, there is clear evidence of discrimination within the systems of housing finance and exchange, affecting estate agents, banks and building societies. These various forms of exclusion will be considered in turn below.

Table 7.1: Housing tenure by ethnic group, Great Britain 1991

Ethnic group	Households (000s)	Owner-occupied (%)	Local authority (%)	Housing association (%)	Privately rented (%)
White	21,026.6	66.6	21.4	3.0	7.0
Black Caribbean, Black African	328.1	42.3	36.8	10.1	9.2
Indian	225.6	81.7	7.8	2.2	6.5
Pakistani	100.9	76.7	10.4	2.2	9.6
Bangladeshi	30.7	44.5	37.0	6.1	9.6
Chinese	48.6	62.2	13.1	3.5	17.0
Other	136.9	54.0	16.5	5.3	21.4
Total minority ethnic	870.8	59.5	21.8	5.9	10.8
Total	21,897.3	66.4	21.4	3.1	7.1

Source: 1991 Census, as reproduced in Owen (1993)

Access to social rented housing

The tenure pattern of minority ethnic groups varies considerably (Table 7.1). Data from the 1991 Census show that the Black Caribbean population, together with the Bangladeshis, have a higher dependence on social renting, with 45-50 per cent of the various black groups and 43 per cent of Bangladeshis renting from a local authority, housing association, New Town or Scottish Homes. In contrast, only 10 per cent of Indians and 12 per cent of Pakistanis are in these tenure categories (Ratcliffe, 1997). The figures suggest that there are perhaps two issues to be considered. On the one hand, where minorities such as the blacks and Bangladeshis have successfully obtained rented housing, is it of good quality and do they fare as well within the housing system as white applicants? On the other, if there are large minority groups such as the South Asians who are not living in social rented accommodation, then is this a matter of choice or is it a result of difficulties in accessing the system in the first place?

There is substantial research which has shown that those minority groups which achieve access to social rented housing do not in fact achieve access to the full range of property types. Henderson and Karn's (1987) work in Birmingham for example, showed that West Indians tended to receive older housing than white applicants, were more likely to be offered flats and had their area preferences met less often than whites. The situation was exacerbated by the transfer system and the cumulative effect was the production of an entrenched pattern of racial inequality and growing segregation. The study also found discriminatory practices within Birmingham housing staff with applicants and properties being deemed 'suitable' on an arbitrary – and frequently racist – basis. Similar studies in Tower Hamlets (Phillips, 1986), in Nottingham (Simpson, 1981) and in various other authorities investigated by the Commission for Racial Equality such as Hackney (CRE, 1984) and Liverpool (CRE, 1989) have all suggested that local housing allocations are discriminatory. Where formal CRE investigations have taken place, as in Liverpool, the study has been followed by the issue of a non-discrimination notice against the council concerned.

Census data allow us to examine the type of properties which were actually allocated to minority ethnic households. Across the country as a whole, in the local authority sector, whereas 28 per cent of white tenant households in 1991 occupied semi-detached houses, only 6 per cent of Black Caribbean, 4 per cent of Bangladeshi and 3 per cent of Black-African tenants did so. Conversely, 73 per cent of Black African, 67 per cent of Bangladeshi and 62 per cent of Black Caribbean tenants were in purpose-built flats, compared with 35 per cent of white tenants (Howes and Mullins, 1997). On the face of it, this would confirm previous research on discrimination in allocations but it would also seem that locality has a significant effect.

Thus, one of the reasons why minorities often occupy flats may be because of their predominantly inner city location. Semi-detached or terraced houses may be regarded as an ideal but their location on housing estates which, as well as being more peripherally located are perceived as being white dominated, may mean that minorities are unhappy at the prospect of living there. Research in Glasgow (Bowes, McCluskey and Sim, 1990) noted that, although harassment seemed to occur across the city, certain areas appeared worse than others, notably peripheral housing estates. There is increasing evidence that many minority ethnic households are choosing to accept overcrowded conditions in the inner city rather than a larger house elsewhere, simply in order to feel safe (Bowes, Dar and Sim, 1997).

Location is not the only important factor and minorities tend to occupy the poorest housing, regardless of tenure. Nevertheless, it is possible that location may help to explain the relatively greater presence of minority ethnic groups in housing association property. Many associations operate within the inner city and as Howes and Mullins (1997) have shown, local authorities may specifically nominate minority households to such associations in the knowledge that they are likely to accept an offer of accommodation. Housing associations are often locally based and are relatively recent creations; this means that they are sometimes seen more positively than local authorities and thought to be more sensitive to minority ethnic needs (Bowes, Dar and Sim, 1998). This impression may be heightened by the activities of black and minority ethnic associations, which are dealt with later in the chapter.

House size and household size

A major issue for at least some minority ethnic groups is that of overcrowding. Census data show that the average household size for whites in 1991 was 2.4 but this rose to 2.6 for black groups, 3.0 for the Chinese, 3.8 for Indians, 4.8 for Pakistanis and 5.2 for Bangladeshis. For South Asian groups, the situation is further complicated by the presence in a number of cases of two households living within the same house. Such 'extended' families may result from the presence of two or more different generations. In the case of Islamic families, there is often a preference within households for separate living rooms for men and women at different times of the day.

Within the social rented sector, it has proved extremely difficult to provide accommodation which is appropriate for these needs. Few council houses have more than three bedrooms and local authorities are in any case affected by the Right-to-Buy which, by reducing available stock, has frustrated their attempts to match houses and households in many areas. As a result, there is often severe overcrowding and Harrison *et al* (1996) have estimated that 31 per cent of Pakistanis and Bangladeshis are one or more bedrooms below the standard required. Given the youthful age structure of these groups (as well as the propensity for extended family living), then it is likely that the living conditions in these households will deteriorate as younger members of the household grow older and have greater space requirements.

The Association of Metropolitan Authorities has previously suggested (AMA, 1988) that the absence of large houses in the social rented sector may constitute indirect discrimination under the race relations legislation, although it is difficult to see how local authorities can rectify this at a time of resource constraint. It is perhaps more appropriate therefore that housing associations take the lead in this area. In fact, however, the average size of housing association property has been getting smaller since the 1988 Housing Act and the introduction of mixed funding. Research by Walentowicz (1992) showed that the space standards being achieved in newly-built housing association homes were below Parker Morris standards and indeed there appeared to be a measurable fall in space standards between the old and new funding regimes. Further work by Karn and Sheridan (1994) has confirmed this trend. It is increasingly difficult for associations to build larger houses for minority ethnic applicants without breaking the cost limits set by funders for new developments and associations must therefore seek to gain extra HAG allocations from the Housing Corporation, Scottish Homes or the Welsh Office.

While appreciating the difficulties faced by housing providers in meeting minority ethnic needs, nevertheless the absence of housing of the appropriate size in appropriate locations must act as a significant deterrent to potential applicants. It illustrates very clearly the way in which minorities are excluded from many of the housing opportunities available to white households.

Housing conditions

Minority ethnic groups living in the social rented sector may live in overcrowded conditions but score relatively well on basic amenity levels. The problem of poor quality accommodation is an issue which affects specifically those groups in the private sector, such as the Pakistanis. A high rate of owner-occupation, far from painting a positive picture of achievement, masks the fact that these dwellings are at the bottom of the market and are often in a state of serious disrepair (Ratcliffe, 1997). Ballard (1996, p144) notes that census data confirm that Pakistanis 'enjoy a substantially inferior quality of housing compared with that occupied by the indigenous majority', while they are far more likely than anyone else to 'be living in overcrowded circumstances, as well as in houses which lack central heating'. Harrison (1995) also refers to the poor quality of Pakistani and Bangladeshi housing, while Ratcliffe's (1996) work in Bradford refers (p40) to the 'particularly poor quality of the properties occupied by the Pakistanis and Bangladeshis'.

These findings suggest that either Pakistani households have found great difficulty in accessing good quality accommodation or, alternatively, in improving substandard housing with the aid of grants. Living in poor housing is unlikely to be a positive choice but households may, at some point, have been forced into making compromises over their housing choices, accepting poor quality inner city property, partly because of low income levels and partly in return for a relatively safe living environment. Thus, issues of choice and preference may be largely irrelevant for disadvantaged groups in society, such as minority ethnic groups, whose housing is often determined by forces outwith their control.

Access to housing finance

For those minority ethnic households who seek accommodation in the owner-occupied sector, previous research has identified a reluctance on the part of many individuals to borrow money from banks and building societies but instead to rely on informal networks of friends and relatives. Shaw (1988) has spoken of the operation of savings clubs known as *kametis* or 'committees', whereby individual households pay in at a rate they can afford, eventually retrieving their savings after an agreed period; many households have used this system to save for the deposit on a house or perhaps even the whole asking price. The operation of these 'committees' is not unlike the early terminating building societies, although there is a strong degree of anonymity involved.

One of the main reasons for this form of saving is the rather negative image which some banks, building societies and estate agents have within the minority communities and there seems to be a belief that many organisations operate in a discriminatory way. Certainly, Sarre, Phillips and Skellington (1989) found that many estate agents stereotyped Asians as being unreliable and devious where property transactions were concerned and two openly admitted excluding Asians from their services. This confirmed the findings by the Commission for Racial Equality (1988; 1990), identifying discrimination by estate agencies in London and Oldham.

A case in the Glasgow area during 1996/97 involved an Asian family who claimed they were blocked from viewing a house in a wealthy city suburb by the estate agents concerned and who later sued for damages, supported by the CRE. They won their case after appeal and the case has received enormous publicity within Scotland. The term 'blacklining' was coined to suggest that certain areas were being unofficially delineated by estate agents as inappropriate for minority ethnic settlement (Bowes, Dar and Sim, 1998).

It may be that such cases achieve publicity because of their relative rarity and there is no clear evidence that there is widespread exclusion of minorities from the processes of mortgage funding and house exchange. Nevertheless, the fact that it happens – even in a small number of cases – is surely a matter of deep concern.

The background to exclusion

The exclusion of minority ethnic households from housing may arise for a variety of reasons. It may of course occur as a result of deliberate discrimination but more frequently it may be the result of insensitivity, inappropriate housing policies or problems of communication. There are perhaps three key issues to be explored. Firstly, exclusion may occur because the housing system has not been made sufficiently accessible or understandable to minority ethnic groups and there may be problems linked to language and knowledge levels which are important. Secondly, housing may itself be of an inappropriate size or location for minority families. We have already made some reference to these but it is important to consider the wider and related issues of harassment and the need for culturally sensitive housing policies. Thirdly, there is the very serious question of how minorities deal with situations where access problems become insurmountable, for financial or other reasons, and there is no doubt that homelessness amongst minorities, for example, is increasing.

Understanding the housing system

Research into the experiences of minority ethnic households, particularly in relation to social landlords, has frequently identified unhelpful and unresponsive agencies. As a result, confidence in these organisations and expectations of a positive response are limited. There is therefore often a twofold problem. In the first place, there may be an inadequate level of appropriate housing provision. Secondly, and more specifically, the providers of this housing have been unsuccessful in communicating what is actually available to the members of minority communities.

One of the major difficulties is language, as many minority ethnic households are not proficient in English. It has long been recognised that there is a need for material to be translated into the main minority languages but this does not always happen, particularly where small numbers of minorities lead landlords to conclude that translation is not cost-effective. Where translated material is available, it may not cover all aspects of the housing system and there may, in any case, be no bilingual housing staff to deal with inquiries and applications for housing.

Given the reliance of minorities on informal sources of information, there may also be a need for information to be disseminated through informal community networks. This may be particularly important for those minority households involved in working unsocial hours and who may find it impossible to contact housing offices during the normal working day. An example is the Chinese community, where many households are employed in the catering trade and for whom some form of outreach work may be necessary. For example, the London Chinese Health Resource Centre, established in 1988, provides Sunday surgeries with bilingual doctors, Sunday being the only day off for many Chinese families. The centre also has an important training role which ultimately contributes to the development of community care for the Chinese (Li, 1992).

Indeed, this form of outreach and community development work may now be more important in helping to extend an understanding of the housing system amongst minority groups. English language proficiency is less likely to be a significant problem amongst younger members of minority families and as the numbers of minorities who are UK born increases, the need for translated material may decline. Ensuring that the system is *understood*, however, is less straightforward and may require imaginative and sensitive solutions.

Harassment

Racial harassment is perhaps most usefully defined by the Commission for Racial Equality as follows:

> *Racial harassment is violence which may be verbal or physical and which includes attacks on property as well as on the person, suffered by individuals or groups because of their colour, race, nationality or ethnic or national origins, when the victim believes that the perpetrator was acting on racial grounds and/or there is evidence of racism* (CRE, 1987, p8).

The CRE argues that the inclusion of the victim's perceptions in the definition is important to counterbalance the tendency of bodies such as the police and local authorities not to acknowledge the element of racism. The collection of detail on racist attacks through a case study approach is also important (e.g. CRE, 1987; Bonnerjea and Lawton, 1988)

Harassment can of course take many forms, from simple name calling or the daubing of graffiti to personal attacks, and ultimately life threatening incidents such as arson. It can occur in any location but seems to be particularly prevalent where minority ethnic families are fairly isolated, such as on some peripheral council estates. In parts of the inner city, there may be 'safety in numbers'.

Where harassment has taken place, landlords may find their opportunities for action limited. Graffiti may be cleaned off fairly easily and victimised families may be rehoused – although this is not necessarily a satisfactory solution – but action against perpetrators may be more difficult because of absence of proof. Some victims are reluctant to press charges or see cases go to court because of the fear of reprisals. For minority owner-occupiers, the only solution may be to sell up quickly and move.

The fear of harassment and the belief that particular housing estates or areas are unsafe leads many minority ethnic households to refuse offers of housing in these localities. Indeed, there are many instances of households giving up secure tenancies on some estates and moving to overcrowded private property, simply in order to feel safe. Thus, many minority ethnic households, through fear of and direct experience of harassment, are denied the range of opportunities afforded to white households. It is understandable that many social landlords allocate houses on a 'colour-blind' basis, as this may seem to be fair and objective but such a policy may and does result in black families being offered houses on predominantly white estates. It emphasises yet again the problem, for many minorities, of social housing being, for them, of the wrong size and in the wrong place.

Lack of access and homelessness

Access to council housing has traditionally been through three main routes, namely slum clearance, the waiting-list and homelessness, although these have varied in importance over the years. Slum clearance was particularly significant in the late 1960s and early 1970s and became a very important route into social renting, especially for inner city Asian owner-occupiers (Henderson and Karn, 1987). Homelessness gained in significance during the 1980s and, as far as minority ethnic households were concerned, an increased incidence of homelessness frequently reflected increases in harassment.

Minority ethnic households have traditionally experienced great difficulty in relation to the allocation system, either through intentional or unintended discrimination. The exclusion of owner-occupiers, or of applicants without a long local connection has militated against minority access to the system while allocators have often expressed racist views or operated in racist ways; requiring minority applicants to produce passports is an example of this. Many minority applicants have not been housed on the basis of need but on the basis of 'suitability' as defined by housing staff themselves. Thus, as Henderson and Karn (1987) point out, offers of property have often been dependent on the 'image' presented by the applicant and have more to do with estate management priorities regarding the void rates in particular estates than with the housing needs of the applicant household.

The housing association sector has also operated in an unsatisfactory way in this regard. The Commission for Racial Equality's investigation of housing associations (CRE, 1993) showed that a number of discriminatory practices existed, including 'sons and daughters' policies, residence qualifications, the giving of preference to transfer applicants and the allocation of new tenants only to flats or maisonettes. Many associations actually changed policies during the course of the study, after receiving CRE advice.

Within the social rented sector, the award of waiting-list points and the relative treatment of the waiting and transfer lists have often been causes for concern. Many local authorities reward waiting time by awarding applicants points for every year spent on the waiting-list. Sometimes the points increase exponentially, positively rewarding those applicants who have the ability to wait. This clearly discriminates against homeless applicants and others in priority need, including those suffering from harassment. It has also been common practice for local authorities to award points to transfer applicants with effect from their original date of tenancy. This firstly benefits existing tenants, who are likely to be predominantly white and secondly, it again benefits long-term tenants and discriminates against those who have to move house quickly. This latter group would include minority ethnic households suffering harassment.

Where harassment has occurred, it has taken many forms. The major problems appear to be verbal abuse, personal attacks and attacks on the home, but other identified problems may include the throwing of objects, rudeness, graffiti and attacks on household possessions such as cars. All landlords would probably see harassment as a serious issue to be addressed but the collection of evidence is often problematic. For this reason, it is often quite difficult to take action against perpetrators of abuse without evidence capable of supporting a court case. It is also not uncommon for perpetrators to lodge counter-accusations against a victimised family, leaving housing staff with the problem of whom to believe (Bowes, McCluskey and Sim, 1990).

One immediate and practical response to racial harassment is to move the victim away by means of a transfer. This has the advantage of offering the victim a potentially safer house, while retaining the option of taking legal action against the perpetrator. Many landlords, however, may offer victims a transfer to an equivalent house in the area, a procedure often referred to as a 'management transfer'. The problem here is, firstly, that equivalent housing may simply bring equivalent problems; secondly, that because of constraints of house size or type and the low availability of equivalent property, a transfer may have to be made within a very small geographical area and the family may continue to feel threatened or insecure. It is unsurprising therefore that some minority ethnic households simply give up secure tenancies in the social rented sector, opting instead for relatively insecure private ones, but in areas felt to be safe.

Although harassment is undoubtedly the main cause of homelessness amongst minority ethnic households, employment problems may also be an increasingly important factor. In certain parts of the country, where minority ethnic households have established their own businesses and levels of self-employment are high, loans on businesses have sometimes been secured on the family home. Business failure can therefore lead to home loss and homelessness (Bowes, Dar and Sim, 1998).

Tackling exclusion

Housing agencies, particularly the housing association sector, have become committed in recent years to looking at the housing needs of minority ethnic groups and there is some evidence that they are altering their practices accordingly. In some cases, research findings have been used in formulating policy, while elsewhere agencies have responded to community and other pressure from outside (such as the CRE), and campaigning work by independent housing bodies. Nevertheless, many issues remain.

Firstly, there are still problems of access to address and this relates partly to the availability of information on the housing system itself but also to the ability of housing agencies to deal sensitively with applications. Some housing commentators have suggested that minority-led housing organisations such as black associations are necessary to ensure better access to the social rented sector and this is an important issue for consideration.

Secondly, there are still areas of minority ethnic housing need where little research has been undertaken and where there have been few policy initiatives. One obvious example is in relation to older people from minority ethnic groups but, even in the case of non-elderly households, needs are often poorly understood with the result that allocations made are not always appropriate. There may be a need for greater consideration of community needs in the lettings process.

Thirdly, in the case of inner city owner-occupied housing, where the bulk of South Asian and Chinese households live, the condition of the stock is generally poor. Policies for tackling disrepair and levels of unfitness in housing are not necessarily likely to help such areas and, if anything current policies on repair and improvement may discriminate against inner city minority home-owners. There has been some discussion recently about the notion of 'Housing Plus' and the contribution which it could make to minority ethnic inner city communities.

Access to housing and the role of black-led associations

The level of understanding of the housing system amongst minority communities is often quite low, and this used to be ascribed to the lack of translated material available for minority applicants and the need to employ interpreters (for example, Working Party of Housing Directors, 1976). With the passage of time, a greater proportion of the minority population is British born and uses English as a first language; the need to translate documents is now perhaps less of an issue than previously. Knowledge of social rented housing is often still sketchy and confused but a larger proportion of minorities seem to be considering it as a possible tenure. In a recent study of Pakistani housing careers, Bowes, Dar and Sim (1998) discovered that half of their sample had at some point applied for council housing – yet Pakistanis have traditionally been regarded as having an overwhelming preference for home-ownership. That the rate of application is not reflected in actual minority tenancies suggests that, when offers of housing are made, they are simply regarded as unsuitable. Thus, the issue of access is not so much one of information as of sensitively matching needs with appropriate houses.

Housing associations appear to have been more successful than local authorities in meeting these needs. The 1991 census showed that 3.1 per cent of the population as a whole was housed in housing association properties, but for minorities the figure rose to 5.9 per cent. Black Caribbeans and Africans and Bangladeshis were more likely to be in association tenancies, Indians and Pakistanis less likely (Owen,1993). Since the Census, Housing Corporation monitoring data show that lettings to minorities by housing associations in England have risen to around 11 per cent and the proportion of lettings by smaller associations was significantly higher. A number of these would have been black-led associations.

The Housing Corporation's first strategy for black-led housing associations began in 1986 and arose from evidence of discrimination and bad housing experienced by the minority ethnic communities. Black-led associations were encouraged as a means of providing housing aimed more directly at minorities and with minority ethnic control of management committees. The programme started with the registration of 18 black-led associations; this rose to 59 by 1991, owning and managing around 4,000 homes. By 1996, the number of associations hardly changed but the stock managed rose to 17,135 (Housing Corporation, 1996).

A detailed review of the programme was carried out in 1996 (Harrison *et al* 1996) and concluded that the establishment of black and minority ethnic-led associations had made a significant contribution towards meeting minority ethnic housing needs. It had also led to a significant increase in minority ethnic committee members and staff. There were, however, doubts as to whether some associations would be financially viable in the long-term because of their small size. In late 1997, however, the strategy received support from Hilary Armstrong, Housing Minister in the New Labour government, who asked the Housing Corporation to relaunch its support for black associations. There was also some debate as to how similar strategies for black and minority ethnic housing can be incorporated into local authorities' Housing Investment Programmes (*Inside Housing*, 19 September 1997, p3).

Housing needs and the wider community

Experiences of social renting by minority ethnic groups, particularly in the local authority sector, have often been quite negative and there appears to be a concern that the allocation system is not geared towards the specific needs of minority communities. The main fear is clearly that minority households will be offered accommodation in an area where they will be vulnerable to harassment, and isolation is heightened if heads of household are unable to speak fluent English. Allocations may be made some distance from friends, community facilities and support networks. In such circumstances, households may simply leave and there are many examples of minority households giving up secure tenancies in the social rented sector and moving into private rented accommodation, purely in order to be within 'safe' areas, close to family and other support.

Research by Love and Kirby for the Department of the Environment (1994) drew attention to the need for preventative measures in relation to racial violence and harassment. Such measures could range from community development work including the encouragement of residents' and tenants' associations, through to improvements in the design of estates to prevent crime. They suggested that communication of the landlord's policies to tenants and other residents, and campaigns to educate and raise awareness also had a role to play.

Bradford provides a useful example of an authority where proactive, preventative work is currently taking place (Bowes, Dar and Sim, 1998). There is evidence that the council is succeeding, in its Canterbury estate, south west of the city centre, in creating an environment within social rented housing, where minority households feel relatively safe. The estate has recently been modernised, using funding from Estate Action, Housing Association Grant and private finance, and there is strong tenant involvement. There is a Tenant Enablement Officer, who has been instrumental in involving tenants as closely as possible and initiating development work. Because the estate is relatively close to the city centre, it has proved to be a fairly popular destination for minorities. This suggests that the city council has succeeded through a mixture of careful allocations, refurbishment work and community development, in creating a satisfactory environment for minorities.

The need for greater sensitivity in allocations to minorities suggests that a community lettings approach is one which may sometimes be appropriate. Recent research at Cardiff (Griffiths *et al*, 1996) defines such lettings as:

> *... social housing allocation policies which operate alongside, or in place of, a consideration of housing need and take account of the potential tenant's contribution to that community in which the vacancy has occurred.*

The researchers point out that, while social rented housing should be offered to those most in need, allocation policies are frequently a compromise between meeting needs, making best use of housing stock, avoiding social polarisation and helping to engender more balanced communities. They suggest that, when allocations are made, there may be benefits in giving preference to rehousing those households who actually want to live there, including those who can show a connection or commitment to the area. Such lettings can help to protect existing communities and keep them stable, protect or amend the social mix in an estate, or prevent future problems occurring in newly developed or newly modernised estates. It may therefore be appropriate in dealing with minority ethnic households who have specific needs in relation to house size and type, and in relation to safety and freedom from harassment.

Renewal policies and minority ethnic groups

There are three issues in regard to the renewal of older inner city properties, many of which are owned by minority ethnic households. First, there is the question of whether minority households have made use of grant aid to improve properties and whether this has been affected by recent changes in the grants system in England and Wales. Second, there is the issue of wider urban regeneration policies and the changes in funding mechanisms in recent years. Third, there is the question of combining housing regeneration with other forms of regeneration which benefit the wider community.

Until 1996, the grants system in England and Wales was as established by the Local Government and Housing Act 1989, the main form of assistance being the renovation grant, which was means-tested. Research suggests that, while the numbers of grants being paid were generally falling, the average value of grants rose because they were being targeted to those most in need and it is believed that minority households benefited (Mackintosh and Leather, 1993). The Housing Grants, Construction and Regeneration Act 1996 removed the mandatory right of people living in an unfit house to a renovation grant and replaced it with a discretionary system, with a strong emphasis on targeted investment to the worst areas. Again, it would appear that minorities would benefit from such an approach. The problem therefore seems to be the long waiting time for a grant, resulting from shortage of resources, rather than a complete absence of such grants.

In Scotland, grants are not means-tested but allocations from the Scottish Office are no longer ring fenced. Many local authorities have prioritised council house repairs and allocated a greater proportion of their allocations for this purpose (Chartered Institute of Housing in Scotland, 1997). There is now therefore less money available for private sector repair and this will pose some problems for the minority ethnic communities.

In terms of area regeneration, recent initiatives such as City Challenge and the Single Regeneration Budget have been based on the concept of competitive bidding for resources. Many of the successful applications were decided not exclusively on the basis of need but on the quality of submission (Oatley and Lambert, 1995). Bids which included opportunities for stock transfer and involved the private sector were more likely to be successful and this tended to favour local authority housing estates where tenure diversification could be put into effect. Research in Bradford (Bowes, Dar and Sim, 1998) has shown how, despite the local authority prioritising the inner city, the successful SRB bids were initially in outer estates, where minorities were unlikely to benefit. There are undoubtedly examples of successful inner city SRB bids but it is far from clear that minority ethnic households have benefited from the process.

While much of the debate on regeneration has focused on the physical improvement of dwellings, there is also recognition that lasting renewal can only really be achieved if there is wider community involvement. The notion of 'Housing Plus', whereby housing programmes can be developed which achieve benefits wider than housing, may be relevant for minority ethnic communities. In Luton, for example, there has been some discussion of Housing Plus in relation to Bury Park, the main area of minority settlement, with local people employed in undertaking housing renovation work (Bowes, Dar and Sim, 1998). If repair and improvement grants become more targeted towards such inner city areas, then the involvement of local people will become very important.

Research undertaken, funded by the Joseph Rowntree Foundation (Taylor, 1995) has demonstrated very powerfully the importance of giving local people a stake in the future of their local area. For minority ethnic households, who so frequently experience exclusion of one kind or another, there is a particular significance. Initiatives such as Housing Plus are likely therefore to be of increased importance in the future.

Conclusions

This chapter has argued strongly that many aspects of housing policy and practice have tended to exclude minority ethnic groups from access to the houses they need and want. It illustrates therefore the need to continue to explore the implications and effects of wider housing policy for minorities.

There is a substantial diversity of minority housing experiences and needs, and it is essential that an appreciation of this diversity is also on the policy agenda. National or local policies which attempt to *include* minorities by treating them homogeneously can generate other forms of *exclusion*. For example, linking all social rented housing applications from minorities to certain areas restricts the choices of minorities as compared with other categories of applicant.

Research has an important role in monitoring housing practice, that is, the effects of policy as it is implemented. Where housing organisations adopt anti-discriminatory practice, for example, the effects of this may require monitoring, as the practice may defeat the principle. In some respects, housing associations (particularly black or minority ethnic controlled ones) may in general appear to be doing somewhat better than local authorities in terms of provision for minorities, but the situation is not necessarily clear-cut and there may still be a number of associations whose policies are inappropriate.

Finally, the links between housing and other areas of disadvantage are important. This is an area which has sometimes been neglected but which is now being recognised in policy terms, in regeneration strategies and in other fields, notably community care, where the provision of linked packages of care is central. For minority ethnic groups, there is a danger that instead of linked services or integrated policies, they receive linked disadvantage, or compounded exclusion. Thus, an understanding of disadvantage in one area has to be seen in the context of disadvantage in others. For housing staff, the challenges presented are considerable.

CHAPTER 8:
Lone parenthood: Two views and their consequences

David Webster

Introduction

The rise of lone parenthood in Britain has been interpreted in two completely
different ways. These different views lead to fundamentally different approaches
to public policy.

The view set out here is based on the full analyses now available of the 1991
census and of geographical employment change in Britain. It also reflects the
mainstream of US academic research, which has addressed the issue of lone
parenthood over several decades. It sees the breakdown of family structures as
mainly due to the stresses caused by prolonged high male unemployment in
particular geographical localities, which has in turn been caused by
disproportionate loss of manual jobs, mainly in manufacturing. Both mothers
and fathers live predominantly in areas with excess manual labour supply, where
it is difficult for either of them to get a job. Due to the loss of their employment
base, these areas are suffering from comprehensive decline in terms of poverty,
outmigration, dereliction and related problems. Because of their manual
employment background, their housing is predominantly council owned and has
suffered from the under investment and residualisation of the Thatcher years.
This combination of circumstances shows why lone parents are poor and why
their housing is bad. It also suggests that little can effectively be done to get
them into work or to raise more money from the non-resident fathers unless
more jobs materialise in these areas.

By contrast, the British government view – which has shown great continuity
between administrations – is derived mainly from outdated analyses and
ideological ideas from the 1980s, supported by some more recent British
research which has overlooked the geography of lone parenthood. It does not
recognise the key role of geographically concentrated job losses, but sees lone
parenthood as primarily an issue of attitudes and incentives. The welfare state is
considered to have been providing perverse incentives, which have encouraged
women to become unpartnered mothers, fathers to abandon their families and
thereafter fail to support them, and lone parents to be dependent on social

security instead of getting one of the jobs which are thought to be readily available in every locality. The main requirement, therefore, is thought to be to reconstruct the welfare state to change the structure of incentives so as to encourage joint parenting and paid work. Improvements in lone mothers' incomes or housing are permissible only if they do not create perverse incentives. As in the USA, there is a strong desire to cut the public cost of lone parenthood.

It is argued here that because they are founded on an empirically mistaken view of lone parenthood, most of the present government's policies will not succeed in reducing lone parents' 'social exclusion' except at the margin. Some will make things worse.

The chapter begins by outlining the scale of lone parenthood and explaining how people come to be lone parents, stressing the dominant role played by relationship breakdown. It goes on to show the weight of US and British evidence that the principal cause of rising lone parenthood in both countries is the exceptionally high and prolonged unemployment experienced in particular places. The origins of the dominant, and contrasting, 'New Right' interpretation are then explained. This leads on to a critical examination of the different elements of the current public policy agenda. Finally, an alternative way ahead is briefly outlined.

The rise of lone parenthood and routes into lone parenthood

There were about 1.6 million lone parent families in Great Britain in 1996 (Haskey, 1998), a million more than in 1961. As a proportion of families with dependent children, lone parents have risen from 8 per cent in 1971 to 21 per cent in 1996. A slightly smaller proportion of children (19 per cent) live in lone parent families, because lone parents tend to have fewer children than couples (1.7 on average compared to 1.9). But the proportion of families affected by lone parenthood is higher than 21 per cent, because in 1996 another 8 per cent had a step-parent (ONS, 1998a). Most of the children in these families will have been through a period of lone parenthood. Lone parenthood therefore affects about one quarter of today's children.

Routes into lone parenthood: the key role of relationship breakdown

The great majority of lone parents (92.6 per cent in 1991) are female. In 1996, around three-fifths of female lone parents were divorced or separated, and about a third had never been married, while only one in twenty was a widow. Among the comparatively small group of male lone parents, far more are divorced or separated (three-quarters), or widowed (one in seven). But these figures overstate the extent of unpartnered parenthood among both male and female lone parents. The general trend towards cohabitation instead of marriage has resulted in many lone parents being classified as 'single' or 'never married' when with otherwise identical circumstances they would previously have been classified as 'divorced or separated'.

Between 1979 and 1996, the proportion of women aged 18-49 who were legally married fell from 74 per cent to 57 per cent, while the proportion cohabiting rose from 11 per cent to 26 per cent (ONS, 1998a). Seven out of ten first marriages in the early 1990s were preceded by cohabitation, compared with only one in ten in the early 1970s (Haskey, 1995). The proportion of births outside marriage has therefore also risen enormously, from under 9 per cent in 1971 to over 35 per cent in 1996. However, almost all of the increase has been accounted for by births jointly registered by mother and father, who in three-quarters of all cases are living together at the same address. Kiernan *et al* (1998) argue that these jointly registered extramarital births have merely replaced previously numerous bridal pregnancies. The proportion of births registered by the mother alone has increased only slightly, from about 5 per cent to about 8 per cent (ONS, 1998b). Nine-tenths of non-resident fathers report that they have at some time been married to, or cohabited with, the mother of their child (Pullinger and Summerfield, 1997); while 85 per cent of lone mothers say they have previously married or cohabited (Haskey, 1998).

Half of lone mothers are aged over 33, and half of lone fathers over 42 (Pullinger and Summerfield,1997). Teenage lone mothers are less than one in 25 of all lone parents. Births to unmarried teenagers have risen only from 2.0 per cent of all births in 1964 to 5.7 per cent in 1993 (Babb and Bethune, 1995). But even this small rise includes the effect of the declining popularity of marriage. The actual number of births to teenagers registered by the mother alone scarcely changed between 1978 and 1996 (Botting *et al*, 1998). Conception rates for teenagers have fallen markedly, from 81.5 per thousand in 1971 to 58.7 in 1995 (ONS, 1998b). The Social Exclusion Unit (SEU) (1999a) highlights the 90,000 teenage conceptions per year, but also shows that these lead to only 42,000 teenage births, of which only 16,000 are to under 18s and 3,700 to girls conceiving under 16.

Lone mothers do not commonly have more children while on their own. Over the four years 1991 to 1995, only one in five of a sample of lone mothers had a further baby and in only half these cases (i.e. one in ten) was there no new partner (Ford *et al* 1998).

The great majority of lone parents therefore are in their situation because of relationship breakdown, with the ancient problem of widowhood still playing a role. Unpartnered parenthood is a relatively minor factor.

Lone parents and their children: how they live

It is well known that lone parents and their children are one of the most disadvantaged groups in today's society. Most fundamentally, they are poor. Lone parents' mean household income in 1996/97 was only £160, half the level for all households (£325) and even lower in relation to that for couples with children (around £410) (ONS, 1998b, p93). In 1996, one third of lone mothers and one quarter (27 per cent) of lone fathers had a gross weekly household income under £100. This was a far higher proportion than the 3 per cent for married or cohabiting couples (ONS, 1998a). The gap in poverty rates between lone and couple mothers widened substantially between 1984 and 1995 (Shouls *et al*, 1999). A new Scottish Executive survey (1999) shows over one third (35 per cent) of lone parents worried about money 'all the time' and 27 per cent 'quite often'; these proportions were much higher than for any other household type. It shows two-fifths (39 per cent) with no bank account, compared to 12 per cent of all householders, and only 15 per cent with any savings at all, compared to half of all households. Berthoud and Kempson (1992) found one 'problem debt' on average for every lone parent, far more than for other household types.

These low incomes and related problems reflect lone parents' dependence on social security benefits, and the inadequate level of these benefits given their extra needs (Berthoud and Ford, 1996). In 1995/96, 1 million of the 1.6 million lone parents were claiming Income Support. This 63 per cent proportion compares to only 10 per cent of couples with dependent children (ONS, 1998b, p142). In 1994-96, 58 per cent of lone parents had no employment income, compared to 34 per cent of married mothers, most of whom will have had husbands in work (ONS, 1998a, p56).

Lone parents' housing circumstances

The *Survey of English Housing* (EHS) 1995/96 came up with the remarkable finding that almost one third (30 per cent) of lone parents with dependent children had experienced homelessness within the previous ten years, compared to only 6 per cent of all households. Three-quarters of these homeless lone parents had been given accommodation by their local council (ONS, 1998b).

Lone parents are particularly dependent on renting. Of the two-thirds who formed separate households in England in 1996, almost half (49 per cent) were renting from local authorities or RSLs, compared to only 22 per cent of all households, and 14 per cent were renting privately compared to 9 per cent of all households. Only 37 per cent were owner-occupiers, far less than the 69 per cent for all households (DETR, 1998c). About one in six lone parent owner-occupiers with dependent children in 1995/96 was in arrears with their mortgage, four times the proportion for couples with dependent children. About one in eight lone parents was in rent arrears, but this was actually slightly less than for couple families, presumably because most had their full rent paid through benefit (Pullinger and Summerfield, 1997).

Lone parents tend to live in the worse parts of the rental sectors. In England in 1996, almost one fifth (18 per cent) were living in 'poor' housing conditions (unfit, in substantial disrepair or needing essential modernisation), significantly higher than the 14.2 per cent for all households. Unemployed lone parents with infants were considerably worse off, over one quarter of them living in 'poor' houses. Lone parents were particularly likely to have poor security, to lack smoke alarms, and, in the local authority sector, to lack central heating (DETR, 1998c). In Scotland, 40 per cent of single parents had dampness or condensation on the surveyor's assessment, well above the 25 per cent of all households (Scottish Homes, 1997). Almost one quarter (23 per cent) of lone parents in Britain lived in a flat compared to only 6 per cent of other families (ONS, 1998a).

Lone parents live disproportionately in poor neighbourhoods as well as in poor housing. In England in 1996, one in seven (13.4 per cent) of lone parent households with dependent children was living in a neighbourhood offering 'poor' living conditions, twice the proportion for all households. Willmott (1994) showed that in 1991 all but one of the British deprived areas had an above average proportion of lone parent households and that between 1981 and 1991 their concentration in deprived areas increased. This concentration is also shown by SEU (1998b, p17).

Those lone parents living in poor housing or neighbourhoods were much more concerned about the poor conditions than other types of household. Almost two-thirds wanted to move, compared to well under half of all households in similar conditions, and they were twice as likely to be dissatisfied with their housing as any other type of family (DETR, 1998c; Pullinger and Summerfield, 1997). There is some evidence that a disproportionate number of lone parents are moving out of council into private rented housing, accounting for a third of such movers (Pawson and Bramley, forthcoming). These moves are presumably to housing of better quality and would make sense given the poor accommodation they are getting from councils and their dissatisfaction with it.

Lone parents who live with their parents

In 1991, over one third (35 per cent) of lone parent families lived with another household (Census, 1991), almost always their family of origin (Haskey, 1998, p12). The proportion of lone parent families sharing accommodation in 1991 varied quite widely, from 18.1 per cent in Westminster to 70.5 per cent in Dwyfor, north-west Wales, although it was mostly within the range 27-45 per cent. The main reason for the variation is probably not the varying availability of social housing, but whether the lone parent's own mother lives nearby. Westminster has a shortage of social housing, but it also has a large furnished private rented sector and many of its lone parents are likely to be in-migrants with no family locally. In rural Wales, social housing is also likely to be scarce but almost all lone parents are likely to be local.

A much higher proportion of these sharing lone parents than of all lone parents are in the council sector. Although it is difficult to obtain exact information, it is clear that these families are often very overcrowded. While lone parent families living separately were less crowded than other households with children in 1991 (Atkins *et al*, 1996, p192), 10 per cent of lone parent families overall in 1995/96 had at least one room less than the bedroom standard, double the proportion for other families (ONS, 1998a). This implies that the minority of lone parent families who were sharing must be much more crowded than this.

The health of lone parents and their children

The health of lone parents and their children is undermined by their disadvantaged living circumstances. Lone mothers consistently have significantly worse health than couple mothers (Shouls *et al*, 1999). In 1991, 15 per cent of a sample of lone parents reported a long-term or limiting illness, and 13 per cent that they had ill children. By 1995 twice as many of these same parents said they were ill themselves, and that they had ill children (29 per cent in each case). There was a strong association between the experience of physical hardship and the development of health problems among both parents and children. In only four in ten of these households had the mother and children remained free of long-term or limiting illness throughout the four years (Ford *et al*, 1998).

The non-resident fathers

It is important to remember the non-resident fathers. They also are a disadvantaged group. In 1997, the Labour Force Survey showed only 76.6 per cent of widowed or divorced men aged 25-49 in full or part-time jobs compared to 91.1 per cent of married men. Of the 530,400 non-resident parents (almost all men) with a Child Support Agency (CSA) full maintenance assessment at May 1997, only just over half (53.6 per cent) were in a job (DSS, 1997b). In 1995/96, most British non-resident fathers had not gone on to another permanent relationship: nearly 60 per cent were living without a partner (Bradshaw *et al*, 1999). There is evidence that, like the lone parents with care of the children, they are particularly likely to be homeless. SEU (1998a) noted that the single most common reason for a first episode of rough sleeping is relationship breakdown, either with parents or partner, and that older homeless people were five times more likely to be divorced than the average for their age group. Of 335 homeless men making contact with agencies in the Glasgow Rough Sleepers' Initiative in 1998/99, half were fathers. From the USA, Lindblom (1991) reported that 'homelessness appears significantly more likely among extremely poor divorced or separated solitary males than among never-married single males'.

Teenage fathers appear to be even rarer than teenage lone mothers. In Allen and Dowling's study (1998), only one fifth of the fathers of teenage mothers' babies were teenagers themselves at the time of birth, the average age being 23.

Why has lone parenthood increased so much? – the link with unemployment

It has long been known that marital behaviour depends strongly on the economy. The English Registrar General pointed this out as early as 1878 and an outstanding statistical study by R.H.Hooker (1901) showed the marriage rate in 1861-95 very closely correlated with the level of trade. Southall and Gilbert (1996) have recently shown that the relationship between marriage and unemployment in 19th century England was so close that parish marriage registers are a better indicator of local unemployment rates than are the available data on unemployment. Dorothy Thomas (1927, pp100-02) showed that the illegitimate birth rate rose and fell in England in 1854-1913 in inverse proportion to the business cycle. She suggested that this was 'probably due to the restriction of the marriage rate in times of depression'.

Unemployment and family breakdown: the American evidence

The Great Depression of the 1930s does not appear to have produced any statistical studies of lone parenthood. The likelihood is that it was too short (around 7-8 years) to produce marked effects on family structure, and of course social restraints on lone parenthood were at that time extremely strong. The Depression did however produce distinguished ethnographic studies (Bakke, 1940; Komarovsky, 1940) showing the severity of the stresses placed on the parents' relationship by unemployment of the father and the consequent severity of the threat of marital breakdown. This evidence was drawn upon by Daniel Patrick Moynihan when he came to write his landmark report on *The Negro Family* (1965).

It was among the black community in the USA in the 1930s to the 1960s that unemployment rates first rose high enough, for long enough, to have a marked effect on family structure. Moynihan was concerned that the prevalence of lone parenthood would prevent the black minority from realising the benefits of the formal racial equality then being enacted under the Johnson administration. He argued that high black lone parenthood was due to the 'fundamental, overwhelming fact....that Negro unemployment, with the exception of a few years during World War II and the Korean War, has continued at disaster levels for 35 years' (p20). Moynihan presented an elegant chart (p22) showing a near-perfect one year lagged relationship over the period 1951-63 between the non-white male unemployment rate and the proportion of non-white women separating from their husbands. He also pointed out (p47) that over the period

1948 to 1962 'male Negro unemployment and the number of new AFDC cases rose and fell together as if connected by a chain ... The correlation between the two series of data was an astonishing 0.91'.[1]

Subsequent to Moynihan's 1965 report, the US problem went on to get much worse, as 'urban-rural manufacturing shift' intensified the shortage of blue collar jobs in the northern cities to which blacks had moved (Kasarda, 1989). Katz (1989, p28) pointed out that 'major newspaper accounts omitted Moynihan's emphasis on unemployment as the great source of family disorganization', and it has often been forgotten. Nevertheless, a large body of American research went on to confirm the strength of the unemployment-lone parenthood linkage. In 1989, McLanahan and Garfinkel wrote (p121): 'Despite some gaps and anomalies, there is now a strong body of empirical research that documents that one of the costs of increased unemployment is increased female headship'. It is important to note that this research includes longitudinal studies of samples of people over time, such as that of Cherlin (1976), Lichter *et al* (1992) and Testa *et al* (1993) as well as aggregate studies such as that of South (1985) and Wilson (1987). The evidence cannot be dismissed on the ground that 'correlation does not prove causation'.

Unemployment and family breakdown: the British evidence

Recent British evidence has confirmed the causal link between unemployment and lone parenthood already seen in the USA. Haskey (1984) found in a cross-section study that unemployed husbands are particularly likely to divorce. A longitudinal study of six British towns (Lampard, 1994) showed that a spell of unemployment during a year raised the chance of marital breakdown during the following year by about 70 per cent. Kiernan and Mueller (1998) made a similar longitudinal finding using the *British Household Panel Survey*. The importance of unemployment is as obvious to researchers on the ground in Britain as it is in the USA. Fotheringham's (1993) comment about Birmingham's Highgate estate in 1993, 'With male unemployment running at almost 50 per cent in the local area traditional male roles as provider had ... been undermined', is essentially the same as Rainwater's (1970) quote from St Louis' Pruitt-Igoe in 1970: 'The men don't have jobs. The woman, she starts nagging. He don't have the money so he leaves. She ADC's it. If he had a job the family unit could come back together'.

However the most powerful evidence comes from the 1981 and 1991 censuses. In April 1981, claimant unemployment in Britain was still under 10 per cent. It had risen above 6 per cent for the first time since the war only in 1977, and then fallen again. But by April 1991, it had been over 10 per cent for 25 of the

---

1   AFDC stands for 'Aid to Families with Dependent Children'. Although this benefit, introduced under Roosevelt, was available to all low income mothers, most claimants in the last few decades until its abolition in 1996 were black lone parents.

previous 40 quarters and over 7 per cent for 31 of them, with a peak of over 13 per cent in 1983. Moreover Beatty *et al* (1997) showed that by 1991 recorded unemployment was seriously below the 'real' level, which they estimated at 13 per cent. Not surprisingly in view of the American evidence, female lone parenthood in Britain as a proportion of all households with children doubled between 1981 and 1991, from 5.6 per cent to 11.6 per cent. Moreover, the higher the rate of unemployment in an area, the greater the increase in lone parenthood[2]. In 1981 there was already a clear relationship between unemployment and lone parenthood across the 459 British local authority districts, but it was not especially strong (correlation 0.48, see Figure 8.1). By 1991 the relationship had become enormously stronger. The correlation was now a very high 0.846, and an increase of 10 per cent in the male unemployment rate was now associated with an increase of 8.5 per cent in the proportion of lone parents – more than four times the effect seen in 1981. By 1991, there were half as many lone parent households again (452,000) in local authority areas with above average unemployment as in areas with below average unemployment (312,300), even though the former group of areas had fewer households with children (2.95 million compared to 3.62 million).

It is sometimes argued that lone parenthood has increased because women have become more financially independent or less willing to put up with unsatisfactory partnerships. Such changes may have played a minor role. There are some more prosperous lone parents whose position owes little or nothing to unemployment. Figure 8.1 indeed shows that lone parenthood has risen even in areas of low unemployment. But the idea that female emancipation has had much to do with most of the rise in lone parenthood cannot be reconciled with its concentration among the poorest women in the poorest areas. Figure 8.2 shows that the areas with the highest male unemployment and the most lone mothers also have the smallest proportions of lone mothers in work, i.e. with independent incomes.

The dominant influence of male unemployment on lone parenthood is also demonstrated by cross-section multiple regression studies of 1991 census data for local authorities (Bradshaw *et al*, 1996; Gordon, 1996; Webster, 1998a). These show the statistical relationship between unemployment and lone parenthood after controlling for other factors. They use different measures of lone parenthood and different explanatory variables, but produce similar results. Male unemployment is shown to be the strongest influence on lone parenthood. Communities with large Afro-Caribbean populations are shown to have somewhat higher rates of lone parenthood, and those with large Asian populations somewhat lower, after controlling for the effect of male unemployment. Webster, like Johnston (1995), shows that higher education is not a significant factor.

---

2   For most districts, male unemployment was almost the same in 1991 as in 1981 so that either figure is a good guide to the level over the decade. See Webster (1998).

Figure 8.1: GB districts – female lone parenthood by male unemployment, 1981 and 1991

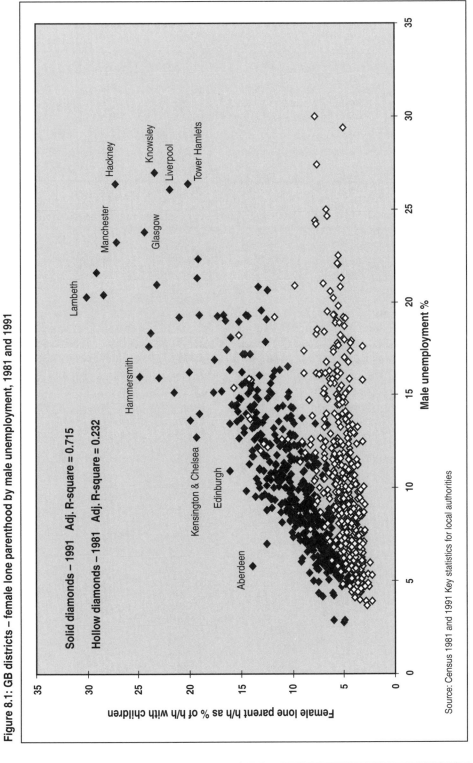

Solid diamonds – 1991   Adj. R-square = 0.715

Hollow diamonds – 1981   Adj. R-square = 0.232

Female lone parent h/h as % of h/h with children

Male unemployment %

Source: Census 1981 and 1991 Key statistics for local authorities

Fig 8.2: Percentage of female lone parents in work by male unemployment – British local authorities 1991

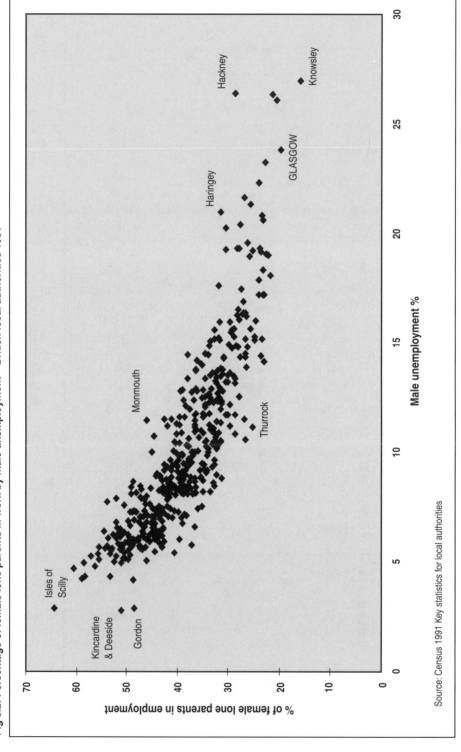

Source: Census 1991 Key statistics for local authorities

As in the USA, unemployment is concentrated in the cities, and for the same reason: their disproportionate loss of manual employment due to 'urban-rural manufacturing shift' (Turok and Edge, 1999). However, all three regression studies suggest that there is a tendency for lone parenthood to be higher the larger the town or city, even after controlling for other factors. In Webster (1998b), big cities have lone parenthood around 2 per cent higher than rural and small town areas, other things being equal, and inner London 4 per cent higher. It is sometimes suggested that this is due to cultural influences, but it seems more likely to result from differential migration after the birth of a child. As Gordon (1996, p418) suggests, couple families can more often afford to move out to the predominantly owner occupied housing in suburbs and exurban areas than can lone parents.

Evidence since 1991 also supports the unemployment-lone parenthood causal linkage. The best measure of 'real' unemployment on an annual basis is the TUC's 'Want Work Rate', which shows those wanting work, whether unemployed or 'inactive', as a proportion of all those working or wanting work. It peaked at 16.2 per cent in 1993 and since then has fallen slowly to 15.1 per cent in 1995 and 14.0 per cent in 1997. If there is a link between lone parenthood and unemployment, the growth of lone parenthood should have levelled off, with some delay, to reflect this fall. This has indeed happened. The number of lone parents claiming Income Support peaked in August 1995 at 1.06 million and since then has been falling slowly, to 982,000 in November 1997. This could in theory be due to falling claims rather than falling lone parent numbers. However, levelling off is also suggested by the *General Household Survey* and the *Scottish House Condition Survey*, although their sample sizes are too small to permit precise estimates. This incidentally implies that current official projections, based on blind extrapolation of trends from 1971 to 1991, are overestimating the future growth of lone parenthood. It should be remembered however that both 'real' unemployment and lone parenthood remain extremely high in many areas, such as Knowsley, Glasgow or Lambeth.

The British debate on lone parenthood – missing the point

The combination of time series, cross-section and ethnographic evidence in support of the view that the rise in lone parenthood has been mainly due to localised mass unemployment is extremely powerful. Unfortunately, the British debate on lone parenthood has not reflected it. In part, this is simply the result of bad luck: minds were made up before analyses of the crucial 1991 census results became available. For instance, the report of the Commission on Social Justice, central to the present government's thinking, was finalised in July 1994.

Much British research has also suffered from weak methodology. In particular, the *Programme of Research into Low Income Families* (PRILIF) by the Policy

Studies Institute, funded by the Department of Social Security, has used small national samples and has not attempted to investigate the impact of varying local labour market conditions. Spurious findings have resulted, to the effect that work is a realistic route out of poverty for all lone parents, that child care is a sufficient rather than merely a necessary condition for lone parents to work, and that receipt of maintenance makes a lone mother better able to work (Ford *et al*, 1995; Marsh *et al*, 1997). A consideration of the geography shows how these findings have come about. Lone parenthood has increased most in areas of high unemployment, where lone parents cannot find work or afford child care and where the non-resident father is unlikely to be in work and able to pay maintenance. But there are also lone parents in areas of low unemployment. They and their former partners find it much easier to get work, and maintenance is much more likely to be paid. This is what produces the observed positive relationships between working, receiving maintenance and having a higher income. But it does not follow that lone parents in areas where jobs are scarce can replicate this favourable experience.

Political ideology has also played a crucial role. The British debate on lone parenthood has been dominated by the ideas of American conservative writers, notably Charles Murray, who argued in *Losing Ground* (1984) that the rise in lone parenthood in the USA was caused by over generous welfare payments, not unemployment. Katz (1989, p152) shows how 'Murray's success illustrates the role of big money in the marketplace of ideas ... the quality of Murray's intellectual goods was not the only reason for his success'. The *Sunday Times* and the right wing Institute of Economic Affairs (IEA) sponsored Murray to apply his arguments to Britain, starting with *The Emerging British Underclass* in 1990, followed by a second visit in 1994 to write *Underclass: the Crisis Deepens*. These volumes have been heavily promoted. The IEA has also published similar work by other authors including Lawrence Mead, whose *Beyond Entitlement* (1986) is the main source of the idea now espoused by Labour ministers that benefits ought not to be paid as of right but should be 'earned'.

It is surprising that so many people have taken Murray's work seriously, given its overtly ideological character, intemperate language, and weaknesses of evidence and logic. Like PRILIF, *Losing Ground* lacked any consideration of the changing geography of employment. Moynihan (1986) commented that Murray had not 'much addressed the data'. He showed that the increase in US lone parenthood was actually accompanied by a fall in AFDC claims, contrary to what was logically required by Murray's thesis. A recent review (Lichter *et al*, 1997, p136) concluded that 'Little evidence exists to support the apparently widely held perception that welfare is largely responsible for the breakdown of the traditional married couple family'.

Murray's papers on Britain have sought to establish the existence of an 'underclass' defined by moral degeneracy, in the form of illegitimacy, violent crime, and supposed refusal to work. As we have seen, births outside marriage are only loosely connected to lone parenthood, and as an analysis of the latter Murray's work is correspondingly weak. His 1990 paper on Britain was written before the 1991 census and does not contain any serious statistical analysis. In 1994, in so far as he did address it, Murray found himself actually confirming for England and Wales the unemployment-lone parenthood linkage discussed here: 'In 1991, the correlation between the male unemployment rate and the illegitimacy ratio in local authorities was a phenomenal +.85'[3]. Unfortunately, he did not allow this evidence to influence his position.

Murray and the 'New Right' have had a major influence on the policies of both Conservative and Labour governments. Margaret Thatcher (1993, p627-9) acknowledged the influence on her of 'conservative thinkers in the United States on the growth of an "underclass" and the development of a dependency culture … We were feeling our way towards a new ethos for welfare policy … comprising the discouragement of state dependency and the encouragement of self-reliance … and, most controversially, built-in incentives towards decent and responsible behaviour'. In relation to the Labour government, it is Frank Field, former Chair of the House of Commons Social Security Committee and Minister for Welfare Reform, who has been the key conduit for New Right ideas. His book *Losing Out* (1989) – its very title a reflection of Murray's – contained most of the ideas which are currently driving Labour government policy. The government's rhetoric has become more restrained since his departure in July 1998: there have been no comments recently to match Field's 'a major consequence of welfare is now the cultivation of idleness, fecklessness and dishonesty' (1997). However, the view that it is social security, not lack of jobs, which is the main cause of worklessness is still present: the 'moral case for welfare reform' is that 'the benefit system … traps people on benefit … And … is now part of the problem – when it should be part of the solution' (Alistair Darling, Social Security Secretary, July 1999).

Lone parenthood: the public policy agenda

The public policy agenda in Britain has focused on removing supposed housing and social security incentives to becoming a lone parent; raising incomes by getting lone parents into work; raising more money from non-resident fathers, which in turn is also intended to deter lone parenthood; and attempting to influence family structures and parenting more directly.

Lone parents and housing

We have seen that lone parents are badly housed. Because they are so dependent on council housing, they need radical improvements to the neglected stock. The present government has raised public housing investment to a modest extent,

---

3   See Webster (1997) for a discussion of Murray's attempt to avoid the obvious implication of this finding.

particularly if improvements via stock transfers, now at a peak, are considered, but investment remains no higher than it was in about 1994/95. Lone parents also need greater preference in housing allocations; at present they tend to get worse housing than other tenants. This is partly because so many of them enter via homeless applications. As McKendrick (1995) points out, homeless families accept worse accommodation because they do not have the same right as others to refuse an offer without penalty. A 'one offer only' rule is very common.

Better treatment of the homeless would therefore particularly benefit lone parents. But the New Right 'incentives' theory of lone parenthood has played a major role in preventing such improvement. Margaret Thatcher (1993) wrote 'most important ... was to reduce the positive incentives to irresponsible conduct. Young girls were tempted to become pregnant because that brought them a council flat and an income from the state. My advisers and I were considering whether there was some way of providing less attractive – but correspondingly more secure and supervised – housing for these young people. I had seen some excellent hostels of this sort run by the churches.' There was an upsurge of such talk by Conservative politicians during 1993 (*Inside Housing*, 1/10/1993; *Housing*, Dec/Jan 1993/94). Shortly thereafter, a DoE Consultation Paper (January 1994) implied that homeless single mothers were taking council houses away from 'couples seeking to establish a good home in which to start and raise a family' (Cowan, 1998).

The attention paid to teenage mothers in council housing has been disproportionate. As shown earlier, there are very few teenage lone mothers; most live with their own parents, rather than in a house of their own (SEU, 1999a); when they do get council housing it is frequently of very poor quality; and teenagers rarely, if ever, get or stay pregnant with the purpose of getting a house (Allen and Dowling, 1998; SEU, 1999a). SEU (1999a) notes that only 2,000 16-17 year old lone mothers have tenancies; including all aged under 20 increases the figure only to 13,000 (Wilson, 1994). An Institute of Housing survey of local authority housing directors in 1993 found 'no evidence that young single parents are being rehoused at the expense of two-parent families', but that lone parents fared less well in the type of properties they received, and that less than half of authorities would offer immediate access to permanent accommodation (Wilson 1994).

Nevertheless, in a detailed historical analysis, Cowan (1998) has shown how the theme of queue-jumping teenage single mothers was used to prepare the ground for the removal of the right to permanent housing from all homeless people in England and Wales in the Housing Act 1996.

The new Labour government has picked up Margaret Thatcher's theme. Local authorities are to be prohibited from giving an independent tenancy to under 18 lone mothers, and the Housing Corporation has been told to divert £10 million to pilots for semi-independent housing with support (SEU, 1999a). There are some obvious objections to this (Winchester, 1999). While it is likely to work for some teenage mothers, it may not work for others. They may be much better off with a council flat near their own mother. We have seen that sharing lone parents – who are particularly likely to be teenagers – are very overcrowded. Limiting their alternative to a hostel, possibly miles away, is likely to induce them to prolong these bad conditions. However, the number of people involved is small. Much more serious is the associated failure to address the issue of preference in housing allocations for lone mothers and the homeless in general. The government, via regulations, not primary legislation, has restored 'reasonable preference' for the homeless in the allocation of housing, and provided that any temporary private sector accommodation should be for a minimum, rather than a maximum, of two years. But as Cowan (1998) comments, these are changes of form, not substance. The government has not committed itself to restoring the right to permanent housing, nor taken any other action to improve the offers being made to lone parents. It has proposed (Home Office, 1998, para.1.60) that 'due weight' in housing allocations should be given to the needs of grandparents and extended families. The issue, however, is not usually the grandmother's housing – she is normally well-established – but the lone mother's.

Lone parents' incomes

The government's approach to lone parents' incomes is to remove supposed incentives to lone parenthood, and to push lone parents into paid jobs of over 16 hours per week.

The key early action of the Blair government was to implement in 1998 the abolition, already planned by the Conservatives, of the additional Lone Parent premiums (based on carefully researched estimates of lone parents' extra costs) paid within Income Support, Child Benefit, Housing and Council Tax Benefits. It was made clear by Mr Blair after the parliamentary vote of December 1997 that the reason was the belief that these additional benefits provided an incentive to lone parenthood. He has laid down the doctrine that 'there will be no return to that approach', i.e. of recognising lone parents' higher costs.

Subsequently, the government has adopted a policy of increasing benefits equally for lone parent and couple families, while removing support for the higher costs of older children. It thinks that lone parents should not stay at home until their child has left school but should get a job. The net effect of the various changes is that a new (or reclaiming) lone parent with one child over 11 will still be about £2.20 per week worse off in April 2000 than she would have been had the 1998 cuts never been made. A new lone parent with one child under 11 will have had her benefits restored to the pre-cuts level only in April 1999. Only in October 1999 will she be better off by more than a few pence. Lone parent claimants who are private tenants have also (in 1998) lost support for any difference between their actual rent and the local 'reference rent'. There is no sign of restoration of single payments for major household items, which would help to keep lone parents out of debt and make rehousing of the homeless easier. Instead, the government remains among lone parents' many creditors via the Social Fund inherited from the Thatcher years.

Mr Brown's three Budgets taken together will have made 15.1 per cent of households with children in the poorest decile of equivalised post-tax household income worse off than they would have been under the policies prevailing prior to May 1997; many of these are lone parents (Immervoll *et al*, 1999). Income Support remains below the Family Budget Unit's 'low cost but acceptable level' (Parker, 1999), and improvements are being substantially financed by redistribution between different categories of lone parent. The doctrine that any extra help for children of lone parents must also go to children of couple families means both that the huge income differential between the groups cannot be closed and that the cost of any given improvement for lone parents is made much higher. Moreover, because lone parents are geographically concentrated in the areas of highest unemployment, cuts to their benefits have a further 'multiplier' effect in impoverishing these areas.

Lone parents and work

The government conceives the problem of getting lone parents into work as essentially an issue of labour supply (whether lone parents offer themselves for employment) rather than of demand for labour by employers. Hence, the supply-side 'Welfare to Work' New Deal for Lone Parents (NDLP). But the evidence shows that lack of jobs is indeed the principal problem. The relationship between the proportion of lone parents in work and the local unemployment rate in 1991 was extremely close (correlation -0.89).[4] The proportion in work varied from three-fifths (60.5 per cent) in booming South Cambridgeshire, where male unemployment was only 4.7 per cent, to one-fifth or less (16.0-20.5 per cent) in the declining areas of Knowsley, Glasgow and Liverpool, where male unemployment was over 20 per cent (Figure 8.2). In other words, lone parents who want to work will get jobs if they are available in their area, otherwise they will not. This is similar to the position in the USA: 'living in states with low rates of unemployment … increases the likelihood of working (of lone mothers) by nearly half' (IWPR, 1995). The problem is compounded by the fact that all of the New Deal target groups which the government wishes to get into work are disproportionately concentrated in the highest unemployment areas, making the strategy unrealistic unless more jobs are created there (Turok and Webster, 1998). But the government has few programmes to promote jobs in these areas.[5]

4   This correlation is between the proportion of lone parents in work and the logarithm of the unemployment rate. The adjusted R2 (i.e. proportion of variation in the percentage of lone parents in work explained by the log of the unemployment rate) is 0.79. The unemployment rate has been logged to produce the straight-line relationship required to calculate a correlation coefficient.

5   The 'New Deal for Communities' does very little to promote jobs as such; it is mainly a labour 'supply-side' programme, like the other New Deals.

There is abundant evidence from the USA that a Welfare to Work strategy for lone parents either does not work, or does so only at the cost of great hardship for the mothers and their children. Pugh (1998) and Ihlanfeldt and Sjoquist (1998) have established that, as in Britain, there is a deficit of 'entry-level' jobs in the cities and that the existence of 'spatial mismatch' prevents their residents from accessing jobs elsewhere. Edin and Lein (1997) show that 'In the present labour market, unskilled single mothers who hold jobs are frequently worse off than those on welfare'. The Nobel prize winning economist Robert Solow has pointed out (1998) that US Welfare to Work programmes, while placing a lot of people in jobs, have only tiny effects on their subsequent employment probabilities. He derides the 'Panglossian error' that all the problems lie on the supply-side of the labour market: the belief that 'kennel dogs need merely act like bird dogs, and birds will come' (a 'bird dog' is a retriever). He argues that there is a need for more relevant jobs to be created in the right places.

The initial results of the UK NDLP have been predictably poor. Over the first six months, 163,383 letters were sent to lone parents, of which one quarter (23.9 per cent) led to an interview, one fifth (19.6 per cent) to an agreement to participate, and – most important – only 3.8 per cent in an actual job (DfEE press release, 99/052, 5/3/1999). Many of the 3.8 per cent would have got a job anyway, so the true success rate was even lower.

In June 1997, when Tony Blair launched the NDLP on the Aylesbury estate in Southwark, Downing Street 'insisted there was no question of single parents being "hauled" into job centres and forced to take part in interviews.' (*The Scotsman*, 2/6/1997). However, by 10 February 1999 the *Daily Mail* was proclaiming 'Mr Blair has been dismayed by the low take up of the government's New Deal package by lone parents. The vast majority – about 94 per cent (sic) – simply ignore invitations to voluntary interviews'. Mr Blair himself, writing exclusively in the same edition, stated 'It marks the end of a something-for-nothing welfare state. The days of an automatic right to benefit will go. It's tough, but the right thing to do … In future, lone parents will have to come for an interview or risk losing their benefits.'

There has been relatively little protest about these proposed benefit 'sanctions' under the new 'ONE' service or 'single gateway'. But evidence from the New Deal for Young People suggests that they could cause serious problems. There, sanctions have risen to an annual rate of 18,500, including a full one quarter of those allocated to the Environmental Taskforce, and are concentrated on the most socially excluded in high unemployment areas (Bivand, 1999). These 'sanctions' will operate alongside those in the government's Sure Start Programme for the under-3s. A maternity grant worth £200 will be paid to Sure Start mothers, but only on condition that they keep appointments for child health advice and check-ups. It is difficult to reconcile this with the reference in the Home Office's consultation paper *Supporting Families* (1998, para.1.41) to 'parents (who) lack confidence initially to visit more formal services'. It is precisely the most disadvantaged mothers who are likely to lose grant.

The direct persuasion of the NDLP and 'ONE' is being backed up by increasingly large financial inducements to work. A new Working Families Tax Credit (WFTC) is to be paid from October 1999 to every family with an earner working over 16 hours a week, giving a minimum income guarantee of £200 per week to those on 35 hours. The WFTC will include more help with child care costs than the existing Family Credit. Lone parents will also now continue to receive Income Support in their first two weeks in a job. Married couple's allowance is to be replaced (after a 12-month gap) by a children's tax credit which will benefit those few lone parents who are both working and earning enough to incur a sufficient tax liability. The 'poverty trap' created by Housing Benefit (HB) for those in work is being considered in a government review in progress at the time of writing. The obvious approach is to reduce social housing rents, which have been raised enormously since 1979 and have been the main cause of increased HB expenditure. But indications are that the government is more likely to reduce HB than to reduce rents.

Bearing in mind their 'supply-side' nature and experience to date, the whole package of government measures seems likely to increase the number of lone parents in work very little. The Institute for Fiscal Studies has estimated that the WFTC, as originally announced, would add only 10,000 to 45,000 workers to the labour pool (*Financial Times*, 11/2/1999). But since the in-work benefits go to all lone parents in work, including those already in a job, they have a high public expenditure cost and will effect a substantial redistribution of income to lone parents in full-employment areas, mainly in the south of England, leaving those in high unemployment areas relatively unaffected.

Even if lone parents can be got into paid work, there is a question whether they ought to. Half of lone parents on Income Support have a child under school age (Hansard, 7/12/1998) and even where children are older, loss of time with the child can be particularly damaging where there is only one parent for most of the time, and where the family is living in a disadvantaged neighbourhood where a parent's presence is especially important in keeping children out of trouble. It has also been argued that work on top of child care can often be too stressful (e.g. Shouls *et al*, 1999). Edwards and Duncan (1997) show that different groups of lone mothers have differing, but deeply held, views on this question.

The government's emphasis on expanding child care provision has been generally welcomed, although it has been objected that it is not being well targeted to lone parents (*Financial Times*, 18/12/1997). But there has been criticism of the idea that 'the government values the act of looking after strangers' children, but puts none on the demanding work by a parent looking after his or her own child' (*Financial Times*, 18/2/1999). Many lone parents cannot earn enough to make paid child care worthwhile; is the combination of

16+ hours' paid work for the mother and professional childcare for the children so beneficial as to justify extensive public subsidy?

The message from lone parents themselves seems to be that many really do want opportunities for work, training, and child care. Almost half (44 per cent) of those voluntarily signing up for NDLP have children under five. However, some think they either ought not to work or should not work so much as to detract from their role as parents; this may mean working less than the arbitrary lower limit of 16 hours a week applied to WFTC and Child Care Tax Credit. It would be sensible to take more notice of what they think.

Non-resident fathers and maintenance

The treatment of non-resident parents is still bedevilled by the misconceptions of the 1980s. Margaret Thatcher wrote (1993, p630): 'I was … appalled at the way in which men fathered a child and then absconded, leaving the single mother – and the taxpayer – to foot the bill and condemning the child to a lower standard of living … So … I insisted that a new Child Support Agency (CSA) be set up, and that maintenance be based not just on the cost of bringing up a child but on that child's right to share in its parents' rising living standards'. The CSA, which commenced operations in 1993, was designed on the basis of these views, before the 1991 census results came out, and in the almost complete absence of research on non-resident parents. None of the key assumptions on which it was based are correct.

Most non-resident fathers do not appear to be irresponsible in fathering their children; only 9 per cent have never lived with the mother (Bradshaw *et al*, 1999). Most do not have 'rising living standards'. The 'drastic decline in levels of child maintenance that occurred during the 1980s' which the CSA was 'intended to stop' (DSS, 1999, p1) was not due mainly, if at all, to irresponsibility but to the fact that the additional lone parent families were mostly the product of mass unemployment of the children's fathers, who thus had far less money to pay. Bradshaw *et al* showed that, far from 'absconding', almost three-quarters (72 per cent) of British non-resident fathers were in contact with their children's mother, with over half (55 per cent) claiming an amicable relationship with her. Two-thirds (68 per cent) were seeing their children at least once a month and almost half (47 per cent) at least once a week.

They were also paying a significant amount of maintenance without any urging from the CSA. Over half (57 per cent) were currently paying maintenance and three-quarters (77 per cent) had ever paid. Only just over half of payers (57 per cent) had ever had a formal arrangement (CSA, Court etc) to do so. Payers were giving £60 per week on average in formal and informal support, 21 per cent of their income. Most non-payers were giving some informal support, with only 14 per cent of fathers having never given some informal support. The fact that three-quarters of current payers had jobs, compared to only a quarter (28 per cent) of those who had never paid, goes a long way to explain why the proportions paying and amounts paid are not higher. Bradshaw *et al.* classified only half (49 per cent) of non-resident fathers as having 'certain' or 'probable' paying potential, and two-fifths (38 per cent) as having none.

The CSA's own statistics for May 1997 confirm the extent of non-resident fathers' poverty. In respect of the better off group of 149,700 lone parents who were not themselves on Income Support, two-thirds of former partners had jobs and one quarter (26.3 per cent) were on social security. However, of the 380,700 former partners of lone parents who were on Income Support, less than half (47.8 per cent) had jobs, and almost as many (46.6 per cent) were themselves on social security. The level of maintenance assessments reflected this. Two-fifths (212,900) were nil, and a further one in seven was for under £5 per week, so that overall, half were for less than £3.34.

The CSA has been one of the greatest administrative disasters of recent times. The proportion of lone parents on Income Support receiving maintenance is no greater now than before the CSA was introduced (DSS, 1998a). In 1997/98, administration costs took 41p out of every £1 collected or arranged – much of which would have been paid anyway. The Treasury received so little (£141 million or about 3 per cent of lone parent IS costs) that the CSA operation had a net public cost of £85m. Over one third (38.3 per cent) of absent parents with an assessment were in arrears or not paying at all, and there was a backlog of 407,000 unprocessed cases. Finally, one quarter (26 per cent) of maintenance assessments were inaccurate (1996/97 figures, *Guardian*, 23/7/1997).

Experience in the USA, which provided the model for the CSA, has been similar; 'Federal efforts to improve the collection of child support from fathers appear to have little effect on payments' (Garfinkel *et al*, 1998). Johnson *et al*, (1999) point out that US non-custodial parents have often been vilified as 'deadbeats' who have dropped out of their children's lives, and have been the target of largely punitive enforcement policies. They argue on the basis of experience that they are likely to respond better to a less adversarial and more supportive approach which gives more consideration to the complex circumstances of their lives. The same is likely to be true in Britain.

However, the government has not seen the need to question the fundamental assumptions. 'We know why (the CSA) failed. The formula for calculating maintenance was too complicated, and too little benefit … went to the children' (DSS, 1999, pviii). It proposes to simplify the maintenance formula, raising more money generally from poorer fathers and bringing more poor fathers into the net; to toughen the sanctions for non-payment, introducing fines and even prison; and to allow lone parents on Income Support, for the first time, to receive some benefit – the first £10 per week – from the maintenance paid. But in the commonest case – particularly in high unemployment areas – the non-resident parent will be on benefit himself and only liable to pay £5, and in many cases he will already be paying at least this much unofficially. In the usual case where there is no second family, the £10 figure will only be reached when the father's income reaches £110-£118. The actual benefit to children, and any reduction in the over 70 per cent of lone mothers on Income Support who seek to avoid making a child support application, are likely to be small. Working lone parents on WFTC, by contrast, will keep all maintenance paid, and will not even have to co-operate with the CSA. This will further widen the gap between poor people in high unemployment areas and better off people in prosperous areas.

A more realistic way ahead

The government has a great deal of policy on lone parenthood. But too little of it will achieve its objectives, while much will be experienced by lone parents as positively threatening, adding new stresses to what is already one of the most stressed social positions in modern Britain.

Whatever other policies are followed, it is essential quickly to raise lone parent benefits: today's generation of children are only young once. With the 'incentives' theory of lone parenthood discredited, there is no reason to fear that this will make the problem worse. In the longer term, the real issue is not the welfare state but the male unemployment and related undermining of men's economic role which this paper has shown is the principal cause of increased relationship breakdown. *Supporting Families* (Home Office, 1998, para.6.6) does in fact get to the root of the issue in a single brief paragraph about the problems facing young men – what is jocularly referred to in Whitehall as the 'lads and dads' agenda. 'Increasingly, boys and young men seem to have difficulty maturing into responsible citizens and fathers. Declining educational performance, loss of traditional "male" jobs, the growth of a "laddish" anti-social culture, greater use of drugs, irresponsible teenage fatherhood, and the rising suicide rate may all show rising insecurity and uncertainty among young men'. With the exception of 'irresponsible teenage fatherhood' – shown above to be rare – this is mainly an accurate list of problematic reactions to men's worsened economic prospects. But to mention the main cause of the problems – loss of traditional 'male' jobs – within this list of effects reveals the lack of a coherent analysis.

Reasons have already been given for thinking that the purely supply-side approach of the government's New Deal is not going to work for the areas where lone parents are concentrated, which are those with the greatest shortage of jobs. An effective policy on employment requires to operate on two levels; first, to address the overall loss of blue collar jobs resulting from the rundown of manufacturing, and second, to deal with the problems which have caused the cities, coalfields and some other places to lose disproportionate numbers of blue collar jobs. The issue of British policy towards manufacturing involves considerations which go well beyond the scope of this book. All that can be done here is to flag up its importance. The same however is not true of 'urban-rural manufacturing shift'. This is a question of spatial planning which is intrinsically related to housing, since any housing system must be based on a well-functioning home-workplace relationship.

Turok and Edge (1999) comment that their study of the geographical pattern of employment change 'has revealed the overriding importance of taking action to increase labour demand in and around the cities ... there is a particular need to expand employment opportunities for blue collar workers, and greater effort and resources should be devoted to this important challenge by all levels of government'. This mainly requires more spending on derelict land and infrastructure, since Fothergill *et al* (1985) and others have shown that the main factor driving blue collar jobs out of the cities is the lack of suitable sites and premises. This in turn would help to relieve the problems of declining demand for housing in the cities, and excessive pressure for new house building in the shires. A reduced rate of family breakdown would reduce household growth, relieving pressure for new house building all round. At the end of the day, policies for lone parenthood are a second-best. Ideally, we want families to stay happily together.

CHAPTER 9:
Housing and young single people

Suzanne Fitzpatrick

Introduction

This chapter examines the position of single young people aged 16 to 24 in the housing market[1]. It focuses on young workers, that is those who are employed, training or unemployed, rather than students. The chapter relates primarily to the position of Scottish young people, but sets this in the British context whenever possible. It is appropriate to use Scotland as a case study of housing and young people for two reasons. First, narrowing the housing market context enables a more precise analysis of young people's position to be undertaken. Second, research on young people and the housing market based on the Scottish Young People's Survey (SYPS)[2] is more extensive than work undertaken elsewhere in Britain (Jones, 1993; 1995a).

The chapter begins by examining young people's role in the social exclusion debate, before turning to consider the deteriorating economic position of this age group. The demand for housing from young people is then examined. The main part of the chapter explores whether the housing market provides suitable accommodation for young single workers on low incomes. Each of the main housing tenures is examined, as well as specialist youth accommodation. The chapter concludes by considering the relationship between these housing concerns and the social exclusion of young people.

Social exclusion and young people

The concept of social exclusion is discussed at length elsewhere in this volume (see, in particular, Chapter 2). However, it is worth highlighting here the relationship between young people and social exclusion.

---

1   By 'single' I mean people who are not living with a long-term partner or dependent children.
2   The *Scottish Young People's Survey* (SYPS) is a longitudinal study of cohorts of young Scots surveyed at around 17 years old and again at age 19. The two cohorts referred to in this chapter were interviewed in 1987 and 1989 (SYPS, 1989) and in 1989 and 1991 (SYPS, 1991).

Academic definitions of social exclusion (e.g. Room, 1995a) generally imply that it is:

- a multidimensional concept, which embraces income poverty but is broader: it also encompasses lack of participation in social, economic, political and cultural life;
- concerned with the processes which sustain disadvantage. The socially excluded are those whose long-term life chances are severely restricted, often, but not necessarily, geographically concentrated in particular neighbourhoods.

Young people are central to debates on social exclusion for a number of reasons. First, youth is a crucial, formative stage in the life course. Opportunities and experiences at this age, and decisions made at this point, can fundamentally affect a person's long-term life chances. Second, the social exclusion debate can be seen, at least to some extent, as an attempt to move on from the 'underclass' thesis and its ethos of 'blaming the victim' (see Murray, 1990). However, some of the emphasis within the underclass debate on the values and behaviour of unmarried teenage mothers and unemployed young males has carried over into the social exclusion agenda. The third, and most important, point is that young people are particularly vulnerable to social exclusion.

Moving from youth to adulthood has been conceptualised as involving three main interlocking 'careers':

- education, training and labour market career (the school to work transition);
- domestic career (from families of origin to families of destination);
- housing and household career (from parental home to independent home).
(Coles, 1995).

Social, economic and policy developments over the last couple of decades have made each of these youth transitions far more complex and hazardous. A key factor has been young people's deteriorating economic position, discussed in the next section.

This chapter will consider a particular dimension of social exclusion amongst young people: namely marginalisation in the housing market. Thus, it focuses on young people's housing and household careers, although these clearly interact with their labour market and domestic transitions. The chapter concentrates on young single workers on low incomes as this is the group with the least favourable position in the housing market.

The most obvious symptom of young people's marginalisation in the housing market is the very high levels of youth homelessness. However, only brief mention is made of homelessness in this chapter, as it is too complex an area to explore properly here. Homelessness is discussed more fully in Chapter 6.

The deteriorating economic position of young people

Young people's economic position relative to adults has declined substantially since the 1970s, and this has seriously undermined their bargaining power in the housing market. The key factor has been the collapse of the youth labour market. The proportion of British 16 year olds in employment fell from 61 per cent in 1974 to 18 per cent in 1984, and by the mid-1990s only around one in eight 16 year olds held a full-time job (Coles, 1995).

This drop in employment is partly accounted for by the steep rise in levels of participation in post-compulsory education, and by the expansion of youth training schemes. But youth unemployment has also grown dramatically since the 1970s, and has consistently outstripped adult rates. Whilst youth unemployment fell in the mid-1990s, unemployment levels of more than 30 per cent persist amongst young people in some deprived areas (Roberts, 1997).

There has been a significant reduction in the social security protection given to unemployed young people over the past decade. Those aged 16 and 17 have been worst affected. They lost their entitlement to Income Support (IS) in 1988, except in certain exceptional circumstances, such as having a child or being disabled, but may apply for a discretionary award of IS on grounds of 'severe hardship'. In place of entitlement to IS, 16 and 17 year olds were 'guaranteed' a youth training (YT) place. However, this guarantee was often not met because insufficient training places were provided in some areas (Maclagan, 1992). Allowances paid under these training schemes are considerably lower than wages paid to young workers by employers.

Since 1988 unemployed young people aged 18 to 24 have received lower rates of IS than those aged 25 or over. The Job Seekers' Allowance (JSA) introduced in 1996 to replace Unemployment Benefit (UB) and IS for those in the labour market has meant that 18-24 year olds who would previously have been able to claim UB have lost money because there is an age differential in contributory JSA.

Young people under 25 have also, since 1988, been disadvantaged in relation to Housing Benefit (HB) because it begins to be withdrawn from them at a lower level of income than for those over 25. Since October 1996 the eligible rent for HB purposes for private tenants who are single and under 25 has been limited to the average local rent for shared accommodation in their area.

Another social security change in 1988 with important implications for young people on low incomes was the abolition of 'exceptional needs payments' for large expenses such as furniture and equipment for setting up home. This system was replaced by the discretionary and budget limited Social Fund. Applicants to the Social Fund have to establish a high priority for their claim to have any chance of an award, and payments usually take the form of repayable loans. Most housing costs, such as deposits, are excluded, and although rent in advance may be awarded it does not constitute a high priority.

Even young people in work are poorer than their predecessors, as the gap between adult and youth wages has widened. For example, in 1979 full-time male employees aged 16 and 17 earned around two-thirds of the average full-time male wage, but by 1995 they earned only a third (Hickman, 1997). Young people under 18 have been excluded from the new National Minimum Wage, and a lower minimum has been set for 18 to 20 year olds.

These labour market and social security trends have extended the period of young people's economic dependency on their families. However, while some parents may subsidise their children until they are 25, numerous studies of youth homelessness demonstrate that not all young people have families willing and able to support and accommodate them. Forcing young people to rely on their parents is particularly problematic for those brought up in 'non-conventional' families. Lone parent families are considerably poorer on average than two-parent families, and there is evidence that young people from step-families experience particular difficulties in obtaining parental support (Jones, 1995b).

The Labour government has not removed age-based discriminations in the social security system, but youth unemployment is one of their policy priorities and 18-24 year olds unemployed for more than 6 months were the first target group for the 'New Deal' programme. However, the New Deal has been criticised as a supply-side measure with no job creation dimension, therefore young people in areas of high unemployment may find it difficult to move on to long-term work (Turok and Webster, 1998). There is also an element of compulsion in the New Deal, with the social security benefit of those who refuse to participate being withdrawn for specified periods.

The demand for youth housing

Central to the demand for youth housing is young people's patterns of leaving home. The factors which influence the decision of young people to leave home and embark on independent living have been divided into 'push' and 'pull' categories (Bannister *et al*, 1993). The pursuit of work, training or educational opportunities, and getting married or moving in with a partner, are amongst the positive 'pull' reasons to leave home. Negative 'push' factors may force some young people out of the family home. These include family conflict, violence or sexual abuse, or simply poverty and a lack of space and privacy. Young people over 16 can also be thrown out by their parents as they are merely 'licensees' in the family home.

The more prominent are the push factors in a young person's decision to leave home, the more problematic the transition into an independent household is likely to be. Young people who leave home for negative reasons tend to leave at an early age, and so are less likely to have the resources and skills required to set up home successfully. During the process of leaving home it is normal for young people to receive a great deal of emotional and practical support from their families (Bannister *et al*, 1993). But for those fleeing family conflict this parental support is less likely to be forthcoming. Jones (1995a) has also argued that these young people do not attract state support for their transition, such as access to housing or income, because their move is not considered 'legitimate'.

Young people's reasons for leaving home are closely related to their age at leaving. There are three main 'waves' of home-leavers:

- the earliest leavers, under 18, tend to leave because of family conflict or to take up a job or look for work;
- the next wave are 18 year olds who leave mainly to go on an educational course;
- older leavers are more likely to leave to marry or cohabit.
(Jones, 1995a).

Women tend to leave home earlier, partly because they are more likely to move away to study and they have a younger average age of marriage (Furlong and Cartmel, 1997). A study of 1981 data highlighted the impact of social class on the leaving home process:

> *The working class may typically remain in the parental home until marriage, when the move will be permanent, one way, and into marital housing. The middle class may leave home for educational reasons, at a younger age, return to the parental home after having ostensibly left it, and live in temporary, intermediate forms of living accommodation* (Jones, 1987, p71).

There have been a number of important shifts in the reasons for young people leaving home in recent years which have amended these patterns to some extent (Jones, 1995a):

- fewer young people are leaving home to move in with a partner;
- significantly more young people now leave to become students;
- there has been an increase in the numbers of young people leaving home due to family problems.

A number of researchers have noted an apparent rise in the age at leaving the parental home in recent years (for example, Holmans, 1996). However, the underlying trend appears to be that the average age at which young people *first* move out of the family home has declined, but they *last* leave home later (Furlong and Cartmel, 1997). In other words, the process of leaving home has become more prolonged and complex in recent years. In particular, working class young people are more likely to be following the middle class pattern of returning to the family home. Some of these young people may choose to return, particularly as increasing numbers are leaving for reasons which are traditionally more 'reversible', e.g. to become a student. For others, however, the difficulties they face in trying to live independently may be forcing them to return.

Household formation patterns have also adjusted. Working class young people are increasingly likely to experience an intermediate stage between living with their parents and living with a partner. Single person households are becoming significantly more common, and the incidence of peer households (sharing with other young people) also appears to be increasing (Jones, 1995a). This latter trend is probably due primarily to an expanding student population, but there may also be an emerging phenomenon of young workers sharing accommodation.

Young people have to compete with other types of households for housing as well as with each other. The overall demand for housing in Britain has increased in recent years, mainly as the result of a substantial growth in the number of single person households. In 1971 only 17 per cent of British households contained a single individual, but by 1996 the figure had reached 27 per cent (*General Household Survey*, 1996). This trend is attributable to rising divorce rates and an ageing population, as well as a growing tendency for unmarried people to live alone (Ermisch, 1990). The number of Scottish households is therefore predicted to increase from 2,067,000 in 1992 to 2,293,000 in 2006. However, there is actually a projected decline in young households throughout Britain over the next decade associated with falling birth rates in the late 1960s and 1970s, although this drop in population may be offset by more young people leaving home earlier. The housing system is ill prepared to meet the growing demand for single person accommodation as both major sectors, public rented housing and owner-occupation, remain overwhelmingly family orientated.

The key points from this section are as follows:

- first, it seems that there is an expanding group of vulnerable home-leavers 'at risk' within the housing market because they are leaving at a young age and for negative reasons;
- second, more working class young people require access to transitional, non-family housing;
- third, young people face increasingly stiff competition for single person accommodation, as the housing market is not geared up to meet the demand from this household type.

Young people in the housing market

The supply of housing

As has been described elsewhere in this volume, government policies since 1979 have brought about a dramatic change in the tenure structure in Britain, including Scotland. Table 9.1 indicates that owner-occupation grew from 35 per cent of the housing stock in Scotland in 1981 to 60 per cent in 1997. Over the same period the public rented sector (including local authorities, Scottish Homes and New Towns) shrunk from 53 per cent to 28 per cent of total housing stock. The private rented sector continued a long-term decline, dropping from 10 per cent in 1981 to less than 7 per cent in 1997. The housing association sector has more than doubled its stock since 1981, but still only accounts for around 5 per cent of housing in Scotland.

Table 9.1: Tenure structure of Scotland's housing stock, 1981 and 1997

Tenure	1981 (%)	1997 (%)
Owner-occupation	35	60
Public rental	53	28
Private renting	10	7
Housing association	2	5

Sources: Wilcox, 1997; Scottish Office, 1998a

The tenure structure in Scotland remains distinct from that of England, where owner-occupation accounts for more than two-thirds of the housing stock and the council sector only about a fifth of houses. Scotland's private rented sector is smaller than in England, which has around 10 per cent of its housing stock in this tenure.

Young people's position in the housing market

Among young people, three 'housing consumer groups' can be identified: single students, families and single workers (Jones, 1993). Each of these groups tend to occupy different sectors of the housing market when living away from the parental home:

- single students often live in accommodation provided by the institution, such as halls of residence, or in the private rented sector;

- families with children, both lone parents and couples, are given priority by the public rented sector. Childless couples have the greatest access to owner-occupation amongst this age group[3];
- young single workers have no clearly identifiable section of the housing market catering for them. The state has traditionally done little to assist this group into independent living, other than those entering particular professions such as nursing or the armed forces.

The SYPS (1989) indicated that 62 per cent of 19 year olds were 'single workers'. However, they were less likely than the other housing consumer groups to be active in the housing market; only 20 per cent were living independently at the time of the survey. This is likely in part to reflect their lack of housing opportunity.

Table 9.2 below demonstrates that young single people (heads of household aged between 16 and 24 years old) have a very different tenure profile from that of the population as a whole[4]. They are significantly less likely to be owner-occupiers than older age groups, and far more likely to be renting from a private landlord[5]. Young single people are also disproportionately represented in the public and housing association sectors.

Table 9.2: Comparison of tenure profile of young, single heads of household and all heads of household in Scotland (%)

Tenure	All heads of household	Young single heads of household (16-24 years)
Owner-occupation	56	27
Public rental	32	36
Private renting	8	27
Housing association	4	10

Source: The *Scottish House Condition Survey*, 1996, deposited in the Data Archive, University of Essex. These figures are weighted.

---

3   Jones' (1993) concept of 'housing consumer groups' may be criticised for placing childless couples and families with children in the same category, as these two groups have very different income profiles which mean that they are in quite distinct positions in the housing market. However, the main purpose of this classification was to highlight the marginalised position of young single workers in the housing system and it is effective in doing so.

4   It should be noted that Table 9.2 relates to all young single people, as it was not possible to get separate data for young single workers.

5   It should be noted that the tenure profile of young single people is likely to diverge even more significantly from the population as a whole than these figures suggest. Table 9.2 is based on young single adult households, and excludes those living in flatshare or lodging situations if they share one meal a day or a living room with the other residents of the house. The proportion of single young people in the private rented sector is therefore probably underestimated, as this is the tenure in which young single people typically share accommodation.

These figures provide a snapshot of young people's housing circumstances at a particular point in time. The route which young people take through the housing market is generally related to their social class. Middle class young people have tended to move from the parental home into the private rented sector or student housing, before moving onto home-ownership. In comparison, working class young people more often move directly from their parents' home into one of the two 'major' tenures, owner-occupation or social rented housing, and stay within that tenure for the remainder of their housing careers. However, these housing careers are likely to adjust in the light of the household formation trends discussed earlier.

Young workers and the housing market

This section considers whether each of the major sectors of the housing market provides appropriate accommodation for young single workers on low incomes. These young people generally require accommodation which is inexpensive; of a small size; in an appropriate location; and which offers flexibility, given their often rapidly changing geographical and family circumstances. Some young people, particularly those who lack parental support, will need help from public agencies to sustain their independent accommodation. This may include material assistance, such as furniture and equipment for setting up home, and practical support with living skills, such as budgeting, cooking and dealing with bureaucracy. A small minority will also have emotional support needs or require specialist help with problems such as drug or alcohol dependency. Whether landlords or other agencies should provide this support and who should fund it are difficult issues; nevertheless support issues are considered below along with other aspects of the suitability of accommodation.

Owner-occupation

The expansion of owner-occupation has been encouraged by successive UK governments through tax and other policies, although state support for home-owners has diminished in recent years (McCrone and Stephens, 1995). Home-ownership suffered a series of setbacks in the 1990s, including unprecedented levels of negative equity, mortgage arrears and repossessions by mortgage lenders. These problems have, however, been somewhat less severe in Scotland than in England.

Access to owner-occupation is determined by market processes, and the most important criterion is the ability to secure and repay a mortgage. Financial deregulation in the 1980s led to mortgages becoming more readily available to young people, but in the most recent housing slump young owners were particularly vulnerable to repossession (Anderson, 1994). In the early 1990s there was a significant fall in the number of young households entering owner-occupation in the UK (Holmans, 1996).

Owner-occupation is not a realistic option for the majority of young single people because their incomes are insufficient to raise a mortgage. Also, they generally do not have the resources to pay for deposits and legal fees, or to furnish and equip an empty house. In any case, young people may not welcome the financial responsibilities or potential barriers to geographical mobility which home-ownership brings (Jones, 1995a). There is, of course, no provision of support for young people within this tenure.

Public rented sector

The public rented sector in Scotland, although still larger than elsewhere in Britain, has been shrinking as the result of the virtual cessation of new building by public sector landlords, and the loss of stock through transfers to sitting tenants and to other landlords (mainly housing associations). By 1995, 310,000 Scottish tenants had bought their homes under the 'Right-to-Buy' provisions (Scott and Parkey, 1996b). Most sales to tenants in Scotland have been of desirable properties in high amenity areas, leaving a residualised council sector containing a high proportion of low demand housing in peripheral schemes. As better off tenants have exercised the Right-to-Buy, the concentration of poor and vulnerable households in the public sector has increased.

Access to the public rented sector is generally on the basis of housing need. There are two routes into council housing: via the waiting-list and through the homeless persons legislation. As regards the waiting-list, public landlords have wide discretion in determining their allocation priorities. Young people can take up tenancies from age 16 in Scotland, and local authorities are not permitted to discriminate against them on the basis of age as regards admission to the waiting-list or allocation of housing. The situation is different in England and Wales, where age restrictions on eligibility for housing are both permissible and commonplace (Anderson and Morgan, 1997).

Allocation policies are usually based on categories of households and points awarded for various 'housing need' factors, and most policies give some weighting to the length of time an applicant has been on the waiting-list. While these policies generally give priority to families with children, Dyer's (1993) survey of Scottish local authority waiting-lists found that 44 per cent of applicants wished to set up a single person household. It also revealed that applicants are generally young, with nearly half aged under 30. Nevertheless, Anderson and Morgan's (1997) research on British local authorities indicates that they often fail to take account of housing need factors which are most likely to apply to young single people, e.g. insecure circumstances such as living in hostels, staying with friends or sleeping rough.

The other route into local authority housing is through the Housing (Homeless Persons) Act 1977 (now incorporated into the Housing Act 1996 and Housing (Scotland) Act 1987). Local authorities have a duty to secure accommodation for households which become homeless 'unintentionally', provided they belong to a 'priority' group such as families with dependent children. Local authorities are required to 'have regard' to a code of guidance accompanying the legislation, although they are not obliged to follow it. The statutory protection given to homeless people was substantially reduced in England and Wales by the Housing Act 1996, but the homelessness legislation remains unchanged in Scotland. However, the House of Lords has ruled that even under this statutory framework the accommodation provided to homeless households need not be permanent in nature, although it must be offered indefinitely (R v Brent LBC *ex p.* Awua [1995] 1 A.C. 55).

Official statistics indicate that young single people aged 16 to 24 are disproportionately affected by homelessness; this age group accounts for only 17 per cent of the adult population in the UK but comprises 25 per cent of homeless applicants to local authorities (Evans, 1996). There were 10,300 single homeless applicants under 25 in Scotland in 1996/7, and, in line with the UK figures, they accounted for just over a quarter of all applicant households (Scottish Office, 1998a).

Most single people are excluded from the protection of the homelessness provisions unless they are assessed as particularly 'vulnerable'. The *Scottish Code of Guidance* issued in 1991 specified that 16 and 17 year olds, care-leavers, and young people over 17 at risk of sexual or financial exploitation were amongst the groups which may be considered 'vulnerable' and thus entitled to 'priority' status. Shelter (Scotland) noted that local authorities had gradually adopted more sympathetic policies towards young homeless people in the early 1990s (Caskie, 1993). However, by 1993 still only 32 Scottish district councils (57 per cent) deemed all 16 and 17 year olds as vulnerable (Dyer, 1993). In 1996/7 almost half of single applicants aged under 18 in Scotland were assessed as being homeless and in priority need (44 per cent), but only 15 per cent of those aged 18 to 24 (Scottish Office, 1998a).

The new *Scottish Code of Guidance on Homelessness*, which came into effect in December 1997 adds involvement in drug, solvent or alcohol abuse as a risk which should be taken into account in assessing vulnerability. A new statutory instrument provides that those under 21 who were 'looked after' by a local authority at school leaving age or later should always be regarded as vulnerable. Also, the Children (Scotland) Act 1995 places a duty on the Scottish unitary authorities (which include both housing and social work services) to provide accommodation for children up to 18 years of age if no adult is providing suitable accommodation and care. This means that even if a local authority does not accept a statutory responsibility to accommodate a 16 or 17 year old under the homelessness legislation, they may have a duty under this Act. It also provides a power (rather than a duty) for local authorities to provide accommodation for young people aged between 18 and 21. These legal developments should substantially increase the protection given to young homeless people, but research suggests that not all Scottish councils have as yet embraced these additional responsibilities (Corbett, 1998).

Young single people have easier access to public sector housing in Scotland than elsewhere in Britain because of the larger stock available, at least in urban areas, and the more favourable legal position. However, this does not necessarily mean that this housing meets the needs of young people. The unsatisfactory quality and location of much Scottish council housing has already been mentioned. As young, single people constitute a low priority group they will often be allocated the least popular housing, particularly those who are accommodated through the homeless persons provisions (Fitzpatrick and Stephens, 1999). Most houses are family sized, and many authorities limit single people's eligibility for such housing to difficult-to-let areas (Pedreschi, 1991). The lack of new building means that public sector landlords cannot develop appropriate smaller properties to meet the growing demands of single applicants (Thornton, 1990).

The vast majority of council and other public sector housing is unfurnished, and it is difficult for young people on low incomes to take up these tenancies because of the restrictions of the Social Fund. Some local authorities, including Glasgow, have developed a stock of furnished, supported scatter flats for young single people. This is a valuable intervention, but the 'unemployment trap' faced by young people, created by the rapid withdrawal of HB as income rises, is exacerbated by the high rents charged to cover the additional costs of these flats. Anderson and Morgan (1997) report that only two-fifths of all British local authorities provide support to vulnerable single people, and in the main this consists of liaison with other agencies on behalf of tenants. Very few provide furnished tenancies or specialist support workers.

Private rented sector

The private rented stock in Scotland is split between tied, unfurnished and furnished sectors. The tied and unfurnished sectors are concentrated in rural Scotland, whereas furnished accommodation consists mainly of tenement flats in urban areas. Most of the recent decline in the private rented sector in Scotland has been in unfurnished rather than furnished accommodation (Kemp, 1994).

Young people are concentrated in the private rented sector, particularly in furnished accommodation. The *Scottish House Conditions Survey* indicates that about a quarter of all household heads in the furnished sector in Scotland are under 25, and the figure for Britain as a whole is very similar (Wilcox, 1997). Private renting in youth has been associated mainly with the middle classes in recent times, but, as discussed above, working class young people are increasingly in need of this transitional accommodation. However, the small size of the stock constrains the number of young people that this sector can accommodate. In any case Kemp and Rhodes (1994) found that young, single people were the type of household Scottish private landlords least preferred to let to.

There are three main economic barriers to access to the private rented sector for young people on low incomes:

- first, the restrictions of the Social Fund have made it much more difficult to obtain payments for deposits or rent in advance which are normally required to secure a private tenancy;
- second, there is evidence that most private landlords would prefer not to let to tenants in receipt of HB (Kemp and Rhodes, 1994), and single tenants under 25 face particular difficulties created by the restrictions on their HB entitlement;
- third, there are now fewer lets available at the bottom end of the market and more accommodation targeted at higher income groups.

(Bailey, 1996).

Private renting has a number of drawbacks for young people. It is expensive as compared with social rented housing, and the accommodation at the bottom end of the market is often of poor quality and insecure. Clearly, there is no social support offered by commercial landlords. On the other hand, the private rented sector has several advantages for this age group. It offers access on demand, and allows geographical mobility, and mobility within localities, not afforded by the more secure tenures of council housing and owner-occupation. Furthermore, furnished private accommodation enables young people to set up home relatively cheaply. Shared housing in the private sector also offers young people company and the opportunity to share living costs.

Housing associations

In 1989, the last government identified housing associations as the main providers of new social rented housing in Britain, and this sector continues to increase rapidly, mainly through stock transfers from public sector landlords. However, associations have had their capital subsidies reduced in recent years, and as a result have been forced to increase rent levels. There have therefore been concerns about affordability in this sector (Anderson, 1994), although the situation is not yet as acute in Scotland where subsidies have remained higher than in England.

Like the public rented sector, housing association accommodation is broadly allocated on the basis of need. However, in contrast to local authorities, associations have traditionally played an important role in housing single people, and Anderson and Morgan (1997) found that housing association policies were generally sensitive to the needs of young people. Households may gain access to housing association accommodation either directly through the association's waiting-list, or indirectly through local authority nominations. As well as offering mainstream housing of an appropriate size for single people, many associations provide hostel accommodation, furnished flats and supported housing for young people. However, the housing association sector is severely constrained in the extent to which it can meet the needs of young people by the small size of its stock.

Specialist youth housing

This chapter is concerned primarily with young people's position in the mainstream housing market. However, it would be incomplete without noting the specialist accommodation which has been developed for this age group.

The SYPS (1989) indicated that just under one third of young people who had left home by age 19 occupied various forms of transitional housing such as nurse's homes, army barracks and student halls of residence (Jones, 1995a). The quality of accommodation and degree of privacy in this sector is frequently low. Nevertheless, these forms of accommodation are important because they allow young people to take up employment or education away from their home area without having to compete in the mainstream housing market.

Two principal forms of transitional housing exist to cater for more disadvantaged young people. The longest established is 'youth residential projects'. These were developed from the 1970s onwards as an alternative to traditional, adult hostels for young homeless people. They are small-scale projects, typically accommodating 10 to 20 young people, which offer support and independence training. Most are managed by housing associations or other voluntary sector bodies, though some are run by social work departments.

The more recent innovation is 'foyers'. These are based on a French network of hostels for young workers which was established in the late 1940s to mobilise labour in the post-war period. A Foyer Federation for Youth was established in 1992 to promote the development of foyers in Britain. The term foyer in Britain has become closely associated with the provision of employment and training services within a hostel environment (Anderson and Quilgars, 1995). Many foyers offer light support and are relatively large, although some new foyers are adopting a more flexible structure, catering for smaller numbers of young people and offering varying levels of support.

There are a large number of foyer projects currently in operation in England, but their development has been much slower in Scotland (Anderson and Douglas, 1998). The Labour government has expressed support for the continued development of foyers. The main advantage of foyers is that they represent a 'holistic' approach to addressing young people's housing and employment needs. However, there are significant concerns about this form of youth housing, particularly the institutional style of accommodation which is usually provided. The limited research which has been conducted on young peoples' housing preferences has made clear their general dislike of hostels and strong preference for dispersed, self-contained accommodation (for example, Snape, 1992). Linking young people's accommodation to their willingness to work or undertake training is also potentially regressive (Gilchrist and Jeffs, 1995). There is some ambiguity about whether foyers are intended to cater for young homeless people. The levels of support provided often seem insufficient for this group, yet it appears that in practice foyers do cater for vulnerable young people, including many who have experienced rooflessness (Anderson and Quilgars, 1995).

Conclusions

A central tenet of this book is that adequate housing is central to a person's well-being, and poor housing has repercussions across a whole range of other aspects of life, such as employment, physical and psychological health, social interaction, and participation in education. The housing market plays a particularly important role in the spatial patterning of social exclusion, through tenure and allocation policies which have often had the effect of concentrating vulnerable households in deprived public sector housing estates.

Marginalisation within the housing system is therefore a key factor in the social exclusion of particular groups within society. Young single workers on low incomes are particularly vulnerable because they have no real niche in the housing market, and generally lack the economic power or social priority of other households. This chapter has demonstrated the difficulties which these young people face in gaining access to each of the main sectors of the housing market, and the drawbacks and advantages of each of these forms of housing for this group. There remains a need to expand the stock of accommodation appropriate to young single workers. These young people's needs are unlikely to be met by owner-occupation because of the high costs and lack of flexibility inherent in this tenure, and so we must instead look to the private and social rented sectors.

One option would be to encourage the expansion of the bottom end of the furnished private rented sector through tax breaks and other such incentives to private landlords prepared to accept young tenants on low incomes. This option would allow young people greater flexibility and geographical mobility than other tenures. Shared housing in the private sector may be an appropriate option for some young people as it considerably reduces their living costs. However, it seems likely that many young people, particularly the most disadvantaged, wish to live alone (see Fitzpatrick, 1997). The HB regulations would have to be revised to allow these young people access to full benefit for single person accommodation in the private rented sector. If young people on low incomes are to have greater access to private renting, the Social Fund would also have to be made more generous to allow them to obtain deposits and rent in advance for private landlords.

Expanding the stock of housing association properties would be likely to benefit young single people given their record of providing appropriate housing for this group. Another option would be to refurbish some of the low demand council stock to be suitable for single young people. Ideally, these houses would be converted into small dwellings, but a more important point is that a large proportion of this accommodation should be furnished as many young people do not have the possessions required to set up home. Alternatively, the Social Fund could supply grants to young people to purchase their own furniture and equipment. There may be some scope for shared housing for young people within the public sector, but young people's natural desire to have some choice about whom they live with may clash with administrative arrangements which allocate places on the basis of housing need.

It is crucial that housing options developed for young single workers on low incomes are inexpensive. Reliance on HB to cover high rent levels is unhelpful for these young people as the resulting 'unemployment trap' prevents them taking up low paid work. One way around this would be for the HB regulations to be made more generous so that young people could keep more of their earnings from employment, or subsidies could be provided to private and public landlords to keep rents low.

A final point is that tenancy support for young people requires greater attention and funding (Anderson and Morgan, 1997). Some young people, particularly the younger home-leavers with problematic family backgrounds, require social support to sustain their tenancies. Without such support these tenancies frequently fail, often exacerbating young people's problems as they find themselves saddled with rent arrears and labelled 'intentionally homeless'. These failed tenancies also contribute to the tendency of many landlords to view young people as 'problem tenants', thus marginalising them even further in the housing market. This support may have to be supplied in a residential setting for the most vulnerable groups, but the provision of floating support for young people living in their own homes should be expanded given the evidence of their general dislike of hostel environments.

CHAPTER 10:
The impact of estate regeneration

Rebecca Tunstall

Introduction

This chapter assesses the impact of estate regeneration efforts within the last fifteen years on social exclusion. It examines four elements of estate regeneration activities, namely Estate Action; local authority housing management initiatives; tenant management organisations; and the cumulative impact of various activities over the last fifteen years in selected areas. It considers the impact of each of these elements in terms of the number of estates, homes and residents which were affected by initiatives; and in terms of the impact in each of these estates and surrounding areas. It also takes account of potential positive and negative effects outside these immediate areas. Crucially, the chapter considers three aspects of social exclusion, namely exclusion from the labour market; political exclusion; and psychological exclusion.

The chapter takes an explicitly English focus and the initiatives described apply, in the main, only in England. But many of the issues identified have applicability in housing estates in other parts of the UK.

Estates and regeneration

Most central government urban regeneration programmes over the last fifteen years have been directed at areas and at property. Within such programmes, there has been a gradual shift from an emphasis on the problems of the inner cities to those of housing estates, which has led some researchers to warn against 'equat[ing] area regeneration with regeneration of council estates' (Lee and Murie, 1997, p39). However, relatively few housing estates have been directly affected by most of the programmes, either through inclusion in the areas targeted or through receiving property investment. Table 10.1 shows the impact of a selected range of central government regeneration initiatives on a sample of twenty unpopular council estates previously studied by the author.

The large programmes of the 1980s, such as Enterprise Zones and Urban Development Corporations, aimed to regenerate by means of levering in private sector investment through improvements to infrastructure. With the partial exception of the London Docklands Development Corporation, they identified infrastructure largely with non-residential property. The Housing Action Trusts programme, announced as a main plank of regeneration policy in 1988, aimed to use demunicipalisation itself as a means of regeneration, and eventually resulted in projects in only seven estates or groups of estates.

Table 10.1: The impact of selected central government urban regeneration programmes on a sample of twenty unpopular council estates 1980-95

Programmes	Number of estates directly affected
Urban Programme	13
Estate Action	9
City Challenge	5
Safer Cities	3
Task Forces	3
Housing Association Grant	3
Enterprise Zones	0
Urban Development Corporations	0
Housing Action Trusts	0
Single Regeneration Budget	0

Source: Power and Tunstall, 1995: Table A5

City Challenge (1992-94) was directed more closely at urban neighbourhoods with residential populations. By the 1990s, Housing Association Grant (HAG) was increasingly used to develop new social housing on the site of demolished council housing or otherwise within existing estates (Crook *et al*, 1996).

The programmes that have funded initiatives in estates have tended to be the smaller ones. For example, a significant proportion of the small-scale funding of voluntary and community sector activities through the Urban Programme, established in 1968, went to groups based in housing estates (Table 10.1). Some of the twelve Community Development Projects established in the late 1960s were located in areas with large proportions of social housing (Loney, 1983). However, the main exception to this pattern of area and property spending outside estates was the Estate Action programme (Table 10.1), which was a central government regeneration programme that ran from 1985 to 1994. It was based on capital borrowing approval and physical change, but it also encouraged local authorities to decentralise and innovate in management and to develop tenant involvement.

The Single Regeneration Budget (SRB), introduced in 1994 to simplify the 'patchwork of complexity' (Audit Commission, 1989) that was British urban regeneration policy, removed the ring-fencing effect of Estate Action and led to a reduction in the net spending on housing and in residential communities.

'Regeneration' is usually understood as a specific activity, and as an activity of government, particularly central government. However, local government, the private sector and the community, as well as the public sector, must all contribute to the processes of urban decline (e.g. Kelly and McCormick, 1998) and must all at least have the potential to reverse them. All have engaged in some regeneration initiatives affecting social housing estates over the last fifteen years.

Local authorities, as the owners and managers of estates, have introduced a wide range of estate improvement initiatives, some taken in the context of central government advice, financial pressure or legislation. Local authorities have also introduced initiatives to improve estate popularity, to reduce population turnover, to improve resident satisfaction, to develop communities and to reduce management difficulty, inefficiency or cost. These can be seen at least partly as estate regeneration initiatives. These have included significant funding of property-based regeneration in estates through ongoing maintenance and refurbishment schemes (Hills, 1998c), changes in housing management, cross-departmental working and initiatives by social services, community education, education and leisure departments which have affected estates. Other public bodies, most notably the police, voluntary agencies including charities, and communities themselves, through local organisations and through participation in regeneration programmes and housing management, have also had an impact.

As well as this changing patchwork of regeneration initiatives over the last fifteen years, there have also been significant social and economic changes, and dramatic changes within housing and social policy. The study of effects over the short-term and the effects of individual initiatives alone may be misleading, because of the changing context and the potential for interacting and cumulative effects.

This chapter examines the impact on social exclusion of the following estate regeneration initiatives:

- Estate Action, the most significant central government regeneration programme for estates;
- local authority housing management initiatives, which are the most widespread, the easiest to identify and the best researched local authority estate regeneration initiatives;
- tenant management organisations (TMOs), which as well-defined institutions incorporating a clear devolution of power are not typical participation or community initiatives but are significant, easy to identify, and have been well researched; and
- the cumulative impact of various regeneration activities, including those above, taken by the range of agencies over the last fifteen years in individual areas.

It does not evaluate the contribution that the private sector, mainstream public services and community organisations can make to regeneration and to the need for it.

Estates and social exclusion

The concept of social exclusion is so broad that it is challenging to define, and contains qualitative and subjective elements that make it difficult to measure (Howarth and Kenway, 1998). However, the breadth of the concept and the ways in which it is different to 'poverty' and 'deprivation' make it particularly appropriate to the analysis of the problems of social housing and its residents in general, to estates in particular, and to the evaluation of estate regeneration.

This chapter considers three aspects of social exclusion:

- exclusion from the labour market and from the related access to higher incomes and material goods and opportunities;
- political exclusion, exclusion from legitimate political power and decision making processes; and
- psychological exclusion, the subjective feeling of being excluded, and the excluding effect of attitudes and expectations, both of the 'excluded' and of the 'mainstream'.

Socio-tenurial polarisation since the mid-1970s (Lee and Murie, 1997; Hills, 1998c) and polarisation within the tenure (Power and Tunstall, 1995), have meant that it is increasingly true that social housing, and estates in particular, are where those who are excluded from the labour market are located. Political and public attitudes contribute to political and psychological exclusion. For the general public, the media and many politicians, social housing, particularly non-traditionally designed social housing, forms one of the most immediate images of at least the location of social exclusion. Residents of the 'worst (social housing) estates' form one of the least politically contested categories of the socially excluded. The current government's Social Exclusion Unit responded to this, and arguably amplified it, through its initial promotion of 'the worst estates' as a priority area alongside street homelessness and school exclusion, although it later reverted to the term 'poor neighbourhoods' (Social Exclusion Unit, 1998b).

Social exclusion goes beyond poverty or disadvantage to imply: extreme quantitative differences in outcomes; qualitative as well as quantitative differences; cumulative, multiplied or interrelated effects; barriers, discontinuities or threshold effects. This in turn implies a re-emphasis of processes, including political and psychological ones. The emphasis on processes is useful and challenging to understandings of estate problems and estate regeneration. Despite decades of interest in the problems of some social housing estates, there has been relatively limited analysis of the causes of problems or the nature of processes. Social work, community development and housing literature and practice have developed a standard list of problematic 'symptoms' associated with social housing estates: for example, levels of unemployment, lone parenthood and child density were quoted as indicators of problems almost twenty years ago (Burbidge et al, 1981). (Incidentally, twenty years ago both absolute levels of these indicators in social housing estates and levels relative to the average or 'mainstream' were much lower.) Causal models have been limited to the 'spiral' model of cumulative effects (Power, 1984; Taylor, 1995) and the repeated assertion of multiple and interacting causes that require multifaceted initiatives. In the late 1970s and early 1980s, rival schools of thought stressed design and physical characteristics (Coleman, 1985), management (Power 1984, 1987b) or social factors (Burbidge *et al*, 1981) as the most significant or catalysing factors in the development of problems and solutions. However, there are special and significant factors or processes associated with social housing and with 'estates'. Some have argued that housing is a 'verb' (Turner, 1976) and should be seen as a process. Estate processes that work through the physical concentration of homes and people include:

- concentrations of particular social groups, particular social networks and particular communal cultures, which may (or may not) link people into job opportunities or opportunities for crime, affecting people through local expectations, role models and patterns of behaviour and enabling identity and reputation and the processes of discrimination and labelling (see Box 10.1a);
- the physical distinctiveness of many estates and individual homes which enables identity and reputation and the processes of discrimination and labelling (see Box 10.1b); and
- interaction with the geographical nature and differentiation of much public service provision, including housing management, and geographical differentiation and discrimination in access to the private sector (see Box 10.1c).

Box 10.1: Evidence from the sample of council estates, of the processes at work

a: You can hold a can of Special Brew and a spliff and walk round in front of the children without being ashamed – what kind of role model is that? 'Joneses' to keep up with do help solve problems, but we haven't got any Joneses. There are so many irresponsible people here (Resident).

b: We want streets with houses on them, not an estate (Resident).

I don't tell people where I live (Resident).

c: We need a supermarket – it's like being on a desert island (Resident).

I visited some local employers and found that they employed no-one from the estate because the youth on the estate were thought to be trouble (Housing Manager).

There is stigma, even within the Council, at member level and officer level. We need to bring people here, literally to force them to see the change (Senior Council Officer)

Source: Interviews for Power and Tunstall, 1995

All these processes may contribute to labour market, political and psychological exclusion of estates and estate residents. They must be addressed by estate regeneration programmes if they are to have an impact on social exclusion. Underlying issues such as labour market failure need to be addressed as well.

The impact of estate regeneration on social exclusion

This chapter examines Estate Action, local authority housing management initiatives, tenant management organisations and the cumulative impact of various activities over the last fifteen years in selected areas. It considers the impact of each of these elements in terms of the number of estates, homes and residents that were affected by initiatives. As a comparison, Department of the Environment research found 1,370 estates or parts of estates (enumeration districts or clusters of enumeration districts) in England which were dominated by social housing tenure and scored highly on the *Index of Local Conditions* measure (Department of the Environment, 1997). It considers the impact in each of these estates, and also takes account of potential positive and negative effects outside the immediate areas. It uses available quantitative evidence for exclusion from the labour market, and qualitative evidence for political exclusion and psychological exclusion.

Estate Action

Estate Action was the central government regeneration programme that has had the greatest impact on council estates. It specifically aimed to regenerate estates. It became increasingly significant over time. In 1986/87 the budget was £50 million and by 1992/93 it was £348 million (Robson *et al*, 1994). In all, over £1 billion was spent between 1985 and 1994.

Through Estate Action, local authorities and estates were awarded borrowing approval on a competitive basis. Proposed schemes had to incorporate physical investment and redevelopment, but also tenure diversification, decentralisation and innovation in housing management, increased tenant involvement and, after 1988, economic and social initiatives. Particularly in the 1980s, many local authorities saw Estate Action as a tool of central government's ideological agenda for council housing (Pinto, 1993; 1995). Authorities argued that it was 'topsliced' from investment funding allocated to them on the basis of need, did not involve additional funding, and concentrated funding in particular areas and according to central government priorities.

Five hundred estates received funding, comprising 100,000-300,000 homes. Department of the Environment, Transport and the Regions records are no longer complete, but available evidence shows that the distribution of Estate Action projects was heavily concentrated in the metropolitan authorities which generally reflects the geographical distribution of exclusion from the labour market (Green,

1994). It is likely that most of the five hundred estates were among the 1,370 'deprived estates' identified by the Department of the Environment (1997).

Available research, case studies and anecdotal evidence suggest that Estate Action had a very limited impact on estate residents' unemployment and income levels (Capita, 1996), even through the effects of the displacement of population through decanting for redevelopment and through tenure diversification.

Estate Action had an influence on local political exclusion, of targeted estates and their residents. This was through the high local political profile, albeit an ambiguous one in some local authorities, which made Estate Action estates local 'flagships', and through the involvement of residents, usually in special liaison committees, in planning and carrying out physical works (Taylor, 1995; Stewart and Taylor, 1995).

Estate Action's greatest and most immediate impact in most areas has been improved physical conditions (Pinto, 1993, 1995; Capita, 1996). Work ranged from basic improvements to fabric, to environmental changes, crime prevention measures and complex estate redevelopment involving demolition of homes and reorganisation of access to homes. A study of twenty council estates that had Estate Action treatment showed that managers felt that capital works were successful in fourteen cases, with mixed effects in four. Residents' assessments were more evenly balanced between successful and mixed outcomes. In non-traditionally designed estates both residents and managers were least positive about the effects of capital spending, although it was these estates that received most funding (Power and Tunstall, 1995: Table 7). Physical changes were associated in various schemes with increased resident satisfaction, reduced estate unpopularity, reduced population turnover and better housing management staff morale, reduced crime and increased community activity (Capita, 1996; Osborne and Shaftoe, 1995; Taylor, 1995). Evidence suggests that these improvements have reduced stigmatisation and acted as a catalyst to tenant involvement and community development (Taylor, 1995; Capita, 1996). These knock-on effects of physical changes contributed to a reduction in psychological exclusion.

It is important to consider the effects of this area-based programme outside the immediate areas it was aimed at. The 'topslicing' argument suggests that estates that did not receive Estate Action lost out in absolute as well as relative terms. Capital funding over the last fifteen years was concentrated in non-traditionally designed and built estates developed in the 1960s and 1970s, largely because of the availability and targeting of Estate Action and increasingly so later in the programme. Some of the psychological gains made by estates which received funding were at the expense of or alongside losses in other local estates, which may have experienced reduced relative popularity, resident and staff morale, local political profile and an increased sense of relative deprivation. On the other hand, in many local authorities with an Estate Action scheme, it provided a model for increased tenant involvement in housing improvement and management that later affected other estates.

Housing management initiatives

Over the last fifteen years, housing management initiatives have been almost ubiquitous. They were certainly more widespread than Estate Action or TMOs. It is very unlikely than any of the 1,370 'deprived estates' identified by the Department of the Environment (1997) went unaffected during that period.

Housing management initiatives were not explicitly seen as estate regeneration initiatives nor targeted directly at social exclusion. Their primary aims were managerial and political. Particularly spurred on by problems in unpopular estates (Burbidge *et al*, 1981; Power, 1984), local authorities took initiatives to reduce management difficulty, inefficiency and cost, to improve estate popularity, to reduce population turnover, to improve resident satisfaction and to develop communities. Housing management initiatives were also taken in the context of central government advice, financial pressure and legislation. Pressure on management performance was, like Estate Action, seen by some local authorities as a tool of central government's ideological agenda for council housing, but they also saw management as a means of defence or counter-attack (Cole and Furbey, 1994). Local authority management was criticised (Audit Commission, 1986). Local authorities were given advice to decentralise and funding for experimental schemes through the Priority Estates Project from 1979 (Power, 1984), and incentives through Estate Action funding criteria, and more experimental funding through the 'Recommendation 9' programme in 1990 and the 'ring-fencing' of Housing Revenue Accounts. Compulsory Competitive Tendering (CCT) for housing management services which affected English local authorities on a phased basis from 1996 forced authorities to devolve budgets and gave powerful incentives to perform. Tenants were given the ability to pressurise landlords more through rights to consultation and information and options to transfer to owner-occupation and to alternative landlords such as tenant management organisations, Housing Action Trusts and 'Tenants' Choice' landlords.

Despite the managerial and political aims of most management initiatives, they should be evaluated for their effects on estate regeneration. Housing management is widely acknowledged as the most important public service in housing estates, as having a 'social role', whether developmental or controlling (Cole and Furbey, 1994; Pearl,1998), and as a necessary and catalysing element in estate regeneration projects and the sustainability of their effects (Taylor, 1995).

Management initiatives have included the physical decentralisation of staff, devolution of decision making and budgetary control, increased emphasis on management goals and performance, increased tenant involvement, and multi-agency consultation, information sharing and co-operation.

Decentralised housing management, advocated throughout the last fifteen years, is no longer an innovative initiative and has become part of orthodox good practice (Department of the Environment, 1989b; Pearl, 1998). Decentralisation of staff and the opening of estate-based offices occurred earliest and to the greatest extent in 'difficult to manage' estates, likely to be those most affected by social exclusion (Power and Tunstall, 1995, p42). Again, it is unlikely than any of the 1,370 'deprived estates' identified by the Department of the Environment (1997) went unaffected.

There is very little evidence to indicate any effect of decentralisation on the unemployment and income levels of residents.

Decentralisation has been shown to improve management performance, tenant satisfaction, area reputation and popularity, through improved information for managers and improved relations between staff and service users (Power, 1984; Power and Tunstall, 1995). These changes are likely to reduce political and psychological exclusion through improved relations and communications, better services and reduced stigmatisation. The physical decentralisation of staff, resources and processes alone can have only limited positive effects, and may have negative effects through greater exposure of staff to pressure and threats (Power, 1984; 1987b). Only twelve of twenty estate-based management offices surveyed in 1994 controlled any budgets although this was an increase on seven in 1988 (Power and Tunstall, 1995). In addition, sources do not usually refer to the fact that most decentralisation initiatives, particularly early ones, have also incorporated greater intensity of service provision, increased tenant involvement, increased multi-agency working and in some cases capital investment. These associated changes may have contributed to benefits attributed to decentralisation. It is possible that the increasing ubiquity of decentralisation may have reduced the local political profile of estates with estate-based management, and reduced the impact of the initiative on political exclusion.

The increased emphasis on management goals and performance has resulted in improved performance by many local authority housing departments, according to available performance indicators. As the greatest incentive to reorganisation and improved performance, CCT has had dramatic effects on council housing management; this has been replaced by 'Best Value' by the Labour government. CCT led to some recentralisation in areas that had well-developed decentralisation, decentralisation in areas that had not introduced it, and greater devolution of budgets and decision making in most areas. Statutory requirements meant increased consultation in most areas. Pressure on local authority in-house tenderers meant that service costs were reduced. These changes have ambiguous implications for social exclusion. Improved management performance and more responsive management are likely to reduce psychological exclusion. Pressure to increase efficiency may mean incentives to reduce social development work, increase 'social control' work, and even to 'cream off' (Le Grand and Bartlett, 1992), and exclude difficult to manage individuals or households. An increasing number of local authorities maintain lists of households that they will not house (Power and Mumford, 1999). These changes are intended to protect residents from the excluding estate processes of anti-social behaviour and crime, but may add to the psychological exclusion of at least some residents and potential residents, and also reflect and may even add to the social exclusion of social housing and estates in general.

Tenant Management Organisations

Local authorities have been able to establish and delegate management of parts of their stock to TMOs since 1975. A board with at least a majority of tenants' representatives takes on responsibility for budgeting and for day-to-day management, according to a formal agreement reached with the authority. The local authority retains ownership of stock and responsibility for capital funded projects and remaining management tasks. Sources do not usually refer to the fact that TMOs are not just involvement initiatives, and that most incorporate decentralisation, greater intensity of service provision, and that many have received capital funding, particularly Estate Action. These associated changes may have contributed to benefits attributed to the participatory nature of TMOs.

By the beginning of 1998 there were over one hundred and fifty TMOs in operation in England, managing more than 70,000 homes. TMOs are operating in about one sixth of the housing authorities in England that retain their own stock, and the distribution of TMOs reflects the geographical distribution of exclusion from the labour market (Tunstall, 1996; Department of the Environment, 1997). A survey of a sample of twenty TMOs showed that levels of exclusion from the labour market were relatively high. 55 per cent of adult residents were not employed according to the 1991 census, compared to 63 per cent in the sample of twenty unpopular council estates identified above (Tunstall, 1996).

There is very little evidence for the impact of TMOs on unemployment and income levels of residents. There is anecdotal evidence at the individual level that some resident board members use confidence, skills and experience gained through involvement to get further training and jobs. However, it is also likely that the majority of TMO boards include resident members who could obtain paid work but feel obliged to prioritise their voluntary commitment.

In most cases, available evidence suggests TMOs improve management performance and resident satisfaction (Price Waterhouse, 1995), although performance is variable. A survey of TMO chairs showed that seventeen out of twenty three felt that their estates had become more popular since TMO formation (Tunstall, 1996). TMOs give estates high local political profile. In many cases TMO development builds groups of residents with unusual level of skill, confidence and contacts, who act as lobbyists and advocates for individual estates. TMO development demands some organisational and procedural changes. In combination, these changes are likely to reduce political and psychological exclusion through changed internal and external attitudes and expectations. A member of a TMO advanced in development said of the local authority: 'They're consulting us more – it's a cultural change. But they don't take us seriously enough … We're not going to struggle when the EMB comes into action, but there's going to be an almighty shock down the civic centre'. This impact is stressed among the non-quantifiable benefits of TMOs that Price Waterhouse recorded (1995). A survey of TMO chairs showed that twelve out of twenty three said their groups were involved in other issues in addition to housing management (Tunstall 1996). These included a welfare advice surgery staffed by volunteer TMO members, parenting and adult literacy projects staffed by residents, a school attendance promotion scheme with incentives negotiated from McDonalds by residents, a bid for lottery funding for community psychiatric nurses and a building co-operative. It seems unlikely that many of these projects would have been initiated without the individual experience, group development and momentum gained in working on the TMO. While Estate Action projects or particularly active neighbourhood housing managers might have produced similar schemes, resident initiated and led schemes are likely to have a greater effect on psychological exclusion.

The effects of TMOs outside the estates in which they were developed are ambiguous. In many authorities, the development of TMOs was part of or even a spur to greater tenant involvement across the stock. However, effects have been somewhat restricted by conflicts between the culture and aims of many traditional tenants' associations and federations and TMOs, and in some cases the existence of TMOs has allowed landlords to 'rest on their participation laurels'. There is some evidence that TMOs' flexibility in the use of labour and some of their particular management practices have been picked up by local authorities and included in mainstream policy. There have been long-running arguments about whether TMOs manage more or less expensively than councils (Price Waterhouse, 1995). Whether or nor management agreements and allowances originally favoured TMOs, they have tended to fix past funding practice over time and are increasingly favourable as finances elsewhere are pressured. In one authority, a tenant participation officer said, 'one day it will only be TMOs that get planned maintenance'.

Cumulative impact

This section draws on a study of developments in twenty unpopular council estates between 1980 and 1995, which has been referred to above (Power and Tunstall, 1995). The twenty estates were slightly unusual because of the early and sustained priority they received from the local authority. However, the study takes account of the cumulative and potentially interrelated effects of different initiatives, which are often stressed in discussions of the processes of regeneration, and by assessing effects over the long term. This means it adds to the three cases above, and addresses the weaknesses of much of the regeneration evaluation literature.

The twenty estates were the subjects of a wide range of regeneration initiatives over the fifteen years of the study (Table 10.2). Thirteen received some Urban Programme finance. Nine received Estate Action funding. There were other physical improvements in a further ten estates. One estate was almost completely demolished, and there was some demolition in five more. Small areas of land or homes were sold to housing associations or developers in four estates. In all of the estates, management was physically decentralised in the late 1970s or early 1980s with local staff and offices, and by 1994 the offices were open longer hours, covered a wider range of functions, and over half controlled at least some budgets. There was increased resident involvement in management. In four of the estates residents explored the TMO option to development stage, and this led to operational TMOs in two estates by 1998. Housing managers felt that education departments and voluntary agencies, including local churches, Groundwork, Children in Need, Save the Children and Barnardo's, also had an important impact in a minority of estates.

Table 10.2: Cumulative regeneration initiatives in a sample of twenty unpopular council estates 1980-95

Initiative	Number of estates directly affected
Decentralised and intensive housing management	20
Increased tenant participation in management	20
Urban Programme funding	13
Changed tenancy agreements (as part of authority-wide change)	13
Strong support from senior councillors and officers	11
Estate Action funding	9
Partial demolition	6
Education department initiatives	6
Involvement of voluntary agencies	6
City Challenge funding	5
Safer Cities funding	3
Task Force funding	3
HAG and housing association development	3
Tenant Management Organisation	2

Source: Power and Tunstall, 1995
Note: All estates had several initiatives

In this case comprehensive information is available on the labour market exclusion of estate residents (Table 10.3). The initiatives did not reduce exclusion of estate residents from the labour market, although it is possible that this effect would have been worse if there had been no initiatives.

Table 10.3: Economic status of residents of twenty estates 1981-91 (%)

	1981	1991
Under 16	31	31
All adults (16 or over)	69	69
Adults: economically inactive	27	30
Adults: economically active	41	39
Economically active adults: unemployed	12	13
Economically active adults: employed	30	19

Source: Derived from Power and Tunstall 1995, p77
Note: Rounding means that figures do not always sum exactly

In 1981, 30 per cent of all residents of the estates were in employment, while in 1991 only 19 per cent were. This was due to a slight increase in unemployment and a significant increase in economic inactivity of adults, going against the national trend of increased activity. These figures match and tend to confirm the weaker evidence from the Estate Action, management and TMO cases above.

However, the initiatives affected local political exclusion of the estates and their residents. The estates had high local political profiles, established by the pioneering, early estate-based management projects, reconfirmed in estates which received Estate Action, and sustained in most estates despite the gradual diffusion of decentralised management through the stock. The estates also had strong traditions of tenant involvement, related to early local management and to Estate Action.

Residents and managers felt that in general terms housing conditions had improved and were still improving in half of the estates in 1994. By 1994, in most estates crime problems were reducing. The absolute and relative popularity of the estates had improved gradually over the period. While at the start of the local management projects, fifteen of the estates had been classified as 'difficult-to-let', by 1994 only five were, and managers felt that demand for eight estates was rising. By the end of the period, the number of estates that had been among the least popular in the local authority reduced from sixteen to eight. These suggest reduced psychological exclusion. However, despite fifteen years of local political profile and sustained initiatives, residents and managers reported continued and powerful prejudice against the estates and their residents in 1994.

The long-term element in this study forces an examination of the context of the initiatives and the long-term structural changes in the position of social housing and these estates. As unpopular estates, the twenty were affected very little by the Right-to-Buy (Power and Tunstall, 1995, Table A8), reflecting the polarisation between tenures and within social housing over the period. Residents and managers referred to the increased pressure of social problems, which some related explicitly to socio-tenurial polarisation. Residents referred to a sense of increasing psychological exclusion through the fact of being estate and social housing residents *per se*.

As a comparison to the sample of twenty estates, a study of twelve estates in England where there were riots in the early 1990s showed very similar levels of exclusion from the labour market (Power and Tunstall, 1997). In comparison with the group of twenty estates, key differences contributing to the disturbances included fewer and less sustained initiatives over the past fifteen years, a lack of local political support, location within smaller towns, where the estates were socially and physically more distinct and stigmatisable, fewer Estate Action projects, later decentralisation of management, less participation in management and only one TMO. All of these suggest greater levels of political and psychological exclusion at the estate level. These two latter points confirm the significance of psychological exclusion as an estate process and as an element of social exclusion.

The cumulative effects of initiatives on the areas surrounding the twenty estates are ambiguous. In all cases, the development of estate-based management and related tenant involvement was part of or a spur to decentralisation and greater involvement across the stock. However, there is some anecdotal evidence that some of the psychological gains made by estates from higher political profile and capital funding were at the expense of other local estates, which experience reduced relative popularity, resident and staff morale, local political profile and an increased sense of relative deprivation.

Conclusions and policy implications

In summary, over the last fifteen years most central government urban regeneration projects have not directly aimed at estate regeneration. However, a range of agencies, including local government and communities have acted to regenerate estates, through a wide range of initiatives, including Estate Action, housing management initiatives, and TMOs.

Most estate regeneration initiatives have not aimed explicitly to tackle exclusion from the labour market, and have had little effect on it. Evaluation using the measures of 'poverty' or 'deprivation' would draw solely pessimistic conclusions. Using the concept of social exclusion, all the estate regeneration initiatives examined have had more significant effects, although as yet unquantifiable ones, on political and psychological exclusion. In addition, understanding of 'estate processes' suggests that reduced political and psychological exclusion may have some knock-on effects on exclusion from the labour market.

Regeneration funders and evaluators should accept the value of the 'unquantifiable', and consider how to record it. This must be done through more sophisticated and open-ended research into attitudes of estates residents than is possible through satisfaction surveys, and should incorporate the views of residents and public and private organisations in surrounding areas.

This is a significant time in the development of estate regeneration policy. The SRB will continue on its current path, but the government's New Deal for Communities will focus on residential areas and will lead to the development of seventeen pilot 'Pathfinder' projects. These will be the first regeneration initiatives to be directed explicitly at social exclusion. What does this chapter suggest the projects should do to maximise impact?

In its 1998 report, the Social Exclusion Unit was rather dismissive about capital expenditure, stating: 'huge sums have been spent on … giving estates a new coat of paint', and arguing that there has been 'too much emphasis on physical renewal' (Social Exclusion Unit, 1998, p7, p9). The experience of Estate Action has indeed shown that some physical problems are not amenable to cheap solutions or alterations short of demolition, and that some capital funding could have been better spent or more knock-on benefits garnered. However, overall the programme had a positive and very significant impact on the estates that received funding. The greater issue is the lack of ongoing planned maintenance and reinvestment in council housing as a whole. The study of twenty estates showed that almost none of the authorities had any planned maintenance programme (Power and Tunstall, 1995). As an external evaluator, Price Waterhouse included as an indicator of TMO performance the extent to which necessary and prudent investment was made. Price Waterhouse had to concede that the measure was not useful because TMOs had very little influence over spending levels, the same being true for the local authorities that delegated power to the TMOs concerned. The Social Exclusion Unit should recognise that through continued promotion of stock transfer, the need for investment forms by default, the main factor behind government policy towards social housing.

The Unit argued that mainstream government programmes have in some cases contributed to social exclusion (1998). The Best Value regime, which will affect housing management services, may not contribute to a reduction in social exclusion if it does not confront the internal contradictions in demands for continued cost reduction, increased social support and increased social control.

The Unit emphasised tenant involvement as positively essential to estate regeneration and argued, normatively, that tenants should take power and responsibility (1998b). Evidence from TMOs shows that resident involvement does not affect all socially excluded areas, and is not likely to. While involvement can affect political and psychological exclusion, it requires support and funding. In addition, increased involvement may also require difficult decisions on trade-offs between developing new groups and sustaining existing ones, and between empowering residents and ensuring fairness, performance minima and stability.

As a final caution, evidence on the cumulative impact of several initiatives over fifteen years did not suggest that the 'initiative-itis' the Social Exclusion Unit referred to (1998b, p38) outweighed the value of a range of approaches, and continued or repeated emphasis in the long term.

CHAPTER 11:
The changing role of housing associations

Ian Cole

Introduction

In 1987 everything seemed possible for housing associations. To adopt the titles of two of the volumes of Eric Hobsbawm's renowned historical work, it was their 'age of empire' and 'age of capital' rolled into one. Their empire was poised to expand, as a result of stock transfers, Tenants' Choice and a stronger development role. After decades perched uneasily between the owner-occupied and local authority sectors, housing associations were moving to the centre stage in the provision of rented and shared ownership housing. And their capital base was to be sheltered from the reductions in public investment coursing through the local authority sector. Private finance would, the government planned, step in to fill the breach.

The prospects of mass transfers out of council housing meant that housing debates in the late 1980s suddenly became infused with piscine metaphors, about minnows, piranhas and sharks – the only point at issue seemed to be the speed with which housing associations would gobble up their bigger brethren, and take over local authority stock. Some of the more voracious appetites were being countered by reassuring signals from within the movement – about the need to preserve the social and ethical foundations of housing associations, with 'friendly' rather than hostile overtures to those local authority landlords facing extinction. But the sector undoubtedly faced a bright, if insecure, future.

By the end of the 1990s, however, registered social landlords (RSLs), most of whom were housing associations, had started to examine their future strategies more tentatively than before. There were strong pressures on affordable rent levels and land supply, and difficulties in assembling development portfolios in the south east of England. By contrast, in the north, the threat of 'oversupply' could be discerned, with some soul searching about the scale of future needs for social housing of any kind. In the north east of England, for example, some housing association properties faced demolition without ever having been let in the three years since they had been built.

In this period of a dozen years, 'social exclusion' had moved from a rather obscure term used by European social policy analysts to the very heart of the housing association movement. The three year strategy set out by the Housing Corporation until 2001/2, for example, placed as the first of its four main priorities the need 'to tackle the problem of social exclusion' (Housing Corporation, 1998b). Four specific challenges were identified – more effective links between housing provision and other policies to produce solutions for deprived neighbourhoods; new partnerships between local agencies and members of local communities; a more affordable and coherent rent structure; and a key role for RSLs in neighbourhood renewal.

In this chapter the transformation of the housing association sector over this period is outlined and the role of social exclusion is considered in terms of the three basic functions of RSLs – development, finance and management. Finally, future strands of policy and provision are explored, along with the main pressures on housing associations to play a leading role in wider strategies to tackle social exclusion.

Links with social exclusion

Other chapters in this book have examined in more detail the concept of social exclusion and its applicability to housing policy. It is undoubtedly a contested and elastic term which can be invoked to describe a whole set of social constructs. Somerville has described social exclusion as something which happens

> ... if the effect of housing processes is to deny certain social groups control over their daily lives, or to impair enjoyment of citizenship rights (Somerville, 1998, p772).

This casts a wider framework for analysis than an emphasis confined solely to one's position in or out of the labour market, or to the social and economic processes which affect this relationship.

The pattern of social exclusion may be mediated by processes of housing production and distribution and by housing tenure, although the relationship is often complex and depends on the nature of the local housing market, or on specific management or allocation practices. The 'ghettoisation' of particular groups in social housing is not an all-consuming or inevitable process, but is contingent on social relations at the neighbourhood level. Those who are 'trapped' in the housing market may equally include private tenants or poor owner-occupiers. There is, in short, no direct equation between the housing association sector and the processes of social exclusion.

Nevertheless much recent policy attention has in practice centred on the extent to which the operation of development activities, financial structures and management practices by housing associations have interacted to compound social exclusion, by coralling those outside the labour market into specific neighbourhoods and then diminishing opportunities for them to get out. This has not been the intended course of events, but the pressures pointing in this direction, the argument runs, have proved impossible for housing associations to resist. This chapter therefore examines how these processes have come about and explores some responses which have been made, or are currently emerging, within the housing association sector, in development, refurbishment and management policy and practice.

Housing association development – mass housing for the poor?

The recent expansion of the housing association sector has been remarkable. Housing Corporation funding, for example, increased from £10 billion in 1988 to around £22 billion ten years later. The amount of private finance being drawn into the sector was £14 billion by 1998 – compared to nothing prior to January 1988. There were 250,000 properties transferred into the sector from local authorities in this period, with the prospect of an annual 40,000 properties continuing to be transferred in the coming years. The total number of RSL homes increased from 400,000 in 1988 to about a million ten years later (Housing Corporation, 1998b). The minnows had indeed grown into something more substantial. Of course these bald figures mask the enduring diversity of the sector – in terms of households catered for, criteria for access, rent levels, and the quality of liaison with other agencies, notably local housing authorities. And the record of steady expansion has not been achieved without some difficulties.

By the early 1990s, it had already become clear that housing associations had completely taken over the mantle of developers of social housing from local authorities. The Conservative central government had announced the impending death of council housing, by supplementing the politically successful Right-to-Buy policy with inducements to remaining tenants to transfer to other landlords – through a variety of increasingly inventive (or desperate) 'exit' options. As local authorities increasingly accepted their fate as residual landlords of last resort, any pretence at holding on to land banks, and awaiting the glorious rebirth of council housing under a Labour government vanished with the Conservative election victory of 1992. Housing associations were now the only option for new socially rented housing.

These development pressures had a clear regional accent. Associations in London and the south east of England came under particular pressure to provide family housing, in view of spiralling rates of homelessness and ever lengthening council waiting-lists. In other parts of the country, the care in community programme placed more pressure on housing associations to build to meet special needs, although this was rarely matched with an equal concern for a support framework to follow on from this (Arnold *et al*, 1993; Arblaster *et al*, 1996).

While there were golden opportunities awaiting the more ambitious housing associations, there were also darker undertones to the promise of expansion and success. The foundations of the housing association movement had been anchored on a bedrock of a century of social responsibility in meeting housing needs, coupled with intensive (not to say intensively paternalistic) housing management. Many housing association stalwarts no doubt feared that Octavia Hill would be turning in her grave at the sound of 'cutting edge' market vocabulary and continual pressures on housing associations from the government to take a more commercially oriented perspective – an approach which reached its peak (or nadir) with the temporary redefinition of homes provided by RSLs as 'social housing product' in the mid-1990s.

In the midst of this uncertain mood, Cassandra's message duly arrived, in the form of the report by David Page, entitled *Building for Communities* (Page, 1993). The report had a major impact on the sector. Page's analysis was not new, but it knitted together several strands of policy and practice in a direct and informed manner. His starting point was the 'spiral of decline' which had already been charted on many unpopular council estates (Power, 1991a). Page suggested that housing associations were rushing headlong into creating spirals of their own. A combination of demographic, social, financial and strategic pressures were encouraging housing associations to build large developments to meet the needs of socially disadvantaged households, while funding constraints were pressing down on environmental, design and construction standards.

Page undertook a tour of larger new housing association schemes and showed how they were producing a population profile characterised by high child densities, high proportions of those dependent on benefits and at risk of vandalism, crime and disturbance. Following a misguided allegiance to economies of scale, housing associations were being compelled to reproduce against their will the worst excesses of council housing in the 1950s and 1960s. And, just as local authorities had attracted public odium for producing drab estates then, housing associations would now find their reputation tarnished as purveyors of specialist rented housing built and managed to high standards.

David Page therefore suggested that housing associations were becoming accommodation agencies for the socially excluded, by default as much by design, through the interaction of financial constraints, allocation priorities and patterns of community and household change. In a follow up publication, *Developing Communities* (Page, 1994), Page set out a broad agenda of ideas, polices and initiatives for mitigating such problems.

There were several development implications of Page's analysis. First, there was concern about the *scale* of such developments, especially as they often comprised a single tenure, just like the mass council estates of the past. Second, estate design and layout often neglected to incorporate adequate security measures and sufficient defensible space, and environmental programmes were often unattractive and mean spirited. In procurement, Page claimed that many new schemes were being bought 'off the shelf' as an a economy measure, with restrictions on the number of property types. Development officers were not consulting housing management staff in the housing association, let alone actual or potential residents. Finally, new housing schemes were rarely accompanied by the relocation of other social amenities and services – such as health centres or leisure facilities.

Page's critique had particular impact because it was published at a time when many associations were in the process of extending their development portfolios, creating consortia or getting involved in organisational take-overs. The move to mixed funding had also made new development a more attractive investment option for private lenders than more complex and riskier rehabilitation projects. Page's report sent out a warning that the excitement in the sector about expanding development portfolios had to be measured against the prospect that islands of social exclusion were being created as a result.

Page rested his analysis on contacts with several senior staff in projects across the country, but especially in the south. It was a telling mixture of interpretation, anecdote and informed prognosis. However, it was not based on primary research, still less on the views of any housing association residents themselves. One study of new housing association developments in the Yorkshire and Humberside region in 1996 provided limited empirical sustenance for Page's analysis. There was little evidence that cut-backs in design standards had begun to bite. Overall, residents on the estates were satisfied with the standards of accommodation, apart from poor sound insulation and a lack of storage space. Residents did complain, however, that housing provision had not been complemented by other services and facilities, especially in amenities for children and young people (Cole *et al*, 1996, p60).

Much of Page's critique rested on the size of new schemes. In practice, the vast majority of new housing association projects since 1988 have contained less than fifty dwellings, as Page himself had advocated. A study of RSL schemes between 1992 and 1995, for example, showed that almost two-thirds accommodated 23 dwellings or less (Farthing and Lambert, 1996). Indeed, the problem of large-scale estates was often greater in *inherited* stock, where RSLs had taken over council property as a result of large scale voluntary transfers. A more pertinent criticism was that new schemes were generally based on a single tenure. Residents on the new housing association estates in Yorkshire and Humberside provided vivid evidence of tenure prejudice from those living in adjacent areas. Furthermore, housing associations rarely consulted with those living nearby to new schemes during the process of development, and as a result incoming residents often found that their cards were marked, as a result of local rumour mills about the apparently unsavoury nature of housing association tenants (Cole *et al*, 1996, pp55-58).

While new schemes in the early 1990s began to incorporate shared ownership dwellings alongside rented properties, there were few examples of full-bodied mixed tenure developments in local neighbourhoods, bringing together dwellings from the owned, rented and intermediary sectors. More recently, mixed tenure has been advocated in various government reports as a key strategy in the fight against social exclusion (DETR, 1997; London Planning Advisory Committee, 1997; Urban Task Force, 1998). The report of the Select Committee on Environment, Transport and the Regions, for example, concluded that:

> ... *new housing must be of a mixture of tenures, and must be suitable for a mixture of incomes; we must avoid social ghettos* (DETR, 1998a, paras 239, p277).

Empirical evidence about the beneficial effects of mixed developments is thin on the ground. Small-scale research in Glasgow and Sheffield has suggested that mixed tenure can indeed have a positive effect on the overall image of a neighbourhood (Atkinson and Kintrea, 1998; Cole and Shayer, 1998) and this in turn may counteract the effects of employer 'addressism' which stand in the way of local residents gaining employment, thereby reinforcing social exclusion. However, there is also research which suggests that tenure diversification can exacerbate the problems of an estate (Wood and Vamplew, 1999). There is less evidence to show that mixed tenure affects the *internal* social dynamics of neighbourhoods to any great extent. The hope that such schemes may broaden the social networks of the unemployed, by causing them to rub shoulders with their employed owner-occupying neighbours (see, for example, Perri 6, 1997), remains an assertion rather than a demonstrable sociological phenomenon.

The development-led orientation of many RSLs is more in check now than in the immediate post-1988 period, perhaps less as a result of fears about the spread of social exclusion than of anxiety about future demand for social housing. Attention has turned to the RSL contribution to neighbourhood renewal programmes rather than the headlong pursuit of new schemes, especially in regions outside the south east of England (Maclennan and Pryce, 1998).

Finance and social exclusion – the crisis of affordability

If there has been a change of emphasis in the focus of development programmes in the housing association sector, the level of rents paid for both new and existing tenancies has proved less tractable. The 1988 legislation had the effect of increasing rents sharply in real terms, as the burden of shouldering the risks of new schemes fell on to the landlord directly. This was coupled with the shift in emphasis from bricks and mortar to personal housing subsidies as a well established trend in the British housing market (Murie, 1997), and the intensification of the 'poverty trap' effects of Housing Benefit which has resulted (see Kemp, 1998 for an overview).

David Page had acknowledged the changing balance of working tenants in the housing association and local authority sectors, but he did not make a direct connection between this profile and the rising pattern of rents. He focused on allocations methods and the nomination system for homeless applicants rather than the possible impact of rent levels on the decision whether or not to accept the offer of a RSL property.

As stated above, it would be misleading to deduce from this that there is a universal pattern of social exclusion becoming concentrated in the social housing sector. Lee and Murie found that neighbourhoods of deprivation did not coincide closely with housing tenure (Lee and Murie, 1997, p39). However the growing differentials *within* social housing – between RSL and local authority rents – have recently raised concerns about the extent to which those dependent on welfare benefits were becoming ever more prominent in the housing association sector.

There is statistical support for this trend. Analysis of household composition in the RSL sector has indicated that between 1984 and 1996/7 the proportion of recently moving household heads in full-time employment fell from 40 per cent to 26 per cent (the comparable figures for the local authority sector were 28 per cent and 30 per cent). The proportion of retired or otherwise economically inactive RSL households increased from 22 per cent to 44 per cent in the same period, and again the position in the council sector had changed little (Ford *et al*, 1998, p4).

In 1996, there was a differential between the rents for new lettings in the RSL and LA sectors of 35 per cent in London, rising to fully 73 per cent in Yorkshire and Humberside (the comparable figures for relets were 19 per cent and 53 per cent) (Ford *et al*, 1998, p1). Figures from the National Housing Federation (1997) have confirmed that the percentage of working tenants in the RSL sector is lower in the north of England, where rent differentials are greater. By contrast, in Scotland, where rent differentials are negligible, a higher proportion of RSL than LA tenants are in employment (Yanetta *et al*, 1997).

Of course the changing composition of RSL tenants can be explained by a host of other factors – such as the level of private rents and the local costs of house purchase, the level and distribution of unemployment, or the proportion of homeless households nominated to local RSLs. In patterns of social exclusion the key point is whether rent differentials deter tenant mobility, so that households are reluctant to take higher rented property, even when it is of a higher standard (Burrows, 1997; Crook *et al*, 1996). To what extent do rent levels affect choices by applicants, by encouraging those in work to turn down an offer of RSL accommodation, so they can enter local authority housing instead?

A study for the Department of the Environment by Prescott-Clarke *et al* (1994), showed the extent to which financial issues could affect applicant preferences.

Among those households not interested in a RSL home, the most prevalent reason given, by one in five, was that they could not afford rents. Maclennan and Kay's study (1994) of transferring tenants, found that local authority officers in all nine case studies said that high rents deterred non-benefit applicants from accepting nominations to RSLs (p43). High rent was also ranked alongside the loss of the Right-to-Buy as a deterrent factor for applicants not wishing to be nominated for RSL property in four of the eight case studies covered in a DETR review of allocations systems (Griffiths *et al*, 1997).

This research evidence still begs the question about how rational and informed decisions made by applicants actually are. It is unlikely that rent levels are the sole or the most important influence on housing preferences, but the subject has been little explored. Statistical comparisons are made complicated by the absence of a data set on new entrants to local authority housing, but overall the analysis by Ford *et al* was:

> ... *highly suggestive of an association between rent differences and the differences in economic circumstances of those entering the RSL sector compared to those entering LA housing* (Ford *et al*, 1998).

The effects of the high rent regime are proving difficult to contain. The government's structural review of welfare benefits failed to produce any fundamental change in the Housing Benefit system, which seals the poverty trap consequences of high rent regimes. There is no shortage of proposals for reform (Kemp, 1998; Wilcox, 1997), but any move to a system such as housing allowances across tenures is unlikely to be introduced in the near future.

There have been some moves to respond to the problem of affordability. Grant rates for 1999/00 have been held constant and a formula has been introduced to limit future RSL rent rises to a ceiling of Retail Price Index +1 per cent, but the changes in the characteristics of those entering the RSL sector are likely to remain fairly constant. Rent caps may also make it more difficult to promote new developments in areas where housing demand remains high. The difficulties in tackling the consequences of high rents will in turn put pressure on the management capability of housing associations, struggling to accommodate those outside the labour market while simultaneously diversifying the social base of their estates.

Management and social exclusion – striving for social balance?

The combination of the development pressures and rent regimes outlined above fed fears that housing associations might end up by 'creating the slums of the twenty first century' (Balchin, 1995, p155). However, the Page reports had suggested that the process of reproducing patterns of social exclusion on housing association estates was not immutable. Steps could be taken to create more diverse, better balanced communities on these estates. A more comprehensive approach was advanced, to confront problems of disadvantage and social exclusion before their effects began to unravel. Page's recommendations had hinged on 'preventative' rather than 'curative' measures, particularly through adjusting the social mix of new estates, and letting the strengthened community dynamics rescue the neighbourhood from the threat of social exclusion. Social balance was thereby presented as an antidote to social exclusion on new estates.

The goal of a balanced community is scarcely a novel aspiration – one can trace a policy lineage from the Garden Cities movement onwards, and more than fifty years ago a prescient Aneurin Bevan was pronouncing on the 'evils' of geographical segregation by income (see Lansley, 1979, p183). While the underlying sentiment was plain enough, the translation of this objective into management practice has been more nebulous. It is not self-evident, for example, what criteria are in need of being 'balanced', nor which wider geographical boundaries form the 'reference group' for a given estate.

While the aspiration for social balance has continued undiminished, the policy focus has changed. At the time of the New Town programme in the early 1950s, for example, concerns centred on the relative proportions of owner-occupied and rented dwellings, and the provision of sufficiently diverse employment opportunities to attract different skills in the local, largely male, workforce. Fifty years later, attention had turned to sectors of consumption rather than production. The most prominent aspects of Page's analysis were the proportion of households dependent on benefit, the proportion of single parent households, and the level of child density on estates. The message for housing associations was to avoid allocating an undue proportion of properties to these groups to prevent estates becoming a locus for social exclusion, detached from wider local social and economic processes.

The question arises about whether the concentration of non-working households on housing association estates makes the management task more difficult or costly. An answer to this question is made difficult, as RSLs rarely collect cost and resource information which is disaggregated to the neighbourhood level. Although average management costs per dwelling unit vary widely across the sector, it is not possible to advance a straightforward explanation for such variation (Housing Corporation, 1997a).

A study of void control by housing associations showed that the level of rents, along with nomination arrangements with the local authority over allocations, could affect demand, and cause an increase in 'casual vacancies' as tenants decided to move elsewhere. However, the accompanying survey of RSLs showed that only 9 per cent mentioned high rent regimes as a major factor behind difficult-to-let problems (Pawson *et al*, 1997). There is only limited evidence to show that a high level of households dependent on benefit increases the difficulty of dealing with rent arrears (Ford 1999). In general, normal housing management procedures appeared to be more influential (Housing Corporation, 1997a).

The concerns about managing social exclusion therefore extend beyond the immediate housing management tasks, to wider issues of social dislocation. A recent study by Clapham and colleagues found that 92 per cent of RSLs felt that the socio-economic marginalisation of their tenants made the management of homes more difficult, but over two-thirds felt there was 'considerable' or 'reasonable' potential to counteract some of the problems through employment creation and linked activities (Clapham *et al*, 1998).

The dilemmas between meeting housing need on one hand, and achieving social diversity on the other, are felt most acutely in the allocations process; especially for new developments, when the cumulative effect of each lettings decision will rapidly shape the character of the area, or indeed where demand for social housing is still strong. David Page's approach rested on the assumption that a needs-based system of allocations would not produce sufficiently balanced or settled neighbourhoods. This diagnosis prompted a flurry of interest in modifications to lettings procedures in the RSL sector, through measures sometimes referred to as 'community lettings', which can be described as allocations which:

> ... *operate alongside or in place of a consideration of housing need and take into account the potential tenant's contribution to that community* (Griffiths *et al*, 1996, p1).

The adoption of such procedures rests on the assumption that greater benefits will arise from 'mixing' the population in an artificial way, overriding the operation of the needs-based system. Community lettings policies have tended to be introduced on difficult-to-let estates, as a local response to problems of low demand. They often rationalise what is happening in any case, with demand emanating primarily from people who already have a local connection.

The involvement of community representatives in the allocations process might exert a conservative influence on offers, by consolidating rather than changing the existing social profile of the neighbourhood. Writers such as Perri 6 have argued that a concept of community, based on maintaining strong ties with neighbours and kin simply reinforces poverty and social exclusion. It has been suggested that instead of 'introverted' social networks, more expansive networks of 'weak ties' with those in work would combat social exclusion by providing better access into employment (Perri 6, 1998).

This kind of approach to social engineering has taken a further step through growing interest in the technique of 'estate profiling' which has been developed in French social housing (Cole *et al*, 1998). Under this method a series of eight key indicators are chosen, to reflect length of tenancy, income level, benefit dependence, and the proportions of single parents, overcrowded and non-European households. The analysis then maps the characteristics of existing households along the indicators through an annual survey, and attempts to match incoming allocations so that there is a broad correspondence between the social profile of the estate and the wider community.

The estate profiling system raises difficult and sensitive questions about policy and procedure, especially as it involves procedures for *excluding* certain applicants simply on the basis of key attributes, if this would upset the balance in the social profile of the neighbourhood. But it does force into the open the extent to which any variations of needs-based procedures need to be informed by clear criteria and subject to continuous review. Modifications to allocations systems thus bring to the fore issues of community balance and long-term support for estates, which was often overlooked in earlier phases of development-led expansion.

The study of new estates in Yorkshire and Humberside, however, suggested that residents did not necessarily share the concern of housing association officers about social balance (Cole *et al*, 1996, pp49-52). Indeed, many residents said they valued living near to people with similar circumstances to their own, particularly as this created opportunities for informal networks to develop (around child care, for example) when formal provision was too inaccessible or expensive. Diversity was not a self-evident bonus.

A sense of community might therefore be preserved by households maintaining *existing* social networks as much as forming new relationships on estates (Young and Lemos, 1997). Residents living on estates of high child densities, for example, were less concerned about the proportion of such households on the estate than the lack of services and amenities for them. A high proportion of children could in fact often enhance a sense of belonging and increase social interaction, especially if the new development was relatively small. These processes challenge a one dimensional approach to social exclusion, hinging on the assumption that the problematic 'excluded' group simply needs to be given a route into the (unproblematic) 'mainstream'. This model has been rightly criticised by Blanc among others in favour of a process of 'social integration' in which minorities and majorities develop new forms of social bonds in an interactive manner (Blanc, 1998). It is still tempting from many policy documents to get a sense of the 'excluded' as an inert mass which somehow needs to be moulded back into the networking realities the rest of us enjoy.

New housing association residents, however, showed more concern about the nature of local provision, the location of services and amenities and the need for responsive housing management, especially in dealing with anti-social behaviour, than with ideas of community diversity. Of course, any balancing exercise has its limits – it is simply not possible to 'read off' a particular set of conflicts or difficulties from a given socio-economic profile. More important is the interplay of allocation policies with resident involvement, tenure balance, intensive management, inter-service working and community development support (Cole *et al*, 1996, p63). This emphasis duly shifts attention to the emerging agenda of 'Housing Plus' intervention as a strategy by which RSLs can deal with social exclusion more effectively.

Beyond landlordism – housing associations and Housing Plus

The need for comprehensive approaches to tackle social exclusion on new estates has produced a flurry of initiatives under the banner of 'Housing Plus' (Fordham *et al*, 1997; Clapham *et al,* 1998; Evans, 1998). The term 'Housing Plus' covers a range of possibilities – creating more sustainable estates, obtaining added value from investment, producing associated benefits in health or local employment opportunities (McGregor *et al*, 1995), using housing investment as a catalyst for wider resident involvement (Cole and Smith, 1996), and building partnerships with other local stakeholders.

Certainly, the extent to which a strict 'bricks and mortar' approach in new development and refurbishment can bring automatic benefits to a neighbourhood has come under increasing challenge. The study by Tony Crook and his colleagues found that improved RSL dwellings on a third of the estates remained difficult-to-let after the period of investment (Crook *et al*, 1996). Given increasing evidence of low demand for social housing in various sub-regions in the north of England (Northern Housing Research Partnership, 1997; Murie, Nevin and Leather, 1998), the changing context has raised questions about the extent to which capital improvements to neighbourhoods had to be supplemented by wider strategies to attain community sustainability.

The benefits of regeneration programmes may be placed at risk by the impact of needs-based allocations systems (Robertson and Bailey, 1996), especially when compounded by high rent regimes (Harding, 1997). Studies of housing association involvement in the regeneration of estates such as Hulme in Manchester and Newcastle's West End (Robinson, 1997) have underlined the difficulty in sustaining momentum through community development. Partnership working and longer-term commitments to intervention now typically accompany economic and social regeneration programmes, but a long-standing negative image can be extremely difficult to eradicate (Cole and Shayer, 1998). A pattern of low overall demand may be impervious to new investment in the housing stock, or changes in tenure and forms of management control. While the principles of 'Housing Plus' have garnered widespread support, the chances of sustained improvement in neighbourhoods are far from certain.

The shift in focus for regeneration programmes under the Labour government has now enshrined many of the trademark elements of 'Housing Plus' into public policy, through measures such as the 'New Deal for Communities' initiative announced in the 1998 budget (DETR, 1998a), and the emphasis in SRB 5 of developing effective partnerships and targeting resources. In this, the central role of housing associations has been confirmed – whether in improving the physical fabric of the dwelling and the estate environment, stimulating resident action and as a potential vehicle for promoting community diversity. The Housing Corporation has recognised the growing diversity of RSLs' roles in recent consultation documents.

Research has not conclusively isolated how far added value has been brought to community regeneration by means of additional investment in housing associations. Anticipated gains may have been placed in jeopardy by the severity of social and economic disadvantage in some neighbourhoods, high rents and benefit traps, and the prospects that renewal will be marred by the lack of demand even after improvements have been completed.

Certainly, the 'develop, compete or perish' idiom for housing associations in the early 1990s now needs to be recast to link into initiatives for community renewal. There are currently moves to link regeneration to techniques for local housing market analysis, examining more critically the demand for different property types and tenures in the light of demographic information, trends in rents and house prices, and waiting-list information. The rationale for housing association intervention needs to be set against the changing shape of the local labour market, and the use of such techniques is increasingly well-developed in some areas. The analysis also needs to incorporate an appraisal of future housing options in new build, demolition or refurbishment.

Future initiatives directed at social exclusion are likely to embrace more partnership planning between local authorities and housing associations, possibly as part of broadly conceived estate contracts or neighbourhood agreements. While the full integration of the two sectors into a single social housing tenure seems an unlikely prospect at present, a closer alignment of the two tenures in neighbour-hood renewal is to be expected, whether in common housing registers, similar funding and investment regimes, or joint marketing and management plans.

Conclusion

The future contribution of housing associations over measures designed to reduce social exclusion remains uncertainly poised. There is no straightforward path to follow. The general drift of the sector's changed role can be discerned – moving away from previous obsessions with ownership changes and development opportunities to the possibly more mundane but fundamental questions of community sustainability. In many areas, this brings housing associations up sharply against social and economic disadvantage which extends well beyond lack of participation in the labour market.

Underlying this change in the sector are questions about the breadth of responsibility which associations have for the social dynamics and problems in those neighbourhoods where they are prominent stakeholders. The future strategy set out by the Housing Corporation points in two potentially incompatible directions – stressing the value of a neighbourhood approach, while also urging lower rents to be charged (Housing Corporation, 1998b). There is an undeniable tension between the need for a 'Housing Plus' approach, where local problems extend well beyond the quality of the repairs' service, and the provision of financial support for such 'additional' responsibilities, especially where there is already pressure on *existing* rent levels.

It has been suggested that the best way ahead might be through a 'care and repair' approach within a neighbourhood-based partnership programme, rather than the traditional 'worst first' approach to prioritising reinvestment programmes, which may simply improve dwellings at the expense of social sustainability (Wadhams, 1998). The other side of this coin, however, would involve housing associations abandoning a commitment to certain areas which are deemed to be 'beyond redemption' – raising questions about the diagnostic tools required to come to such a judgement, let alone the more obvious sensitivities about making such decisions in the first place. For a sector weaned on expansion and broadening of the role, 'walking away' from areas of severe disadvantage may prove a rather unpalatable option.

The fact that the housing association movement has absorbed the shock waves of the past twelve years or so is a testimony to its resilience and flexibility. However, in the light of the growing segmentation of the housing market, questions about overall housing demand, the 'Best Value' regime, and the increasing emphasis on neighbourhood regeneration are being raised, these qualities of resilience and flexibility will be put to an even sterner test in the future.

If one takes the broader and more interactive view of social exclusion outlined here, the potential contribution which housing agencies need to make goes far beyond simply hanging on to the coat-tails of the latest Welfare to Work initiative. It remains to be seen whether the same RSL organisation can continue to juggle these new kinds of responsibility with more directly commercial functions, or with specialist management and care activities. If not, the age of anxiety may shortly be superseded for housing associations by the age of fragmentation.

CHAPTER 12:
Housing abandonment

Stuart Lowe

Introduction

This chapter focuses on the question of why some inner city neighbourhoods enter a spiral of decline which depletes the area of population leaving behind only those unable or unwilling to move. In these streets housing is increasingly abandoned and normal housing market logic collapses – properties are valueless and because of the lack of demand for any form of property, public or private, moving is easy, leading to bizarre behaviour as people become prey to fraudsters, organised crime, disturbed neighbours. From such communities services rapidly disappear, and economic and social life ebbs away with remarkable speed making it difficult to create and sustain stable personal relationships. All of this happens despite multi-million pound investment programmes through SRBs[1], City Challenge or other government schemes, and so it is apparent that centrally inspired and designed policy may not be the best way of tackling this form of social malaise.

At the very heart of such a scenario is the problem of abandoned housing. For various reasons – outlined later in the chapter – this has been until very recently a publicly unspoken issue despite the fact that quietly and privately, housing officers in local authorities and housing associations have been grappling with its consequences for some years now. Strangely there has been until the last few months almost no published literature or research on housing abandonment despite large-scale spending in recent years on studies of urban regeneration and the problems of void, vacant and difficult-to-let housing.

Housing abandonment is the process by which residential units in either the public or private sectors become detached from the housing market and eventually fall into disuse. It is a situation several stages removed from the property simply being vacant or a void tenancy. Sometimes the deterioration of the property can be very rapid especially in the private sector when owners simply walk away from a more or less valueless asset. Quite often public sector abandoned properties are in good, even excellent, condition. They have benefited from expensive refurbishment and in some cases are literally brand new. By no stretch of the imagination are we talking about slum housing in either the private or the public sectors.

---

1   Single Regeneration Budget projects

In neighbourhoods afflicted by housing abandonment it is clear that social cohesion is threatened. Once a property is abandoned the immediate neighbours quickly come under pressure from vandals and burglars. The value of their own property is affected and with sometimes astonishing speed a whole street becomes infected by a range of problems – any remaining corner shops close, people able to leave move out while the going is good, drug abusers colonise the area and petty criminals move in, unscrupulous private landlords desperate for income from their property manipulate the Housing Benefit system. And thus, the life blood of a community drains away and is replaced by a kind of twilight world.

Not only do house prices collapse but the large number of vacant private sector properties or void rental housing enables people to move relatively easily inside the area. Under threat or stress, young couples, single parents and other families move around with increasing rapidity. Quite often they do not leave the area but look for a solution locally, with relatives, in the PRS, or with a housing association. Young single mothers and young partners often appear to adopt unconventional solutions and, contrary to orthodox wisdom on moving behaviour, relationship breakdowns do not seem to lead to an increase in demand for social housing. This may indicate that the PRS plays a much greater role in such areas than might have been thought, or that their behaviour patterns are not as we think. At any rate one feature of these events is that attachment to housing tenure becomes completely instrumental. Evidence of this, drawn from a study in Newcastle, is presented later in the chapter.

These processes are closely associated with the problem of low demand, which affect towns and cities all over the country, particularly in the north. Oversupply of housing in some places is very difficult to admit to when local and national housing projections universally argue that there is a significant national under-supply problem. Nevertheless, at its heart, one key reason, but not the only one, for abandoned housing is that in some parts of the country there are surplus properties. The effects of low demand are dramatic. Landlords compete with each other for tenants, threats of clearance creates blight, housing providers think twice before investing in their properties, residents from all tenures face problems of drugs, crime and social malaise as we have seen. It is also a principal reason why, stealthily, some local authorities have been demolishing council housing for a number of years now. DETR data, based on HIP returns, suggests that demolitions have doubled between 1992/3 and 1996/7 to 7,700 dwellings, although this is likely to be an underestimate. In a recent paper it was shown that between 1994 and 1997 in three north of England cities – Leeds, Manchester and Newcastle – over 3,500 council properties were demolished or sold to housing associations for demolition or development (Keenan, Lowe and Spencer, 1998, p1). These were not slums. Some of them had been refurbished with SRB or City Challenge money and, in a few cases, were brand new properties.

These problems put many inner city communities under such severe stress that whole neighbourhoods in effect become detached from the mainstream of society. It is a central argument of this chapter that the processes leading to housing abandonment, with the associated breakdown of the market and of day-to-day administration of public housing, are embedded deeply in the development of housing policy in recent decades. There is a very real sense in which the policy process has played a significant part in the creation of this form of social exclusion.

The link to the social exclusion debate will be made more fully in the concluding section of the chapter, but that housing more generally plays a central role in shaping peoples' way of life is abundantly obvious. At its most extreme this is why homelessness is such an appalling state because it cuts people off from services, security, community and all comforts and aspects of daily life that constitute 'home'. Indeed, following this argument, it is one contention of the chapter that the sense of belonging associated with home life is deeply disturbed in areas where abandonment of housing occurs, even to the point where behaviour is affected, on occasion quite dramatically.

The bulk of this chapter is spent outlining the causes of housing abandonment and the closely associated question of low demand. It begins by reviewing such literature as there is, then, in a preliminary way, addresses the reasons for low demand and, finally, considers evidence of what happens to people in inner city areas that have entered this seemingly inexorable spiral of decline. A key theme in all this is that what is happening in these communities is changing much more rapidly than policy planners have, until recently, known about. The social exclusion of our fellow citizens in the inner cities is thus partly explained by policy failure.

Evidence of housing abandonment

In fact there is little direct reference to abandonment in the UK literature although in the US the issue has been recognised and documented for many years. Here mention is made of a small selection of the best US papers. In a seminal study Hoover and Vernon (1962) showed how abandonment could be a threat to the economic and social fabric of US cities. Sternlieb and Burchell's study of Newark (1974) and Van Allsberg's work on Detroit (1974) both pointed to issues of market failure as the root of this problem. Tobier's analysis of New York related the phenomenon to suburbanisation, inflexible rent structures and 'red lining' by banks leading to a pattern of disinvestment and neglect of property (Torbier, 1974). Wilson *et al* showed that in Cleveland abandonment '... spread in a contagious fashion beyond a dilapidated core' (Wilson *et al*, 1994). In all these situations, whole areas of inner cities were left to decay and became virtually uninhabitable. The structure of the housing system and pattern of housing tenure in the UK is, of course, different to the free market American city. Nevertheless, it is strange that when city officials in this country have been concerned about this issue for some time, there is no UK evaluation study to turn to[2].

The UK housing literature has concentrated on two closely associated concepts; 'voids' and 'vacants'. Void properties are a particular problem for public rented housing and here the research effort up to now has been concerned to explain the incidence of void property and how management systems can be improved to shorten void duration. For example, the recent large-scale study commissioned by the Housing Corporation focuses on 'void management' and despite collecting a great deal of evidence from housing associations about the growing problem of difficult-to-let housing there is only a short reference to abandoned housing (Housing Corporation, 1997b). However, the terms of reference of the commission may have constrained the focus of the research.

The nearest to defining the issue is the study by Fielder and Smith (1996) who identify two types of vacant properties, 'transactional vacants' and 'problematic vacants'. The latter they described as '… often in poor condition and the vacancy is likely to be prolonged'. According to these definitions the *English House Conditions Survey* 1991 identified up to 250,000 problematic vacant dwellings, mostly older and unfit properties in inner urban areas and likely to have been in the privately rented sector. In several studies Smith and Merrett found no evidence of problematic 'voids' or a nascent problem of abandonment (1987; 1988). They were concerned to calculate void durations and concluded that most voids were concerned with property improvement. They found no evidence of speculative withholding or abandonment of property (Smith and Merrett, 1987; 1988).

A later study for the (then) Department of the Environment, examined the reasons for private sector voids in five local authority areas in England (Finch *et al*, 1989). In common with the EHCSs they found that voids were in poor repair, and the longer the property remained empty the worse, on the whole, the state of repair. Owners of such property were discovered to be heterogeneous and the reason for voids varied, with an interplay between factors related to the property and the personal situation of the owners. As with Smith and Merrett, Finch *et al* did not define abandonment and neither study recognised the phenomenon as a problem. No doubt these researchers were working to fairly specific briefs and this comment does not undermine their valuable findings. But secondary analysis of their published data shows, however, that several of them were close to identifying the problem of abandonment more than ten years ago. For example, a

---

2   At the time of writing, a study of low demand housing has been commissioned by the government's Department for the Environment, Transport and the Regions. The study has taken a broad view of the issues and incorporates a number of detailed local case studies. The report, due in late 1999, will be the first time the low demand issue and the associated social problems have been thoroughly investigated. The link between low demand and abandonment is likely to be an important part of the study.

re-examination of the data gathered by Finch *et al* suggests that, of the cases they cited, as many as 30 per cent of 'problematic vacant' properties were *de facto* abandoned, and, in Blackburn, nearly 50 per cent. It is, of course, difficult to talk about other people's research data in this way and such evidence is not proof. But it seems to be indicative, in hindsight, of a deeper level of problem than originally was supposed.

The most direct evidence of housing abandonment is found in a small-scale, unfunded study conducted by an environmental health officer in Leeds (Bell, 1996). Bell found that a significant proportion of the problematic vacants in the Chapeltown Urban Renewal Area of Leeds were abandoned. Moreover, there was evidence that a contagion effect was helping to shape the pattern of events. This was an important finding because for the first time it presented direct evidence of abandonment. Bell identified 182 vacant properties in Chapeltown, which represent over 6 per cent of the housing stock. Using Fielder and Smith's definition, she discovered that over 70 per cent of these vacant properties were 'problematic vacants'. Further investigation of a random sample of 50 of those properties revealed that 20 of them had been abandoned '… these properties have been left to decay with no hope of them ever being reoccupied' (Bell, 1996, p51). One of her conclusions is that if this pattern was replicated across the country, using the narrow definition of problematic vacants in the EHCS, then there might already be some 100,000 abandoned properties across England as a whole. Grossing-up from one small area in this way is a questionable research method but the recognition that a significant proportion of problematic voids were *de facto* abandoned is an important finding from Bell's study.

More recently a number of projects have studied aspects of inner city regeneration and evidence of housing abandonment begins to become more apparent. Four neighbourhoods in Newcastle and four in Manchester were investigated by Power and Mumford (1999). They confirmed the view (see below) that the main cause of abandonment was the depopulation of large cities and the loss of manufacturing jobs (Power and Mumford, 1999). A report from the Northern Consortium of Housing Authorities (NCHA) investigated the low demand issue with an emphasis on more accurate modelling of the problem (Wood and Bryan, 1997). This study confirmed the large number of empty homes in the north of England and that they are found in both the public and private sectors.

A useful discussion paper (*Low Demand for Housing*) was written by the Chartered Institute of Housing (CIH, 1998b) as a contribution to the research and consultation process behind the Social Exclusion Unit's strategy document *Bringing Britain Together* (Social Exclusion Unit, 1998b). The CIH paper referred briefly to abandonment and indicated that it was an extreme consequence of low demand. In the Social Exclusion Unit report, a major part of the 'Housing' section was devoted to low demand and incorporated a useful summary of the evidence which linked housing abandonment to low demand.

Surplus housing is a growing problem and in some areas leads to near abandonment. This may be due to a chronic mismatch of supply and demand, the unpopularity of neighbourhoods with very poor housing or high crime, or rapid increase in the numbers of people moving in and out of different households....figures for housing association property considered hard to let, shows that the problem is worse in the north though not confined to it. One recent study suggests that almost a quarter of local authorities are struggling with areas of surplus housing. On its visits the Social Exclusion Unit encountered problems of actual or potential abandonment in Coventry, Liverpool, Sheffield, Leeds, Manchester and Newcastle. And yet in other areas, particularly in parts of London, demand remains high. Problems of low demand and abandonment can affect relatively new housing ... [emphasis added] (Social Exclusion Unit, 1999b, p27).

Thus, over the last 18 months there has been growing evidence of the problem of abandonment of housing and many of the studies relate the issue to that of low demand.

Abandonment and low demand

Abandonment is possible, of course, in areas of high demand but it is much less likely. What little evidence there is points to the problem of difficult-to-let council estates and housing abandonment in all housing tenures as a product of a housing surplus in certain localities. Abandonment and low demand are very closely related. Evidence of low demand is quite easy to find, particularly in locally based reports. In Newcastle, for example, the 1996 Housing Strategy Statement identified a major issue of lack of demand, particularly in the 'West End' area of the city, 57 per cent of all empty council dwellings concentrated in a part of the city which contained only 20 per cent of the council's housing stock. This serious state of affairs has occurred despite a very large-scale spending programme through the City Challenge initiative between 1992 and 1997. City Challenge had as one of its key strategic objectives the encouragement of greater stability on existing housing estates, and made possible the clearance of derelict houses, renovation of older private sector properties, improvement to local authority dwellings, energy efficiency work, and the provision of some new homes. Some 37 per cent of the budget was dedicated to this new provision (around £4.3 million) and this was supplemented by the city's capital fund.

A review of Newcastle's City Challenge programme stated that '... improvements to the existing stock, in all tenures, and new housing developments, have been of substantial benefit to residents ... (but) *people are still leaving the West End or are reluctant to move there with the result that there is a growing number of void properties, in all tenures*' (Robinson, 1996 [emphasis added]). Voids in City Challenge neighbourhoods in 1997 ranged from 3.5 per cent to 25 per cent with two areas over 20 per cent. An analysis of other tenures revealed that housing associations were experiencing voids at the rate of 11.9 per cent in the City Challenge area compared to 8.2 per cent over the city as a whole, and that vacancies in the private sector were running at similar levels. As was the case in Manchester, housing associations were finding it hard to let even new properties in some parts of the West End of Newcastle (Keenan, Lowe and Spencer, 1998).

Thus, what has happened in many northern cities has been a common pattern of low demand leading to increased void rates, which in some pockets has reached a scale well beyond the orthodox means of housing management to solve, and some of which, in any case, is not public sector stock. There are some neighbourhoods in which void rates exceed 20 per cent and it is here in particular that the abandonment syndrome sets in, sometimes followed by a demolition programme with other void stock being transferred to housing associations for demolition or redevelopment.

The study that does most to advance understanding of the relationship between social exclusion and inner city housing is Lee and Murie's research on the geography of urban deprivation (1997). They show that patterns of multiple deprivation in English cities is characterised by a very differentiated spatial pattern. Poverty and social deprivation is not only a feature of some council housing estates, as has often been thought, but affects pockets of housing involving all tenures. In inner city Birmingham and Bradford, for example, they document areas of owner-occupation or primarily of private renting where indices of deprivation are greater than some of the worst council estates in those cities. They point *inter alia* to the key role the privately rented sector plays in housing poor people. This is a most useful study because it shows that nationally designed, top-down, blanket solutions are inappropriate when localities are so fundamentally differentiated in the ways they describe. Lee and Murie end with a series of questions about the social processes that underpin their findings. They wonder why housing turnover is so high, suggest that little is known about why people move so rapidly in these areas, where they go when they leave and whether their situation has improved when they move out (Lee and Murie, 1997).

In a more recent paper Lee and Murie (1999) emphasise that low demand in social housing is both a cause and a consequence of the residualisation of this housing stock. But they stress that there are closely related sets of problems in the private sector, 'Low demand and high voids rates, low and falling prices are evidence that parts of the home-ownership sector are equally unattractive' (Lee and Murie, 1999, p637). The question remains, however, as to how low demand can be explained.

Explaining low demand

The patterns of differentiation and some of the other findings described by Lee and Murie, and the incidence of long-term voids and vacant property described above is partly explained by low demand. The idea that there is an oversupply of social housing in some parts of the country needs to be carefully considered in the light of the conventional projections about housing demand and supply. Virtually every 'housing needs' study asserts that there is a significant need for new provision. The best known and most influential study estimated a need for about 100,000 new social housing units per annum, in a context in which actual new provision was only 30,000 (Holmans, 1995). The government's official household projections have recently been reduced somewhat (1991 - 2016 projection reduced from 4.4 million to 4.1 million households) and the number of new properties, in all tenures, to be built on green-field sites revised downwards. The need for such a large programme of building based on current assumptions is not in doubt, despite the evidence of surpluses in some parts of the country. As will be shown, this disparity is largely a factor of imbalances in *regional* housing markets.

Compelling evidence of the regional picture has been presented recently by Bramley (1998) who devised a model of housing need based on demographic projections and housing market analysis. His headline figure for new social/affordable building was close in absolute terms to the estimates made by Holmans but was strikingly different when the figures were broken down at local authority level. Bramley showed that a large number of local authorities had a social housing surplus for 1997, with the top 20 on his list containing surpluses equivalent to the total national average new build rate. He argued that this reasserted the position in the 1980s of the north/south divide in the housing market and it is clear from his tables that most, but by no means all, of the oversupplied areas were in the north of England. Bramley's analysis clearly showed that most of the low demand localities coincided with areas where traditional manufacturing industry had declined. His list included Tyne and Wear, Teeside, the Yorkshire conurbations, most of Merseyside and Greater Manchester, cities in the East Midlands and three east London boroughs. In a recent revision of his earlier studies Holmans also accepted that there was a 'strong regional divergence' in the demand for social housing although the overall figure for new housing provision remained largely unchanged (Holmans and Simpson, 1999).

Thus it is clear that some areas of the country have a significant surplus of social housing and it is the problem of regional imbalances in housing supply that is almost certainly the main context in which housing abandonment occurs. Housing in the private sector is also affected as the Lee and Murie studies indicate. There are, of course, other possible explanations for low demand in some vicinities, such as the unpopularity of certain estates or neighbourhoods, particularly associated with the residualisation of council housing. There is also the likelihood that in some areas the supply of housing in the current stock over-represents dwellings built for certain types of households, for example, where there is too much 'family' housing and insufficient property for single person households. There is thus a surplus of larger dwellings compared to demand. But the explanation for the widespread pattern of low demand is likely to encompass more fundamental/structural reasons as well as these more localised factors.

The explanation for the regional disparity is, of course, complex but at one level simply reflects the patterning of the regional economies of the UK. Webster argues that the collapse of manufacturing industries in the north of England and the Scottish industrial heartland has had a dramatic impact on housing (Webster, 1998b). As people moved away from the traditional industrial areas in search of work or simply to escape the decline of their neighbourhoods, so empty property was left behind. Moreover, the new white-collar and service industries, with fewer locational constraints, gravitated towards the suburbs, further depleting the inner cities. According to Webster, 'Most big cities have lost two-thirds of their manufacturing employment since 1979, compared to a national loss of around a third' (Webster, 1998).

In Manchester, demographic change of this type clearly underpinned the problem of low demand, as was apparent in the reduction in numbers of people registering on the rehousing list. Between April 1994 and April 1996 there was a fall of 35 per cent in applicants on the general waiting-list and 22 per cent overall. Population decline was clearly reflected in this process, with a drop of 21 per cent in Manchester between the 1971 and 1991 censuses, although the inter-censal estimates suggested a slowing in this pattern more recently. Nevertheless over the last two decades many cities, not only Manchester, have seen an acute decline in population, and these areas tend to correspond to those in which demand for housing is at its lowest. In addition, the evidence of the modest reversal in this trend over recent years shows that in-migrants have been of smaller household types (in Manchester, 1.9 persons per household compared to 2.2 for out-migrants), and more likely to be unemployed and to live in the private sector (Keenan, Lowe and Spencer, 1998).

Another part of the explanation for the lack of prominence of the low demand issue and its failure to surface until recent years lies in the policy process itself. For example, the subsidy system created a perverse incentive for local authorities not to be open about the problem. With large amounts of 'top-sliced' subsidy available, local authorities were forced to bid against each other, for example, for SRB and City Challenge funds. In these circumstances it was inevitable that the problems of low demand would be minimised or concealed because a successful bid for development funds would be unlikely to succeed if premised on a scenario of low demand. There may well be echoes here of past problems with northern authorities and housing associations fearing a shift in the balance of subsidies to the under-supplied south.

Concealment of the issue of low demand in this way became a 'Catch 22' for the authorities. On the one hand it was difficult to be open about the problem and on the other they were harshly criticised for their failure to manage their downwardly spiralling estates. 'Difficult-to-let' estates and high and seemingly inexplicable void levels were treated as housing management problems, with the implication of poor management performance. It is apparent, however, that the scale of the problem and its somewhat random nature make this a difficult conclusion to sustain. Poor stock management may be part of the problem in some areas, but low demand is a much more broadly based issue. Low demand involves demographic change and the wider restructuring of the economy, with jobs shifting away from the heartland areas of the old manufacturing industries and towards the new hi-tech and service industries based in the suburban periphery. Moreover, monitoring of housing management performance indicated that some of the *best* performing authorities were precisely those areas in the north of the country suffering from low demand and 'worst estates' problems.

The impact of social processes

The idea that housing abandonment and low demand results from population change and economic restructuring is only a partial view. The spiral of decline in some inner cities is often highly localised and so is less amenable to explanations restricted to purely demographic or economic restructuring arguments. For sure these are key parts of the underlying process. But it is very striking in the Lee and Murie study that deprivation operates at almost a micro-level with individual streets, even clusters of houses, affected but round the corner the situation seems much less problematic. At this micro-level abandoned housing is more obviously related to patterns of social behaviour. For example, one factor, which is not sufficiently recognised, is the changing pattern of household composition in these areas, notably the increase in single parenthood and transient relationships, but little systematic research is available.

One of the clearest illustrations of where the economic and social factors coalesce is shown in the pattern of rapid mobility of large numbers of residents *inside* the inner cities. Where low demand is endemic in the structure of a local housing market, there is often a large amount of vacant property and it is relatively easy for households to move both within and between housing tenures. The existence of one or two abandoned houses can create a kind of contagion, spreading out from the empty properties until clusters of dwellings or a whole street are affected. Evidence in Leeds, Manchester and Newcastle suggest that neighbourhoods with a high incidence of abandoned housing often contain large numbers of transient households, moving frequently within the area.

The pattern of rapid mobility is graphically illustrated in a study conducted by Paul Keenan in the West End of Newcastle, a classic inner city area sandwiched between the River Tyne and the city centre (Keenan, 1998). Working for the city council Keenan sought to find out why households gave up council tenancies with increasing frequency. The aim of this work was to find out how often people moved, the type and tenure of dwelling involved in these moves and the distances involved. The results of this monitoring were very surprising.

During the course of twelve months, over 700 moving households were tracked. Keenan found that 88 per cent of households moved less than one mile, with nearly half of these movers going less than half a mile. This was quite a high figure in itself, compared to census data and other moving behaviour studies. Perhaps the most astonishing finding was that 52 per cent of the original movers moved again within six months and once again distances involved were short, with 70 per cent moving less than a mile. Of these 319 households, 212 had moved *for a third time* before the end of the study period. Once again 70 per cent of this group moved only a short distance. Serial moving of this frequency, and involving local moving, was graphic evidence of a community under extreme stress. Some of the most frequent movers eventually left the area, although mostly moving only a few miles. In purely housing terms, relatively few (only about 15 per cent) actually improved their housing situation. Most changed to like-for-like properties and in a minority of cases the housing conditions were worse, usually due to overcrowding (Keenan, 1998).

Keenan subsequently interviewed a sample of movers to find out what was going on. He found that the movers, especially the serial movers, were subject to multiple pressures, the combined effect of which was to cause them to move. They reported problems of crime and vandalism. The high stress arising from the threat of burglary round the clock was a significant problem. Often this combined with mounting personal debt, especially fuel debt. Frequently the final, often decisive, factor for almost half the group was disputes with neighbours, or a perception that their neighbour was a nuisance or a problem. These interviews make it clear that in a majority of cases the purpose of moving was to find a more secure position, drawing on their families, friends and neighbours as a source of support. Rather then becoming resigned to their fate and ruled by fear, they tried hard to find somewhere else to live *within* the West End. The high frequency with which neighbourhood disputes, crime and lack of safety is mentioned might indicate a contrary pressure to leave the area and the prominence of these sorts of concerns makes the pattern of short distance moving all the more remarkable. It was also apparent from the data, that at the time of the move most had expected it to be a relatively permanent solution; only 40 out of the original 728 described the move as temporary.

Clearly the aim was to find a permanent and settled arrangement. They tried desperately to cling on to the area despite their problems. After a short respite many realised the new arrangements were not working and after a period involving several moves some were forced to quit the West End area altogether. (A more detailed account of this study is published in Keenan's chapter in Keenan, Lowe and Spencer, (eds) 1998.)

Evidence drawn from only one or two places should, of course, be treated with caution when drawing general conclusions. However, rapid turnover and mobility have been identified in a number of recent studies of national data. Very high turnover rates in council housing have been documented by Hal Pawson (1998b). He shows that turnover rates in local authority stock has doubled since the late 1970s despite the 35 per cent reduction in council housing since the Housing Act 1980. Lettings remained at about the same level throughout the 1980s and 1990s. He also concluded that such high rates of turnover implied growing residential instability and a weakening of social cohesion. Pawson noted from his analysis that patterns of increasing mobility varied considerably around the country and over time, raising questions about the regional and local distribution of this issue. Rates of increase appeared to have been fastest in southern authorities with the pattern in the north rather less spectacular. Pawson showed that over two-thirds of new voids in the council housing stock arose because tenants moved out of the sector, at least for the time being. A high proportion of these households moved into owner-occupation or the privately rented sector, although recent evidence indicated a contrary movement back into council accommodation (Pawson, 1998b). 'Churning' within the social rented sector was also identified by Burrows who argued that rapid movement into and out of, and within, council housing made it more difficult to sustain stable communities (Burrows, 1997).

Keenan's local study and Pawson and Burrows' analyses of national data all suggest that moving behaviour in some sections of the housing system no longer conforms to stable or predictable patterns. In some parts of the country, particularly in areas of low and declining demand, social housing in general has become almost a parallel universe.

Housing abandonment and social exclusion

An important lesson from this chapter is that a malfunctioning housing system creates social exclusion. There are four closely related dimensions discernible in the mechanics of what happens. The first two are general points. First, people dependent on state benefits, the unemployed, and those working in low paid or insecure occupations are excluded by lack of income from many housing market choices. Furthermore, being dependent on rental housing, they suffer from the vagaries of landlords and housing managers who act as 'gatekeepers' to their homes. By default these people do not have the full range of opportunities available to better off people.

Second, the property itself can be a cause of exclusion. For example, poorly maintained and badly heated dwellings are unhealthy and cause illness; children living in overcrowded houses do less well at school; those living in poor neighbourhoods may suffer anxieties as we have seen even though the dwelling itself is in good condition. Lee and Murie write extensively about these issues in their study and conclude that it is important to recognise that social exclusion occurs not just as a result of being deprived of housing (homelessness) but also *through* housing, by living in areas of multiple deprivation. They caution, however, against labelling areas and so cutting them off from possibilities of self-generated and supported renewal. 'If the perspective of social exclusion is to be useful in this area, it has to be a trigger to further debate about choices ... rather than being part of the process of defining, managing and controlling these neighbourhoods' (Lee and Murie, 1997, p55).

A third way for social exclusion to occur is as the result of policy failure. It has been argued in this chapter that the train of events leading to the exclusion of some inner city communities from the mainstream of society resulted from the abandonment of housing, in the context of low demand. A number of features of the policy system *per se* have contributed directly to this situation. Specific features identified here include a number of orthodoxies, which stem in part from the national housing needs assessments. Further, damaging policy 'games' at the implementation level – especially to do with the distribution of housing subsidies and the disjuncture between the central policy apparatus and the very local level also contribute to exclusion.

A fourth part of the explanation in the chapter is that assumptions about how conventional housing markets operate often appear to breakdown in inner city environments. Not only do house prices collapse and rental property become unlettable, but assumptions about peoples' attachment to housing tenure disintegrates and patterns of unorthodox moving behaviour become endemic. Under the weight of these problems, relationships between partners, neighbours and friends can become strained. Unconventional solutions are perversely created by the choices available to move, or even to occupy than one house, possibly with different partners or possibly none. If people become unable to conduct stable, long-term relationships then the glue that sticks society together starts to weaken. The contagion effect associated with housing abandonment can thus be a cause of 'melting' in the social fabric. It is a source and not a consequence of social exclusion because the lack of social cohesion and the withering away of the foundations of stable social life, often in the shell of poverty, in effect, detaches people and communities from the mainstream of society. Other comparable communities not affected by housing abandonment appear to be much less stressed-out.

Conclusion

It has not been the purpose of this chapter to advocate 'solutions', although one or two general lines of thought do emerge. The first is that the sheer scale of the abandonment problem and the surpluses of housing in some parts of the country suggest that greater attention needs to be paid to regional economic policy. The option, occasionally proposed, of decanting people away from 'declining' regions is clearly untenable. Most people who can leave of their own volition may already have done so. This would suggest a second related point; that some care needs to be taken with the implementation of future building programmes because adding to the housing stock in areas of surplus housing, or even elsewhere, may induce a further residualisation of the inner cities. The economically weak do not have the choice to move to greenfield housing. The creation of new choices for some people may be directly at the expense of others, serving to tighten the screw on vulnerable inner city communities. A great deal more needs to be known about the causes and consequences of low demand, otherwise the building programme has the potential to be socially divisive.

At the macro-level it is clear that housing abandonment is principally, but not exclusively, a function of low demand and housing surpluses. Economic restructuring and demographic change are the main causes of this. But why some neighbourhoods rather than others enter the spiral of decline is more intimately connected to local factors. As we have seen, the abandonment of even one or two houses in an area can trigger the chain of events which eventually, and with alarming speed, drains communities of their economic and social viability.

Thus, understanding the reasons for the social exclusion process now affecting many inner city areas requires the macro and the micro-levels of analysis to be much more closely connected analytically. This necessitates greater awareness of the complex sociology of communities under severe stress. In addition, it is important to have a heightened understanding of the policy networks, particularly the relationship between central and local government, that at the moment are failing to deliver solutions and may indeed be a net contributor to the problem.

When, in December 1997, the Labour government established its Social Exclusion Unit, within the Cabinet Office no less, two of the three immediate priorities set down by the Prime Minster concerned housing. One was to rid the country of street homelessness and the other was to mount a co-ordinated assault on the so-called 'worst estates'. The problems of abandoned inner city housing and more generally of low demand should be a central part of this 'housing' agenda. They raise very fundamental questions about the development and shape of future housing policy. Meanwhile, in small neighbourhoods and on our inner city streets, people are grappling day by day with spiralling decline in their communities, a decline which they seem powerless to control. These streets contain a very large number of the most socially excluded of all our citizens and are where the brunt of economic decline and restructuring, and of housing policy and housing market failure are most acutely felt.

CHAPTER 13:
Developments in housing management

Pauline Papps and Robert Smith

Introduction

During the last few years there has been a growing interest in the related issues of poverty and social inclusion, not only in the UK but elsewhere in Europe. Whilst the concept of social exclusion remains contested, the adoption of the term by central government has brought some of the non-material aspects of social inclusion into sharper focus (Social Exclusion Unit, 1998b). Perhaps one of the clearest definitions is provided by Duffy who refers to social exclusion as:

> ... a broader concept than poverty, encompassing not only low material means but the inability to participate effectively in economic, social, political and cultural life and in some characteristics, alienation and distance from the mainstream society (Duffy, 1997 cited in Walker, 1997, p8).

It is not our purpose in this chapter to examine why individuals and households experience such disadvantages, and whilst others have related the social exclusion agenda to broader housing and regeneration policies (Lee and Murie, 1997; Brown and Passmore, 1998), our intention is to focus attention on the linkages between housing management policies and practices at a local level, and the extent to which these have generated or reinforced social exclusion and the degree to which changing such policies and practices might contribute to achieving greater social inclusion and promoting neighbourhood and community stability.

However, before examining the relationships between housing management policies and practices and processes of social exclusion, we would stress that there is no simple relationship between social exclusion and social housing. Whilst many of those affected by poverty and social exclusion live in the social rented sector, as others have shown, such features of social exclusion are neither limited to the social sector, nor uniform across the social sector within the UK (Lee and Murie, 1997). Changes in housing management policies and practices may be appropriate responses to the problems engendered by social exclusion, and housing management should be linked effectively to other services in order to develop local strategic approaches to tackling social exclusion. This paper concludes that, in themselves, initiatives focusing on issues of access and allocation and anti-social behaviour, are unlikely to be sufficient to address the problems without tackling the underlying causes which explain the increasing concentrations of disadvantage and deprivation in the social rented sector. Areas of social rented housing have been primary targets for housing management initiatives over the last 20 years, and some have been more successful than others, but the evidence that they have overcome the problems on some of the UK's more difficult to manage estates is perhaps rather limited.

What is social housing management?

There has long been debate over the tasks that constitute social housing management. In 1939 the first Central Housing Advisory Committee (CHAC) report defined housing management thus:

> ... management must include far more than rent collection and the ordering of repairs, for unless some steps are taken so to educate the tenant as to secure his co-operation, the landlord, striving to maintain his property, and the tenant destroying it by his neglect, will remain warring parties. Hence good management additionally postulates the application of skill in treating the person who is paying for the use of the commodity so that he too may do his share in preserving its value; it is in effect a form of social education and aims at teaching a new and inexperienced community to be 'housing minded' (CHAC, 1939, p10).

The report clearly accepts that housing management should include tasks beyond those of lettings, rent collection and repairs, but their conclusions failed to recommend one model of housing management above another (for example, the 'welfare' model of Octavia Hill or property management model of the then Institute of Housing and some local authorities), arguing that different circumstances demanded different methods (CHAC, 1939, Brion, 1995). Throughout the following four decades the continuing lack of statutory guidelines resulted in many different approaches to management of local authority, and latterly housing association housing being adopted, with very little consensus on the wider tasks to be included.

Debate over the scope of housing management continues today with competition between welfare and contractual frameworks (Pearl, 1998). The contractual framework eliminates 'social objectives' from the definition of housing management, with the social needs of individuals seen as independent of housing tenure and therefore the responsibility of the social service function of local authorities. The major government reports on the management of social housing (Centre for Housing Research, 1989; Clinton *et al*, 1989; Bines *et al*, 1993) have defined housing management within the property management (or contractual) model: 'The definition covers the collection of rent and recovery of arrears, lettings to new tenants and transfers of existing tenants and the management of voids ... On the maintenance side, it includes response to repairs and planned maintenance ...'(Bines *et al*, 1993, p13). The only other functions considered are tenant participation and consultation (Bines *et al*, 1993).

However, the professional body for those working in housing, the Chartered Institute of Housing (CIH), argues that the welfare of tenants and the provision of an acceptable environment in which to live are an important part of the housing management role. They have listed a number of tasks which constitute the 'social role' of housing management:

- debt counselling and benefits advice;
- racial harassment prevention;
- dealing with aspects of alcohol and drug abuse;
- liaison with social services over community care, children at risk or the mentally ill;
- dealing with environmental problems such as dogs, traffic or litter;
- helping to develop community projects such as play schemes or 'good neighbour' schemes;
- arranging adaptations for people with disabilities;
- wider aspects of neighbour disputes;
- working with police to improve security or deal with anti-social behaviour;
- welfare aspects of wardens' work;
- supported accommodation;
- community alarms;
- community development;

Source: CIH, (undated).

In this chapter the wider definition of housing management is adopted as many of the problems of social exclusion and the responses to it go far beyond the property management tasks identified by the contractual framework.

Housing management in context: the development of public housing

As stated above, although social exclusion cannot be considered synonymous with social housing, the majority of the areas identified by the SEU (1998b) as experiencing social exclusion, are social housing estates. Housing management can in no way be considered the sole cause of social exclusion for other social and economic changes outside the influence and beyond the control of housing managers have made major contributions to its existence. This said, the service provided to social housing tenants has been criticised for its shortcomings, many of which have compounded the effect of other factors in creating, sustaining or reinforcing social exclusion. Prior to outlining the main criticisms of housing management and identifying its role in the process of exclusion, it is necessary to recognise the influence of past housing policies on the type and condition of the stock that has to be managed. Finally, the increasing incidence of anti-social behaviour among tenants is outlined, as an example of the wider problems now facing housing officers and its contribution to the social exclusion of whole estates.

In the first five decades of large-scale public housing provision (1920s-1960s) the emphasis was placed, by local authorities and central government, on the building of large quantities of new dwellings to meet huge housing shortages and to enable the clearance of large areas of slum properties. The use of new, and untested, building systems and materials left a lasting legacy of badly designed and located, poor quality housing, in need of huge investment in repairs, refurbishment, replacement or demolition. In the 1960s central government encouraged local authorities, through successive subsidy regimes, to build large peripheral estates or more problematically high-rise blocks of flats (Dunleavy, 1981) thereby helping to create 'problem' estates which are difficult to manage, difficult-to-let and difficult to inhabit (Coleman, 1990; Morris and Winn, 1990; Spicker, 1987). It is the tenants of such areas that are more likely, although not exclusively, to suffer from social exclusion (Lee and Murie, 1997). The problems they face, e.g. poor health, education and employment opportunities may be compounded by the poor service they receive from their landlords.

More recent government policies have had a major effect on the type of housing available to rent from social landlords, the most important of which is the Right-to-Buy (RTB) legislation introduced in the 1980 Housing Act and Tenants' Rights etc (Scotland) Act. The outcome of this major privatisation of public assets, and the restrictions on the building of replacement stock by local authorities, has been the loss of the higher quality, better located and more popular stock to the owner-occupied sector. Local authorities have been left with the poorer quality (and therefore the most expensive to maintain), badly located and unpopular properties, with a disproportionately high number of flats. The impact of these policies on social landlords has been to make the management task more difficult, and for tenants, they have led to a reduction in choice and quality of property. At the same time central government policies have encouraged the development of housing associations (Registered Social Landlords in England and Wales) as the main providers of new social housing, as well as providing opportunities for local authorities to transfer their housing stock to such bodies, creating a diversified set of social landlords, with responsibility for housing management.

The organisation and effectiveness of the housing service

For many years successive governments and official reports have recommended that local authorities should establish discrete housing departments which have comprehensive control over all housing management and related functions (e.g.

CHAC, 1939; CHAC, 1969; HSAG, 1978; Audit Commission, 1986). However, few local authorities have adopted this approach completely (Audit Commission, 1986, Centre for Housing Research, 1989 and Clinton *et al*, 1989). For example, in 1993 only 29 per cent of local authorities claimed to have a housing department which dealt with all housing management functions, and on average 30 per cent of housing management was dealt with by other departments (Bines *et al*, 1993, p22).

Such centralisation of housing services in distant town halls, and the dispersal of functions between departments, has led to charges of remoteness, over bureaucratisation and inaccessibility (Legg, 1981; Power, 1987a). The growth in the scale of local authority stock combined with the rationalisation of local authorities in the 1964 and 1974 local government reorganisations has also led to large housing authorities which, it is claimed, are incapable of responding to the different needs of local situations (DoE, 1981). There have been some moves to counter these claims through the adoption of various forms of decentralisation, but few local authorities have passed complete autonomy to area or estate-based offices (Bines *et al*, 1993).

Inconsistency in service organisation and remote housing departments are only two, of many, criticisms of social landlords, particularly local authorities. The variations in level of service provided, by all social landlords is also an area of concern, for those tenants in the worst estates may not necessarily receive a good quality service.

Allocations policies have long been linked with the creation and sustaining of difficult areas of public housing, with social landlords accused of discriminatory practices, over use of discretion by housing officers and political interference in letting decisions (Morris, 1958; Ryder, 1984; DoE, 1981; Reynolds, 1986 and Henderson and Karn, 1987). The change in emphasis to needs-based allocation policies (CHAC, 1969) prompted by these criticisms has created a different set of problems. Many applicants with the greatest housing need, and therefore with little or no choice, are often offered the least desirable properties in the most problematic areas, thereby creating estates with high levels of vulnerable and excluded tenants.

To enable the most efficient and effective housing service to be delivered, it is necessary to control rental income. This means setting economic rent levels and ensuring efficient rent collection, and also ensuring that the greatest number of available properties are let at any one time. Without such control it is impossible to provide a level of service that maintains the property and surrounding environment in good order. In 1986 the Audit Commission reported that some authorities were charging rents that were below the level needed to cover outgoings; at the time this placed a burden on all rate payers, but now results in insufficient income to the Housing Revenue Account, which was ring-fenced in England and Wales following the 1989 Local Government and Housing Act.

It was also found that rents did not reflect the value of the property to the tenant (i.e. the same rent was charged for a house and a flat, and the condition of the property had no bearing on rent paid) (Audit Commission, 1986). Local authority rents have risen substantially since this 1986 report.

Problems arising from uneconomic rents are further compounded by non-maximisation of rental income because of high levels of void properties and high levels of rent arrears. Despite good practice among many housing organisations, there is evidence that some authorities still have unacceptably high levels of void properties. In 1993, 18 per cent of inner London authorities and 32 per cent of metropolitan authorities had greater than 3 per cent of properties empty (Bines *et al*, 1993, p115), and high levels of rent arrears, with local authorities averaging 37 per cent of tenants in arrears (housing associations 28 per cent) and 6.1 per cent (4.8 per cent) gross arrears (arrears as a proportion of rent due) (Bines *et al*, 1993, p84).

Without greater control over the financial aspects of housing management, coupled with the collection and collation of the necessary indicators to monitor performance, many organisations fail to deliver a service that can help alleviate the worst aspects of social exclusion. High levels of void properties on an estate not only reduce rental income but also create a feeling of abandonment. Poor rental income makes adequate repair and maintenance programmes difficult and the provision of services that would foster a process of inclusion impossible.

As we have noted, social exclusion involves interrelationships between a whole range of factors, which may reinforce each other, and explanations which emphasise the failings of housing management (or its potential to promote social inclusion) over other factors may be both partial and distorted. Since the focus of this chapter is housing management, we do wish to explore two areas of housing management policy and practice which have been highlighted as contributing to social exclusion, and where initiatives have been developed to respond to these problems, both to reduce the difficulties of the management task and to address social exclusion.

Many social landlords have over recent years faced increasing problems with difficult-to let and difficult to manage estates. The Department of the Environment's investigation of difficult-to-let council housing (DoE, 1981) identified a number of causes of unpopularity in the public housing sector. These included estate size, high density, multi-storey dwellings, housing costs and rents, social isolation and poor housing maintenance and management. In seeking to address these problems, some have emphasised issues of design and the need for physical modification to address the problems (Coleman, 1990). Others have placed much more emphasis upon the nature and quality of housing management, and in particular the need for local management (Power, 1991b). We would propose to examine the relationships between housing management and social exclusion by looking at two particular aspects of housing management: access and allocations, and anti-social behaviour.

Allocating social housing

Whilst it has long been argued that social housing allocations should ensure that priority is given to those in housing need (CHAC, 1969; DoE, 1978; Housing Management Advisory Panel, 1995), it has been argued that over the last 20 years or so, and particularly since the Housing (Homeless Persons) Act of 1977, the prioritisation of allocations has concentrated the most disadvantaged into particular communities. Page has argued that housing associations should find ways of letting new estates to households seeking rehousing via different routes; local authority nominations, council and association transfers and referrals, in order to achieve a more 'balanced' community (Page, 1993). Others have pointed to stigmatised local authority estates with concentrations of vulnerable and dependent households (Power, 1987a). The prioritisation of allocations to families, the vulnerable and others in the greatest need may have reinforced the concentration of deprivation on to particular estates and in to specific areas, which may have reinforced processes of social exclusion.

Social landlords have had duties to address needs but this has been within a context of a declining social rented sector, reinforced by sales, and where the outcomes of social rehousing policies are a result of individual household choices, as well as the operation of allocation policies. It is not always easy to see, therefore, how the concentration of disadvantaged households through needs-based allocations could have been entirely avoided. However, arguments have emerged more recently to suggest that allocations policies should seek to promote more cohesive and settled communities. This should not replace the key objective of meeting housing needs, but figure as a legitimate additional consideration.

Some social landlords have adopted local lettings policies designed to counteract the trend towards concentrating the most disadvantaged into particular areas. However, they have mainly been introduced for difficult-to-let estates, experiencing severe management problems and frequently, they have been introduced to influence the household composition on new or redeveloped estates or to protect communities from problems arising from lifestyle differences between generations (Griffiths *et al*, 1996).

The debates have tended to focus on those parts of the social rented sector which have been marked out as the most problematic. However, more recently the debates have been widened to consider broader issues of changing demand for housing, high turnover, increasing levels of vacancy, abandonment and housing surpluses within a context of continuing housing needs (Murie, Nevin and Leather, 1998; Lowe, Spencer and Keenan, 1999).

Low demand for social rented housing in certain areas may present opportunities to extend allocations to groups other than families and those in the greatest need, to attract other types of household such as childless couples, single people and multi adult households. In some areas there may also be a case for allocating housing to local key workers in order to integrate them into the communities they serve. However, it must be recognised that, whilst allocations may have a role to play in improving the quality of life on estates and addressing issues of social exclusion, their potential contribution should not be exaggerated. Social mixing is constrained by household choice, amongst the housing options available to individual households, whilst many of the problems associated with some of the least popular estates are beyond the scope of housing management. At the same time, prioritising according to criteria other than needs may disadvantage some households, or even exclude them from the process.

The concept of local lettings is underpinned by a number of assumptions. These include the view that it is desirable to improve the social balance on estates (reducing high concentrations of the most disadvantaged), that there are advantages in giving a degree of preference to local people in rehousing decisions, that there are benefits to be gained from involving tenants in the formulation and implementation of policies (although not necessarily in the selection of individual tenants) and that applicants and tenants known to be engaged in anti-social behaviour should be excluded from social housing. This last point leads us to consider how social landlords have responded to this particular problem.

Neighbour disputes and 'anti-social behaviour'

A growing concern of housing managers has been the real and perceived escalation of neighbour disputes and 'anti-social behaviour' among social housing tenants. It has been estimated that housing officers can spend up to 20 per cent of their time dealing with nuisance or anti-social behaviour complaints (Aldbourne Associates, 1993). The type of behaviour complained about can range from the minor (e.g. a one-off noisy party) to violent or criminal acts. An official definition argues that:

> Anti-social behaviour by a small minority of tenants and others is a growing problem on council estates ... Estates can be stigmatised by the anti-social behaviour of a few. Such behaviour manifests itself in many different ways and at varying levels. It can include vandalism, noise, verbal and physical abuse, threats of violence, racial harassment, damage to property, trespass, nuisance from dogs, car repairs on the street, so-called joyriding, domestic violence, drugs and other criminal activities, such as burglary (Welsh Office, 1995, paras 1.1-1.2).

It is difficult at present to gauge the nature and extent of the anti-social behaviour among tenants of social landlords as few authorities have been recording and analysing the complaints that they receive. However, among the research completed there seems little disagreement that noise is the most common cause for complaint amongst neighbours. A survey of local authority and housing association tenants in 1989, by Salford University, found that 25 per cent of all complaints related to domestic noise, with 7 per cent to children's noise. Other common causes were nuisance by pets (16 per cent), vandalism (12 per cent), litter (11 per cent), and harassment (9 per cent). Less common were drug taking/drinking, racial disputes, car repairs, and parking disputes (Karn *et al*, 1993, p2-3). Data collected as part of the baseline study of housing management in Scotland (Clapham *et al*, 1995) found that 20 per cent of tenants surveyed claimed to have experienced neighbour problems; of these 43 per cent had experienced problems with domestic noise, 14 per cent poor soundproofing and 14 per cent noisy parties. Other commonly experienced problems were violence/verbal abuse (26 per cent), children/teenagers (24 per cent), drink/drugs (17 per cent) and pet related (17 per cent), (Scott and Parkey, 1996a).

Anti-social behaviour is in no way restricted to areas of social housing but responsibility for dealing with it falls more heavily on social landlords because they have a duty to ensure that tenants have 'quiet enjoyment' of their homes. Also, high incidence of anti-social behaviour can reinforce the 'bad reputation' of already stigmatised estates, creating greater social exclusion for those who have no choice but to continue living there.

In response to the rising incidence of anti-social behaviour there has been a proliferation of good practice literature (Power, 1991b; Karn *et al*, 1993; CIH, 1999) and a strengthening of legislation. Emphasis is placed on tightening tenancy agreements, cross-department strategies, multi-agency working and staff training in legal procedures and conciliation and mediation skills (CIH, 1999). However, despite evidence of many innovative strategies, local authorities have tended to concentrate on the legalistic remedies such as tightening tenancy agreements; greater use of possession orders and injunctions (NACRO 1996; Papps, 1998), although in practice the numbers of evictions for anti-social behaviour remains relatively small. Only a minority have formal mediation services available to tenants. Legal options in England and Wales have been strengthened by the 1996 Housing Act, with the introduction of housing injunctions and strengthened grounds of possession for nuisance behaviour, and the 1998 Crime and Disorder Act which introduces community safety orders.

The legalistic approach adopted by many authorities have a number of implications for wider housing policy, the role of housing managers and the promotion of social exclusion. First, is the differential treatment of residents of the various tenure types on council estates. Council tenants, who are the perpetrators of anti-social behaviour face more punitive treatment than other residents who may indulge in the same behaviour. Even if the council enforce by-laws and statutory powers more vigorously, the non-council tenant will not be threatened with loss of their home.

Second, what happens to the tenants who are evicted? Are they to be treated as intentionally homeless and therefore ineligible for rehousing? Are they to be excluded from housing waiting-lists indefinitely because of their past behaviour? Re-entry into social housing for previously anti-social tenants is likely to become more difficult in future with the increase in sharing information on disruptive tenants by the various social housing providers in an area. Many anti-social tenants will be forced into the private rented sector, perhaps causing disruption to neighbours who will have little recourse to remedial action. Also, the instability inherent in this sector may only compound the many problems experienced by the evicted tenants.

Third, there must be a question over whether dealing with anti-social behaviour is within the remit of housing managers. During the last two decades, as the emphasis has moved from building as many dwellings as possible to managing a rapidly deteriorating stock with ever smaller resources, the role of housing management has come under close scrutiny (see Pearl, 1998). Through housing legislation in both the 1980s and 1990s, central government has attempted to impose a contract ethos on social landlords with the role of housing management being seen as mainly that of property management, e.g. allocations, voids and rent-collecting (DoE, 1992; NFHA, 1995). Many social housing landlords argue that their role extends beyond bricks and mortar and must include the well-being of the tenants if they are to have sustainable communities on their estates (Power and Richardson, 1996; Fordham et al, 1997). If the environment in which the properties are situated is neglected and intimidating, then controlling allocations and voids becomes much more difficult. It is within this scenario that the way housing managers deal with anti-social behaviour becomes important.

Should this extended role of housing officers include dealing with criminal activity? Possession for conduct likely to cause a nuisance and criminal activity has been made easier by the new provision for repossession included in the 1996 Housing Act, although the required exchange of information from the police is not always forthcoming. The new Crime and Disorder Act increases the role of English and Welsh local authorities, if not housing departments, directly in the control of crime in their communities (Home Office, 1997a; Home Office, 1997b; Home Office, 1997c). Guidelines on community safety strategies and community safety orders give lead roles to local authorities. Community safety orders are obtainable by either the police or the local authority, with the knowledge of the other. Much of the behaviour targeted by this policy is perceived as a problem facing social housing, so it would seem likely that housing officers will be asked at least to take responsibility for gathering evidence; this is a task which it could be said they undertake already. This is yet another step in encouraging housing managers to adopt a legalistic and punitive approach to anti-social behaviour rather than encouraging a more diverse and holistic approach, which could include community and economic development within these areas.

As Lee and Murie (1997) have noted there have been two different perspectives on the relationship between housing and social exclusion. The first sees housing as a consequence of exclusion, whereby an individual's housing options are restricted by their lack of resources. The alternative view is that housing itself generates and reinforces social exclusion, and that housing disadvantage reinforces disadvantage in terms of access to other services.

In reality these two perspectives are inextricably linked. Those with limited resources and bargaining power may find themselves concentrated in the least popular sectors of the housing system. We have sought to show in the last two sections how housing management policies and practices may reinforce problems in the social rented sector and, through an analysis of policies towards allocations and addressing issues of anti-social behaviour we have highlighted how changing policies and practices may change the composition of areas of social housing and thus the nature of process at work in these areas, such as social exclusion.

However, whilst changing housing management policies and practices may be appropriate responses, they may not be adequate in themselves to address the underlying social and economic problems which have also contributed to the concentration of disadvantaged households into particular areas.

Redefining the role of social housing

In the previous sections we have examined the evolving role of housing management and in particular management responses which have emphasised changes to the way the services are delivered, the processes of access and allocation and approaches to tackling anti-social behaviour. However, whilst changing housing management policies and practices may have a role to play in improving or maintaining the quality of life on housing estates, the potential contribution should not be exaggerated. There are two reasons for this. Firstly, many of the very difficult management problems faced by social landlords are not the result of social ownership, poor design, management failures or inappropriate allocation policies; they have their origins in the wider social and economic environment (e.g. poverty, inequality, crime and unemployment), and can only be tackled at these levels. Secondly, given the changing position of the social rented sector within the UK housing system, landlords are constrained in what they can do to influence the choices and behaviour of social tenants.

Over the last 20 years the role of social housing has changed considerably. General housing policy has been designed to encourage home-ownership as the preferred tenure, to transfer existing stock from public to private ownership, to reduce public expenditure on housing and to substitute private for public finance in housing investment. However, as policies have encouraged those who are able to exist in the social rented sector, other trends have pointed to an increasing need for social rented housing. Demographic projections indicate a significant increase in households over the next 15-20 years, with particular increases amongst elderly households, lone parent families and single people living alone (Ford and Wilcox, 1994). Coupled with increasing levels of marital and relationship breakdown and labour market changes which have highlighted a decline in secure employment and an increase in casual and short-term work, these trends are changing the relationships between household incomes and housing costs. At the same time, shifts towards sustaining more people living 'independently' in the community (as opposed to institutionally) have given rise to a need for additional supported housing and move-on accommodation from temporary housing. Taken together, these trends have reinforced social and economic segregation between tenures within the UK housing system, with social housing increasingly catering for those with the least resources.

The work of those such as Forrest and Murie (1988), particularly in relation to the local authority sector, has pointed to the increasing residualisation of public housing in Britain. This can be seen in terms of two key flows into and out of the sector there; the removal from the sector of more 'traditional' council tenants, who have been encouraged into owner-occupation, most notably through the Right-to-Buy (RTB) and, secondly, the drawing in of households who were previously not well served by local authorities (Forrest and Murie, 1988). They place the process of residualisation firmly within a context of economic, political, social and special restructuring which has resulted in growing social and economic polarisation within Britain. They have characterised the changing nature of council housing in terms of a decline in the number of economically active heads of households, multiple earner households and higher income households and, conversely, an increase in the number of economically inactive, benefit dependent households, in elderly households, in young persons (particularly those under 25) and in female headed households. At the same time as a decline in the absolute size of the council sector has been a reduction in the proportion of family houses and a concomitant increase in the proportion of flats and small houses, within an overall context of an ageing and deteriorating public sector stock, whilst an increasing share of lettings have been made to the homeless and those dependent on state benefits.

Page (1993) noted a similar increasing residual or welfare role for housing associations. Using data for lettings on recently developed estates to show high proportions of allocations to the unemployed, those wholly dependent on state benefits and to households whose average income was less than one third that of the national average net disposable income.

Alongside a developing residual role, the social rented sector has become increasingly stigmatised, attracting negative media attention, for example in relation to the growing number of lone parents and rising levels of crime and violence.

Investment in social rented housing has reduced both for local authorities and through housing associations (Wilcox, 1997). Over the last 20 years, social housing investment has often been subsumed within broader policies concerned with economic regeneration. Gross social housing investment in Britain has fallen by more than 60 per cent in real terms since 1979/80, and the virtual disappearance of local authority investment in new build and acquisition, coupled with the loss of stock, has not been compensated by increases in housing association capital investment or investment through various community regeneration activities. Together with the trends of increasing rents and declining subsidies, the financial prospects for the social rented sector remain far from encouraging.

In many areas there is a serious shortage of permanent socially owned housing available for renting. However, in some localities there are mismatches between unmet needs and housing supply and expressed preference for social housing. We have already noted that the profile of applicants for social rented housing is changing, with an increasing emphasis on single people, the elderly, small family households, those with special needs (including a requirement for support or care) and those dependent on welfare benefits. Conversely, much of the available social rented housing (particularly via relets) is of an inappropriate type, size, standard or location, such that a significant proportion of the social housing stock may be unpopular or undesirable. Despite the decline in the overall size of the social rented sector the level of lettings has generally been sustained, as a result of increased turnover within the sector (Pawson, 1998a). Social landlords often find themselves in the seemingly contradictory position of having serious unmet housing needs and difficult-to-let stock (and high vacancy rates). In some localities there may be an excess of low demand, unpopular rented housing, although this does not necessarily mean that in the same area there may not be rehousing pressures.

Where households have choice, there is evidence that those in the social rented sector may exercise this choice and elect to move. At the same time households on local authority and housing association rehousing registers may be unwilling to accept tenancies of particular properties in particular areas. With low-demand estates it appears that even those in considerable housing need are choosing not to take up available tenancies. Often only those in the most desperate housing need may be willing to consider rehousing opportunities in certain localities, reinforcing the concentration of disadvantage and social exclusion.

Redefining the role of housing management

Against a background of a changing role for social housing it has become appropriate to consider how to redefine the role of housing management. We have noted above that the housing management function has usually been defined in relation to the traditional landlord functions of rent collection and arrears control, repairs and maintenance, voids and allocations, tenant participation and tenancy management (Bines *et al*, 1993). Others have widened the definition to include Housing Benefit administration, local budgeting management and the co-ordination of housing management with other aspects of social policy such as social service provision (Power, 1991b).

We have already highlighted earlier in this paper the view of the previous Conservative governments as to the failures of housing management, particularly in the public sector. In its 1987 Housing White Paper, the Conservative government argued:

> As the quality of housing and its environment has declined, so a wide range of social problems has emerged; crime and violence have increased; many people have left for better opportunities elsewhere; local enterprise and employment have disappeared; and whole communities have slipped into a permanent dependency on welfare system from which it is extremely difficult for people to escape (DoE, 1987, pp1-2).

In part the response of the Conservatives from 1987-1997 was to encourage improvements in housing management, placing emphasis on increased accountability of housing managers, enhanced opportunities for consultation and tenant participation, improving the efficiency of service delivery, and giving greater attention to performance indicators as a measure of the quality of the service delivered to customers. At the same time investment has been targeted at 'problem' estates and areas through initiatives such as the Priority Estates Project, Estate Action and the financial mechanisms such as the Single Regeneration Budget (SRB) and Estates Renewal Challenge Funding (ERCF). However, this investment has to be seen in the context of a long-term decline in social housing investment and increasing central government control of revenue budgets, which have often made it very difficult to improve the effectiveness of housing management.

However, alongside central government policies designed to address the failings of management within the public sector, have also been a set of policies aimed at encouraging the privatisation of the housing management functions. Some of the housing policies of the Conservatives in the period 1987-1997 represent a loss of patience with local authorities, despite the evidence of progress being made through the decentralisation of housing management services (Cole, 1993) and through the adoption of best practice approaches to housing management. Whilst housing management failures may have been concentrated into a limited number of organisations and estates/areas, policies such as Tenants' Choice, Large Scale Voluntary Transfer (LSVT) and Housing Management Compulsory Competitive Tendering (HMCCT) have all promoted the privatisation of housing management, without necessarily addressing the root causes of the problem.

In relation to HMCCT, whereby local authorities are required to put their housing management service out to competitive tender, the incoming Labour government have indicated that this is to be replaced by a new duty on local authorities to achieve Best Value for their services (DETR, 1998b). Changes have already been introduced to the compulsory competitive tendering regime to give greater flexibility in advance of the introduction of Best Value. Labour's approach to Best Value is to expect that local authorities will deliver and continuously improve services to clear standards, covering both cost and quality, by the most economic, effective and efficient means available. Specifically in relation to housing the Best Value framework has been set out in a recent consultation paper (DETR, 1999), which indicates coverage (and Best Value is not only concerned with core housing management functions, but also the local authority's housing role in relation to the homeless, the private housing sector, community care and the development of sustainable communities), process, arrangements for inspection, timetable, evaluation and possibility of intervention to remedy failure. It should also be noted that housing associations (or Registered Social Landlords to give them their more recent title in England and Wales) will also be subject to the application of a similar set of Best Value principles (Housing Corporation, 1998a).

However, the redefinition of the housing management role is not purely being driven by concerns with performance, competition and the ethos of Best Value. Concern with issues of social exclusion, regeneration and sustainability are placing an increasing emphasis on the concepts of partnership and community involvement, as well as the desirability of adopting a strategic approach to the regeneration of housing estates (Taylor, 1995). Whilst short-term initiatives such as the Priority Estates' Projects may have an impact, it may be more important to change the nature of mainstream housing management services. It has been shown that local authority housing managers are often working in multi-agency teams, including tenants and residents, to address wider issues than those traditionally defined as estate management (Zipfel, 1994a). More recently, attempts have been made to add 'Housing Plus' as an extra dimension to housing management in the social sector (Power and Richardson, 1996), with housing associations leading the way in this respect (Clapham, Evans *et al*, 1998). The implication is that housing management needs to go beyond housing, and to develop the skills and linkages necessary at a local level to work with others to address the problems which reinforce social exclusion.

We have argued throughout this chapter that housing management policies and practices in the social housing sector may play a part in the process of social exclusion, and thus in addressing the problems. We have highlighted some of the criticisms which have been levelled at the housing management service, particularly in relation to the public sector, and some of the responses which have been made by social landlords in terms of developing more localised services and through specific estate-based initiatives. In focusing on the specific aspects of allocations and anti-social behaviour, we have attempted to show that policies and practices can be developed at a local level which seek to overcome concentrations of disadvantaged households and deal with highly disruptive behaviour by a minority of tenants. The evidence suggests that innovative approaches to housing management, together with a multi-agency approach to complex problems which exist in some areas of social housing, can begin to address issues of social exclusion. However, the housing management service has to be seen in a wider context, with a need to develop broader strategies at both national and local levels, if the worst effects of social exclusion are to be ameliorated.

CHAPTER 14:
What constitutes a 'balanced' community?

Ray Forrest

Introduction

What constitutes a balanced community and would we recognise one if we saw
it? This book has examined essentially the consequences of a coalescence of
processes, namely, widening social inequalities amidst economic restructuring
and technological change and specific developments in housing such as tenure
restructuring, new problems of accessibility and affordability, the growth of
home-ownership and area degeneration. In this context certain groups have
suffered disproportionately, particularly minority ethnic groups, the low paid, the
less educated and less skilled. Some of the consequences are seen in the growth
of street homelessness, hidden homelessness and the visible social polarisation
evidenced by concentrations of disadvantaged households in particular parts of
towns and cities. In this latter context, the contemporary urban experience is one
in which we may not be able to define a balanced community but we recognise
its opposite when we see it.

These are the disconnected places. They may be on the urban periphery or in the
inner city. Typically, they are or have been mainly council owned or managed
but not exclusively so, (and owner-occupied and housing association areas have
suffered similar problems). Unemployment and underemployment is endemic, as
is child poverty. Crime rates are higher than average and the social and
residential fabric is crumbling. Property values are relatively low, in some cases
there are abandoned and empty dwellings. Despite years of regeneration policies,
little seems to have changed. The shops have closed. The bank and post office
have gone. Attempts to reverse decline, through mainly housing related
investment, appear to have been swimming against a tide of general
disinvestment and decline. Those groups which have been most severely
disadvantaged by the social and economic transformations of the last two
decades or so find themselves progressively trapped within, or channelled into,
these neighbourhoods. This concentration of those with limited economic
resources and weak networks of opportunity adds a further layer of spatial
exclusion, and neighbourhood effects further exacerbate processes of social
exclusion occasioned by poverty, unemployment, marital breakdown or ill

health, and typically a combination of factors. In Paugham's (1995) terms the socially precarious find themselves increasingly concentrated and stigmatised. Moreover, social relations and ways of life in these neighbourhoods may produce social norms perceived to be increasingly distant from the mainstream (see, for example, Cars et al,1998). These are then the socially excluded places which lack social cohesion and which require greater social mix or balance.

These are all highly contested concepts and, as many have pointed out, the inclusive society is not synonymous with one in which the norms of the majority dominate or oppress. And cohesion is not the opposite of exclusion. There is cohesion in adversity. There is the cohesion of the defensive community (Suttles,1972; Forrest and Kearns, 1999). And as has been emphasised in this book, the experience of social exclusion in housing need not have a strong spatial dimension or, at least, the experience of street homelessness in the City of London or Manhattan is a qualitatively different experience from living on a poor, peripheral council estate. In this chapter, however, we are concerned with notions of community and balance, with the idea of a residential neighbourhood as essentially a relational web of individuals and households.

We shall also concentrate mainly on the housing dimension of these debates. It would be relatively easy to drift from a concern with housing and housing management to a broader consideration of societal imbalance – from the cohesive neighbourhood to the cohesive society. In a fundamental sense, housing problems are embedded in these broader questions. And, indeed, the current policy emphasis on 'joined up thinking' in relation to 'neighbourhoods that don't work' runs the risk of posing questions which will generate the same kinds of answers as did the Community Development Programmes of the 1970s (Atkinson and Moon, 1994). Compartmentalisation may produce policies that don't work or at best ameliorate. Holistic approaches may, however, produce the answers at the level of the social structure rather than the neighbourhood.

Constructing the balanced community

So, where did we come in? In housing policy terms explicit references to balance and mix are most closely associated with the immediate post-war period, what might be termed the pre-privatisation period of the mid to late 1970s, and the current period focused on issues of social exclusion. Before discussing these periods in greater detail, it is appropriate to dismiss any preconceptions that some optimum mix exists in terms of age, ethnicity, income or occupational class or some other social characteristic which differentiates successful neighbourhoods from others. Homogeneity is as likely to be a feature of stability and cohesion as is heterogeneity. The classic occupational community of miners or steelworkers was hardly a model of social diversity. Few seriously suggest the need to break up rich enclaves because of the negative consequences for those who live in them. Residential concentrations of minority ethnic groups may be highly supportive neighbourhoods of choice. Nor should we assume that neighbourliness and reciprocity are essential features for a neighbourhood that works. Baumgartner (1988) for example has observed that:

People in the suburbs live in a world characterised by non-violence and non-confrontation, in which civility prevails and disturbances of the peace are uncommon. In this sense, suburbia is a model of social order. The order is not born, however, of conditions widely perceived to generate social harmony. It does not arise from intimacy and connectedness, but rather from some of the very things more often presumed to bring about conflict and violence – transiency, fragmentation, isolation, atomization and indifference among people. The suburbs lack social cohesion but they are free of strife (p134).

Specific concern with the residential segregation of the poor has re-emerged relatively recently in the post-war period. When we refer to social polarisation in the contemporary urban context we generally think of the stigmatised estate on the urban periphery or the declining inner city area. But concern with the socio-spatial dimension of residential segregation and differentiation and with notions of mix and balance, have their origins in more general observations about the processes of sifting and sorting associated with the spread of urbanisation. As Drewett and Heidemann (1973) observed, 'Social polarization is a major concern of much writing in urban sociology in the period since the Second World War. Broadly, the thesis of this literature is that different socio-economic groups are becoming increasingly segregated from each other in geographical terms' (p385). Indeed, it was precisely these processes of residential change which were at the heart of the early Chicago School studies of urban growth. Was the contemporary urban form contributing to a less cohesive society? How were individuals and groups adapting to this new urban environment?

The post-war New Towns programme represented, among other strategic concerns, an explicit attempt to construct communities and overcome the haphazard, organic growth of urban centres. Beveridge saw the New Town ideal as an opportunity to 'think out in advance the development of a town as a whole, so as to avoid the waste, the disorder, and the needlessly uncomfortable living that has developed through the haphazard growth of many old towns' (Beveridge, 1950, p6). For Heraud (1968), New Towns were an attempt to 'change the whole character of urban class relationships' (p33). Class distinctions were to play a role in establishing the social structure of these planned spaces. They were not to be eroded or diminished but instead 'every type and class of person' (Committee on the New Towns, Final Report, Cmnd, 6876 p10) was to be represented. 'Social mix' and 'cross-cutting alliances' (Heraud, 1968, p38) were to be encouraged through the development of neighbourhood units each with a variety of housing provision and a range of facilities such as the local pub and the community centre in an attempt to avoid the alleged social evils of 'one-class neighbourhoods' (Goss, 1961).

As Cole comments earlier in this volume, the notion of social balance as a policy objective can be traced back at least to the Garden Cities movement but its translation from a desirable sentiment to a set of clear criteria for implementation has remained more elusive. For the New Town planners social balance and self-containment were intimately linked. Thus, neighbourhoods were to contain a mix of dwelling types and therefore households at different stages in the family life course and in different occupational classes, but these new communities were also to be complete in the sense of transport links, local employment opportunities and leisure facilities (Thorns, 1976). Balance was not framed simply in terms of social composition but critically in relation to sources of employment and broader ways of life. A balanced community in this context was one where the layout and facilities on an estate encouraged social interaction among a wide range of people and where housing and employment were symbiotically related. These were the antithesis of 'estates on the edge'. In the main, the residents were moving from lower quality housing in overcrowded and blitzed London, from parental homes or rooms to relatively spacious houses which represented a quantum leap in condition and location. And they were relocating in the context of an expanding post-war economy where jobs for skilled workers in particular were plentiful. These were communities which worked, literally. Whether they worked in the broader sense as neighbourhoods of conviviality is more debatable. Or, more pertinently, the open plan front gardens, the community centre and the neighbourhood pub were perhaps less important to sociability than the shared circumstances in which households found themselves. The early settlers of the New Towns were by definition non-locals and, in the main, young couples and families with the male breadwinner in a skilled working class occupation. New Towns were 'pram towns'. The men left for work on buses or bicycles, often returning for lunch, leaving their wives to care for the children. The daytime space of the New Town neighbourhoods was almost exclusively the domain of women and children. The point is that homogeneity in terms of stage in the life course was a strong feature of these planned, 'balanced' communities. New estates generally are typically associated with young and growing families and it is precisely that imbalance in age structure which acts as a unifying factor. The children act as pivotal points of contact for adults. The quality of schools and child care are common concerns. Neighbourliness and mutual aid focus on child care and the nature of these bonds evolve as families mature together.

Now this is a slightly idealised version of the neighbourhood of young families but it draws directly on recent research carried out on some of these early post-war council and New Town estates (Forrest and Kennett, 1999a,b). These were not balanced communities in terms of age or occupational structure. And they were not balanced in the sense that certain groups were actively excluded – namely the less skilled and those deemed to have undesirable social characteristics. These were the communities of strategically important workers with standards of cleanliness and behaviour deemed suitable for these new residential areas.

Breaking up council housing areas

We can leap forward in time to the mid-1970s before notions of social mix and balance emerge again as important policy preoccupations. Up until then, home-ownership and council housing grew in parallel at the expense of the private landlord. As quantitative concerns in housing policy gave way to more qualitative concerns, issues of tenure came to the fore. In particular, the promotion and expansion of home-ownership as a social policy required new inroads into social housing rather than private renting. This is well trodden ground (see Forrest and Murie, 1988) but it is arguably at this juncture when fundamental economic restructuring begins to combine with widening income inequalities and privatisation policies that processes towards the creation of residual enclaves of public and mixed tenure housing areas were accelerated if not set in train. The housing privatisation policies of the 1980s, and particularly the Right-to-Buy, have undoubtedly been primary factors in the shaping of the policy and management problems in housing which we face today. It is worth recalling that such policies were justified in part by the argument that tenure transfers would break up one-class ghettos. An injection of home-ownership into areas which were exclusively rented from Councils or New Towns would help create more balanced, socially mixed communities. It is also worth recalling that many critics argued that the policies were more likely to have the opposite effect. Those estates which contained the greatest mix of incomes and occupational profiles were likely to be amongst those which had the highest levels of sales. The poorest estates would have low levels of sales, higher levels of turnover and become even more residual in character. In the simplest version of events, that is pretty well what has happened. This is not to suggest that policy makers and urban managers would now be faced with a relatively benign social environment in the absence of a Right-to-Buy and associated policies of privatisation. After all, the problems of increased urban poverty and disconnected, run down estates are commonplace across Europe despite very different policy regimes, tenure structures and histories (Power, 1997). But if the question is, have the privatisation policies of the 1980s and 1990s contributed to, or detracted from, social stability and social balance? – then, on balance, the answer would probably be negative.

There are different perspectives on this and, given the importance of this policy shift in the post-war period, it is appropriate to review briefly some of the processes that have contributed to current concerns about social exclusion and housing. A primary process of exclusion for lower income households concerned their ability to enter home-ownership through the Right-to-Buy itself. In the absence of replacement new building, which has been a feature of similar policies in many other countries, the Right-to-Buy was a once only offer. Those who were not in the public rental sector and who could not afford home-ownership through the normal market processes were inevitably excluded from the opportunity. And within the public rental sector those tenants with insufficient earnings were effectively excluded. This would have been less of an issue, had it not been for the relationship between lower quality and less desirable public sector dwellings and tenants in less secure and vulnerable circumstances. Higher turnover dwellings, and thus those most likely to be offered to homeless households, tended to be less desirable dwellings in less popular estates. Higher income households and those in more secure financial and family circumstances were more likely to be occupying higher value dwellings. The overall effect was therefore to widen the gap between lower income and higher income households between and within public sector housing areas.

With the maturation of such policies, the processes exacerbating exclusion and disadvantage are cumulative. First, the best dwellings are sold. Second, the best maintained dwellings, typically those occupied by higher income households, command the highest prices on the open market. Third, among those resold, the highest value dwellings in the most desirable locations are more likely to be bought by middle class households. Dwellings which were previously potentially available to poorer households are no longer part of a pool of properties for allocation according to some measure of need. Bureaucratic systems of allocation may have been flawed and may themselves have produced socially unjust outcomes. However, when the best of the public sector stock is resold on the open market it is inevitable that few, if any, of these dwellings remain available to the types of households which would have been allocated to them, had they remained in the council or some other version of non-profit rental sector. The poor are therefore progressively displaced to fewer and less desirable locations in the inner city or on peripheral estates. The logical conclusion is a greater concentration of poor people and continuing downgrading of those estates where that concentration is occurring.

Of course, these processes have been mediated by a range of local and cyclical factors. The picture painted above is most appropriate to higher demand, 'southern' regions (see Forrest, Gordon and Murie, 1996). Nevertheless, in the context of a general widening of income and social inequalities since the late 1970s the loss of the most affordable and better quality state rental dwellings has inevitably limited the housing opportunities of the poorest sections of the community in whatever context. The aggregate consequences are well known. The income profile of those in the social rental sectors has become progressively skewed towards the bottom two income deciles. On that measure at least the social composition of large parts of our cities has become less balanced.

Have the more popular, more saleable estates become more stable and socially mixed as a consequence of privatisation policies? In this context, Best (1996) has suggested that Right-to-Buy sales have:

> ... led to a mix of tenures on most council estates, thus retaining people within these communities who might otherwise have moved out to gain advantage of owner-occupation elsewhere. In terms of creating social mix

and balance within such estates and helping to develop leadership skills in
people who have a direct interest in the quality of the estate, the outcome
appears to be generally positive (p541).

However, research has consistently shown that those who bought houses as
sitting tenants generally wanted to continue to live in them. Relatively few were
speculative purchasers. The early cohort of purchasers were typically committed
to the areas they bought in rather than the tenure they bought into. In many cases
they could have afforded to move out to buy but had chosen not to. They were
areas where their friends lived and where they had brought up families. It is hard
to argue in that context that privatisation policies stabilised such areas. They
were stable already.

When former state owned properties change hands on the open market issues of
social mix and stability become more complex. The new purchasers may be
more likely to see former council homes as a transient type of accommodation.
They may not have a long-term commitment to the area. This is, however, as
much a matter of demographics as tenure. Stable residential areas inevitably pass
through life cycle stages. At some point, long-term residents are replaced by a
new cohort of young couples and families. The extent to which that process is
destabilising will depend on the degree to which the area is somewhere to aspire
to or as a necessary stepping stone to somewhere else – whether it is in decline
or on a stable or upward trajectory (see discussion of social capital in next
section).

The higher quality council and New Town estates built after the Second World
War provide a good example of this process. Recent research shows that such
areas have gone through both a demographic and tenure transformation (Forrest
and Kennett, 1999). People moved there after the war and generally stayed there.
As families matured, some bought under Right-to-Buy and prior discretionary
schemes. Many did not. The major changes, however, in relation to social mix
and balance did not occur with tenure change but with demographic change.
Estates of young couples and families became estates of mature families and
ultimately of ageing couples and single people. The effect of privatisation has
been to alter the nature of turnover as the original cohort die or move into
residential care. If these estates had remained as exclusively or predominantly
tenanted, the new cohort would have been drawn from among the lowest income
groups. With access via the market rather than via bureaucratic allocation, on the
more desirable estates the new residents have many of the characteristics of
those they are replacing – merely younger versions.

Moreover, these new entrants are often escapees from the less desirable and
mainly tenanted estates elsewhere. It is these areas which have become most
fully exposed to the differential recruitment from low income households into
the council or social landlord sectors. While the more desirable estates have
become effectively insulated from that recruitment by tenure transfers, the low

sales estates have felt the full force of differential recruitment. The changed reputation of the sector as a whole has meant that more affluent households will not even contemplate renting in such areas. And those households which have bought are more likely to do so in order to escape. The evidence for this is clearest in relation to sales of flats in England where the turnover of such properties has been much higher than among houses. Moreover, in some cases ex-council flats and less desirable houses have proved difficult to sell and have been bought by cash and let by private landlords. Sub-markets of multi-occupied private rented houses have developed with the former council sector introducing new elements of transiency and instability and often lower standards of maintenance and repair. This is tenure diversification but not of the type originally envisaged by policy makers.

After more than two decades of attempts to engineer social mix and stability through tenure, it is clear that neither tenure status itself nor manipulations of tenure status are likely to be the key. Stability or balance relates to a wider range of social institutions and the way these institutions integrate people into neighbourhoods and society more broadly. They relate in particular to integration through work, through family and kinship networks, through education and leisure pursuits and through shared activities and interests. Stability is not principally about tenure. Home-ownership can be associated with increased commitment to an area and neighbourhood. But it can also be associated with transiency and onward movement. Housing therefore has a contingent relationship with social balance or stability. Tenure and changes in tenure will neither secure nor erode social stability but changes in the housing market may well trigger significant social changes. The underlying causes for such changes may be elsewhere but the trigger for change and the most evident symptoms may be strongly associated with housing.

Social capital, social cohesion and the balanced community

Current concerns with social balance focus on a rather different set of issues. They are less tenure specific (though council housing is strongly featured) but less all encompassing. Whereas post-war utopian planning sought the creation of residentially mixed neighbourhoods and an integration of work and residence, and the era of privatisation sought the societal balance achieved with the social glue of home-ownership, we are now concerned with places and people left in the wake of social and economic changes. The emphasis has shifted from broad based policies aimed at majorities with assumed shared social norms and characteristics to those assumed to be on the margins and increasingly disconnected. Areas of chronic poverty, low reputation and physical decline are argued by some to lack certain key ingredients of cohesion and stability. References to social balance and social mix now sit within a general discourse of social cohesion and social exclusion. Disadvantaged neighbourhoods may be internally disorganised and unstable but are themselves symptoms of a wider social imbalance and a divergence of opportunities, living conditions and lifestyles. What is to be done and where does housing fit this time?

The developing responses take us back to the remarks made in the previous section about processes of integration within neighbourhoods and the way people in their local areas are linked into the wider urban fabric. There has been a progressive disillusionment with attempts at community regeneration which placed too much emphasis on the physical upgrading of housing conditions and tenure change. Often the results have been simply to transform an area of poor people in poor housing into an area of poor people in better housing. That is not a negligible aim or achievement but offers limited possibilities of longer-term and secure regeneration. It is more likely merely to delay the downward trajectory of an area rather than reverse it.

The new vocabulary of regeneration uses terms such as reciprocity, mutuality, and trust. This is about more than 'Housing Plus', the idea that housing programmes can be developed which achieve benefits wider than housing. It is about pursuing policies which encourage and build upon the networks of formal and informal social relations within a neighbourhood. The balanced community from this perspective is one in which residents have a strong sense of local identity, where there is a vibrant and healthy level of interaction and where there are strong linkages with the world beyond. These and other qualities are subsumed within the concept of social capital.

Social capital incorporates ideas of social networks but as part of broader patterns and qualities of civic engagement:

> *By analogy to physical capital and human capital, social capital refers to the norms and networks of civil society that lubricate co-operative action among both citizens and their institutions. Without adequate supplies of social capital – that is, without civic engagement, healthy community institutions, norms of mutual reciprocity, and trust – social institutions falter* (Puttnam, 1998).

Puttnam has argued elsewhere that there is a decline in the stock of social capital in contemporary USA and that poor neighbourhoods in general lack the necessary qualities of self-help, mutuality and trust which could assist in their regeneration – and in part explains, and is a cumulative product of, their decline (Puttnam, 1993; 1996). These ideas have now entered the policy and political arena in Britain. Regeneration strategies have increasingly come to be seen as working with and building on the stock of social capital in a neighbourhood. A key implication is that without sufficient social capital, regeneration policies will not take root or be sustainable. Neighbourhoods where existing relations of trust and reciprocity are weak will lack the qualities which can create and sustain voluntary association and partnership.

Temkin and Rohe (1998) have argued that two constitutive elements of social capital, socio-cultural milieu and institutional infrastructure, are key determinants of neighbourhood trajectories. The socio-cultural milieu refers to these qualities of local interaction referred to above. The institutional infrastructure 'is a concept that measures the level and quality of formal organisations in the neighbourhood' (p69). In a detailed empirical study of social capital and neighbourhood stability they assert the significance of these qualities as follows:

> ... *every neighbourhood at a given point in time can be categorised into a particular quality level based on the status of the area. Potential causes of change to that status originate from at least two sources. First, broad social trends may alter a region's employment base and social structure. Trends such as the loss of manufacturing jobs or the influx of a new ethnic group may have a general impact on a metropolitan area's economic and demographic characteristics. Second, changes occur within the neighbourhood itself. Neighbourhood residents age, marry, and experience other transformations as they move through their life cycles. Therefore, even without large-scale structural changes, neighbourhoods must cope with internal sources of change. The forces of change, however, do not affect every neighbourhood in the same way. The effect of these forces, we argue, depends on the strength of the social capital in the area* (p67).

That is a fairly major claim. And before we all take up the latest policy mantra we should be cautious about possible interpretations of this position. First, there is a danger that the search for, and promotion of, social capital replaces real investment or becomes an attempt to regenerate on the cheap through a greater emphasis on self help. Second, it is debatable whether poor areas lack social capital. Many studies show contrary evidence. Close family ties, mutual aid and voluntarism are often strong features of poor areas. It is these qualities which may enable people to cope with poverty, unemployment and wider processes of social exclusion. As Portes and Landeholt (1996) point out, 'There is considerable social capital in ghetto areas, but the assets obtainable through it seldom allow participants to rise above their poverty' (p20).

What poor neighbourhoods have are high proportions of residents who may have restricted social networks and action spaces. Contacts tend to be between people with networks which do not extend into the world of work. Because of high unemployment, high levels of lone parenthood and perhaps a high number of poor pensioner households, residents of poor neighbourhoods spend more time in their local areas than do residents of wealthier neighbourhoods. Thus, what Friedrichs (1996) refers to as the context effects of neighbourhoods, are particularly marked in the most disadvantaged areas. These context effects include the restricted opportunity structure of the neighbourhood (lack of formal and informal employment opportunities) and the development of deviant social norms – or at least social norms outside the mainstream.

This perspective on social balance focuses therefore not on issues of housing tenure, occupational class or demographic composition but on factors such as the quality and strength of the ties between neighbours. And these contacts may not need to be of any great material or emotional significance. In this context, Henning and Lieberg (1996) report on an interesting study of a Swedish residential neighbourhood. Henning and Lieberg are interested in the role of weak ties between neighbours, that is, 'unpretentious everyday contacts in the neighbourhood' (p6), They stress, as have others, that their neighbourhoods are not physically bounded places but social group relations. For Henning and Lieberg the significance of the neighbourhood is partly as an important arena for the development and maintenance of weak ties. These kinds of contacts range in their terms from a nodding acquaintance to modest levels of practical help (such as taking in a parcel). These kinds of contacts are, however, not only an important source of general well-being but may provide important bridges between networks of strong ties. For this reason, according to Henning and Lieberg weak ties are of particular importance for vulnerable and marginal groups.

The contemporary version of the balanced community therefore emphasises neighbourly contacts, trust, reciprocity and social relations which are supportive but not introverted. A balanced community must combine continuity with dynamism, solidity with fluidity. Social networks must reach beyond the local neighbourhood. The community must be neither physically nor socially isolated. Most of all, perhaps, there must be jobs and facilities such as banks, local shops, quality schools and, of course, decent housing. This version, of course, runs the risk of romanticising the past, the community lost which we seek to regain. But it also reflects a more general unease concerning an apparent weakening of social ties and social cohesion in modern society. It is this unease which is central to the work of social capital theorists such as Puttnam. The unease is not limited to poor or disadvantaged areas but it is these areas which are seen as being most at risk of becoming disorganised and anomic places in the contemporary city. Ironically, however, it may be in precisely such areas where mutual assistance and reciprocity are most evident, where collective and reciprocal coping strategies develop as ways of dealing with adversity.

Concluding comments

Ideas of social balance and social mix have emerged in different social, economic and policy contexts. In the immediate post-war period, these ideas were embedded in a more pervasive utopian idealism. The New Towns programme was one of the most visible expressions of a new corporate and planned approach to urban development and represented perhaps the high point of state intervention in the housing and labour markets in Britain. This was social engineering on a grand scale. The architects, planners and housing managers had tremendous scope to influence the shape and social composition of residential areas. The strategic objectives were not only to control urban sprawl and achieve a decentralisation of employment and employers from central London but to create towns with less residential class segregation than was apparent in the less regulated forms of urbanisation which had previously dominated. Lewis Silkin, introducing the New Towns Bill stated, 'I do not want the better off people to go to the right and the less well off to go to the left … I want them to ask each other, 'Are you going my way?'' (quoted in Schaffer, 1972, p184).

Although such aspirations were only fulfilled to a relatively limited extent with more familiar forms of class segregation soon emerging as the New Towns developed, it was nevertheless a very different set of political and policy objectives which lay behind notions of social balance then, when compared with subsequent periods. For a start it was about majorities not minorities. It was about achieving a greater residential mix of the middle classes and what might be most appropriately termed the labour aristocracy, the skilled and respectable working classes. Most pertinently to the focus of this book, it involved the active exclusion of some of those groups which would now be labelled 'socially excluded'.

In the second phase, the mid to late 1970s, ideas of social balance and social mix take on a different set of meanings. This is social engineering of a different kind, motivated primarily by political expediency and ideology. Housing tenure has become central. Baldly stated, a balanced community becomes one in which there is a greater mix of tenants and owners – at least within the public rental stock. Tenure diversification, at least within the public sector, becomes the primary policy element. In this context the housing manager's role is not the allocation of new dwellings in a pristine social environment. Rather it is dealing with increasing complexity in relation to management and maintenance. This complexity takes on its most complicated form in flatted blocks. Here social mix is perhaps at its most intense and most problematic. Within one block there may be new owners, old Right-to-Buy owners, older established tenants, new, younger lone parent families – even younger unrelated sharers in private tenancies (Forrest, Gordon and Murie, 1996). This is social mix with a vengeance. On the more popular housing estates, the issues, as we have discussed, have been rather different. Tenure mix precedes any social recomposition which occurs more gradually as properties change hands on the open market. But issues of social balance and stability are less to do with tenure and more connected with demographics and labour market change.

In the current, third, phase, questions of social balance are derived from broader concerns with concentrated poverty and threats to social cohesion. It is about disconnected people and places. This debate is less about social engineering, the creation of the 'good city' or the spread of middle class norms and lifestyles through the promotion of home-ownership. Issues of dwelling mix, household variety or occupational diversity are not in themselves perceived as the key problems or indeed the basis of the solutions. While concentrations of council housing have become almost by definition a sign of an imbalanced community the spread of home-ownership to encompass a wider variety of households and dwellings has also created problems within that tenure. As the characteristics of households within different tenures have changed, so inevitably have the characteristics of tenures. At the end of the century, compared with the post-Second World War middle phase, housing of whatever tenure sits within a less stable social and economic environment. For many, jobs and relationships are less secure. The imbalanced community becomes one in which these risks and insecurities are concentrated and where the poorest and those with least bargaining power in the contemporary labour market find themselves increasingly cut off from the social norms and cultural expectations of the majority. The imbalance derives not from some particular occupational mix or demographic composition. Those kinds of factors are not nor ever have been, problems in themselves. The imbalance, if that is indeed the appropriate terminology, comes from a lack of employment, poverty, high turnover and the loss of commercial, retailing, educational and leisure infrastructures. It is an imbalance of power and resources reflecting broader processes of social polarisation. The problems are multidimensional and interrelated – 'joined up' in the current terminology. In this context the housing manager is likely to find her or himself involved in more subtle forms of social engineering in new attempts to integrate disadvantaged areas and combat social exclusion. The need to accommodate greater diversity and difference, to allow greater control and participation will involve a difficult balance between specific interests and those of the wider community. In our three ages of social balance, the emphasis for the housing manager has shifted from being predominantly social planner through efficient accountant to sociologist. The search for, and definition of, a balanced community may remain elusive. Fortunately, most of us know decent housing when we see it.

CHAPTER 15:
Social exclusion and housing: conclusions and challenges

Isobel Anderson

Introduction

In drawing conclusions from a volume on social exclusion and housing, it is worth considering to what extent the concept of social exclusion is of value to policy development and to practice. It can be hypothesised that if the idea of social exclusion aids policy analysis, it should be applicable to a range of social issues and should facilitate a greater understanding of the nature of social problems and the development of appropriate policy responses (Anderson, 1999). The examination of contemporary housing issues in relation to social exclusion, contained within this volume, has facilitated the analysis of housing in the wider context of economic and social change and the development of social policy. Housing issues have been set within 'the bigger picture' of well-being or 'quality of life' (Seed and Lloyd, 1997) in contemporary Britain. The contributions have also adopted a long-term, reflective approach, as a complement to short-term policy oriented evaluations.

Poverty, social exclusion and housing

In Chapter 2, the debates around social exclusion were characterised as moving beyond, though building upon, historical developments in the analysis of poverty. The contributions to this book leave little doubt as to the close association between poverty, poor housing and the conditions which are commonly referred to as social exclusion.

Social exclusion has also been described as comprehensive (Berghman, 1995) or compound (Lee *et al*, 1995), in that it incorporates disadvantage across a whole range of dimensions of welfare. Exclusion from the labour market is a key feature, but *comprehensive* exclusion also embraces health, education, democratic participation and family support. Exclusion from housing has been notably absent from much of the broader social policy literature, and has tended to be addressed primarily by housing specialists (e.g. Lee *et al*, 1995; Lee and Murie, 1997; and the chapters in this volume).

The analysis presented in the preceding chapters has confirmed the relationship between poor housing (and homelessness) and changes in the labour market associated with economic restructuring. The sustained high unemployment levels of the late 1980s and early 1990s, and the residualisation of social housing, may have resulted in a culture in which housing staff increasingly assumed that the majority of their clients would be outside of the labour market, with working clients the exception, rather than the rule (Anderson, 1999).

Family problems are also commonly associated with homelessness, housing abandonment and social problems on housing estates, but it is not accurate to assume that all excluded individuals are totally estranged from their families (Chapters 6, 8, 9 and 12). Family relationships are fluid and can change over time. Housing professionals may be more likely to interact with individuals at times when family friction coincides with a housing crisis, rather than when they engage in household formation or reconciliation. Similarly, while homeless people may be excluded from the types of community contacts and networks associated with a residential neighbourhood, they can be part of alternative social networks. Further, though it would be counter-productive to minimise the impact of homelessness on health and well-being, it is *not* the case that *all* single homeless people have severe health problems or need intensive support services (Chapter 6).

Many households face disadvantage in the housing system which serve to reinforce and perpetuate other dimensions of social exclusion related to employment opportunities and a lack of income for the basic necessities of life (Chapters 6, 7, 8 and 9). Nevertheless, the analyses show that people's experience of social exclusion remains variable and differentiated. With respect to housing, social exclusion may be better characterised as *multifaceted* or *multidimensional*, rather than comprehensive. The notion of comprehensive exclusion fails to encapsulate the diversity and complexity of circumstances discussed throughout this book, and also conflicts with the notion of social exclusion as a *dynamic* process. It may be more fruitful to think in terms of varying *degrees* of inclusion/exclusion in relation to different aspects of welfare (including housing), than a simplistic duality between inclusion and exclusion from 'society'.

Notwithstanding these limitations, the idea of comprehensive or multidimensional exclusion has proven valuable in emphasising the links across different components of welfare policy (promoting 'joined up thinking'). Nevertheless, while the comprehensive approach to acknowledging the links between, for example, poverty, lack of educational attainment, unemployment, poor housing and poor health is constructive, it remains equally important to disentangle the separate and combined roles of different policy areas (Whelan and Whelan, 1995). With respect to housing, this means keeping sight of the inadequacies and inequalities in the housing system, as well as the other social and economic factors which contribute to poor housing and homelessness. For example, there would be little point in providing health care and employment opportunities for homeless people, without simultaneously addressing their housing needs.

The material presented throughout this book consistently shows that the multidimensional notion of social exclusion fits well with the trends in policy and practice towards partnership working and comprehensive approaches to tackling social problems. Most notably, area economic and physical regeneration strategies have developed within the multi-agency partnership approach (Chapters 10, 11, 12, and 14). Tenancy support issues also reflect the multidimensional nature of exclusion (Chapters 6 and 13). Issues to do with the provision of care and support have been identified as being particularly dependent on joint working across policy and practice areas. While the notion of multi-agency strategies to tackle multidimensional problems is attractive, it also carries the risk of conflict and competition rather than partnership and co-operation. Excluded households are still too often left stranded between such conflicts. Despite the recognition of the multifaceted nature of social exclusion, for some people, their housing problems remain primarily a reflection of poverty and exclusion from social housing. For example, exclusionary allocations and property management procedures (Chapter 13) are fully within the remit of social housing providers.

The importance of *process*: towards a dynamic analysis

It has been argued that the dynamic nature of social exclusion remains much less well understood than the notion of multidimensional exclusion (Anderson, 1999). Longitudinal analysis of movement in and out of poverty has been conducted by Walker (1995), Leisering and Walker (1998) and Gardiner (Chapter 3, this volume) and analysis of long-term trends in housing mobility has been conducted by, for example, Burrows (1997). However, there have been no large-scale, longitudinal surveys of movement in and out of homelessness in Britain, although it is known that a high proportion of new social housing tenants have previously been homeless. Life history interviews, as used, for example, by Bowes, Dar and Sim (1997) can provide an insight into the dynamics of housing careers, but there remains a lack of large-scale, longitudinal analysis of pathways in and out of poor housing and homelessness, across household types.

Lee *et al* (1995) characterised social exclusion among tenants of social housing as persistent, spatially concentrated and resistant to change. The evidence presented in this book suggests some caution in the application of these notions. Poor housing and homelessness have certainly remained persistent social issues throughout the 1990s, indeed, over a much longer time-scale. However, the problems are not necessarily unchanging, or resistant to change. Access to suitable housing is determined by a combination of household formation and housing availability. The failure of national and local policy makers and practitioners to predict and respond adequately to changing social trends compounds both the difficulty of matching supply and demand in housing, and the associated social problems (Chapters 10, 11, 12, 13, and 14).

The housing and labour markets, and changes in social security policy, have also been important influences on the scale and nature of exclusion from housing and within social housing (Chapters 3 and 4). A key conclusion, which can be drawn from the evidence presented throughout the book, is that housing and other aspects of social policy need to respond to long-term social changes, rather than try to manipulate social structures (for example, by favouring one type of household over another, or making value judgements about idealised lifestyles). Social exclusion may not necessarily be resistant to change, but appropriate policies and provision to ensure a long-term solution to the issues raised in this book had not been sufficiently developed by the end of 1999. Undoubtedly, as some households were assisted into better housing, jobs etc, new cohorts of people experienced exclusion from housing and other dimensions of well-being.

Political ideologies and the policy process

Chapter 2 introduced some of the established conceptions of social exclusion in relation to welfare regimes and political ideologies. From 1979-1997, British economic and social policy was dominated by the New Right ideology associated with the free market (specialisation) paradigm. While social policy analysis in Britain has traditionally focused on the neo-liberal and social democratic ideologies, the evolving debates on social exclusion have been influenced by comparative analysis and the continental tradition (Room, 1995a) or the democratic socialist (solidarity) paradigm (Silver, 1994).

After the 1997 general election, Britain's New Labour government embarked on a programme of welfare reform founded on the vision of a 'third way' between old style Labour and the extreme liberalism of the previous Conservative governments. However, it is not yet possible to assess how far New Labour's approach will match, say, the solidarity paradigm (Silver, 1994), as opposed to merely representing a re-positioning of the specialisation paradigm, albeit with a higher priority on social justice than that of the prior Conservative administrations.

The prevailing ideologies of successive national governments influence and constrain the practices of local agencies, including the local state. Local strategies to tackle exclusion may be determined as much by the broad socio-economic characteristics of the area and the resources at the disposal of local agencies, as by prevailing local ideologies (Chapters 10, 11, 12 and 13).

Ultimately, the scope for creative initiatives to meet housing needs at the local level remains severely constrained by prevailing ideology and policy at the national level[1].

The social exclusion experienced by the groups identified in Chapters 6, 7, 8 and 9, reflected the long-term dominance of a neo-liberal ideology of a minimal welfare state and the inherent requirement to exclude some groups in order to reduce the state's commitment to welfare. Historically, decisions as to who was given priority in the provision of welfare rested on a balance between acknowledged *need* and some criteria of *legitimacy* for assistance. The latter was principally determined by prevailing social attitudes towards different groups within society. In contrast, in Sweden for example, where the dominant ideology over the long-term had been one of social democracy, the goal of central government housing policy was a decent home for *every citizen* (Turner, 1996, emphasis added).

It could be argued that the very visible increase in street homelessness of the late 1980s/early 1990s represented a key 'breaking-point' for public sympathy towards the least well off, and intolerance of the extremes of inequality which had taken root in British society. A broad public consensus on the need to eradicate street homelessness does not, however, equate with a consensus for 'equal citizenship' or any broad notion of 'social inclusion' (or a right to housing for all citizens). Arguably, the majority of the nation's citizens would need to be persuaded of the benefits to the better off, or to society as a whole, in order to gain majority support for comprehensive policies to combat social exclusion. After the May 1997 election, the New Labour government prioritised reducing 'rough sleeping' and the renewal of run down housing estates. By the end of 1999 however, there was still no policy commitment to the provision of adequate, affordable housing for all citizens.

It has been suggested that a weakness in British housing and social policy during the 1990s has been the tendency to focus on 'special initiatives' to address specific problems, for example, the Rough Sleepers' Initiatives or challenge funding for renewal of housing estates (Anderson, 1999). Such 'problem' based policy analysis only responds to 'problems' which are identified and are placed on the policy agenda, rather than working towards a positive vision for housing provision, or welfare. For example, it cannot be denied that homelessness is a problem for many citizens and that street homelessness is a severe and damaging experience. However, there is a need to move away from the narrow overemphasis on street homelessness, towards a conception of what is an adequate and appropriate housing standard for contemporary British society.

---

1   A further dimension to central-local relations was added to the British policy arena in 1999 with the creation of the Scottish Parliament, the Welsh Assembly, and the stalled introduction of a Northern Ireland Assembly. The degree to which these institutions resulted in increased regional autonomy with respect to tackling social exclusion could not be assessed at the time of writing.

Policy should seek to achieve that standard for all citizens, rather than merely to ameliorate the worst outcomes by providing something that is only slightly better (e.g. hostels for single homeless people). A comprehensive, inclusive policy process then, would start from a clear vision for well-being, from which a strategy (or set of strategies) to achieve that vision would be developed. Local policy making would also benefit from incorporating a vision for the local community.

Focused initiatives, such as the Rough Sleeping Initiatives or the New Deal for Communities may be valuable in times of crisis and it is likely that a combination of targeted and comprehensive strategies would be most effective. However, the complex nature of social exclusion from, and within housing certainly suggests that policy and practical responses needed to be comprehensive, even if the experience of exclusion is not comprehensive for all marginalised individuals. Nevertheless, some New Labour initiatives do appear to represent at least a move towards a more comprehensive approach to tackling deeply entrenched social issues which are often most clearly manifested through housing (or lack of housing).

A comprehensive overview of the policy process must also acknowledge that the process takes place both within, and between, a range of actors in a policy community or network. Within the housing policy community, different actors have varying degrees of power and influence over the policy process. Different policy actors may also have varying goals, decision making processes, strategies and programmes of action, which may complement each other or produce conflict. The overview of social exclusion and housing presented in this book has helped illustrate the complex interaction of social processes, the need for sophisticated policy responses, and the potential contributions of a wide range of actors from the statutory, voluntary and business sectors, as well as communities and individuals. Co-ordination of policy across the wide range of potential policy actors and spheres of welfare will remain a major challenge for central and local government in the foreseeable future.

Since the 1980s, policies to develop tenant participation in housing policy have been widely advocated (Cairncross, Clapham and Goodlad, 1997). Subscribers to the New Right philosophy advocated freedom of choice, while those on the Left recommended empowerment of users in the decision making process. Throughout the 1980s and 1990s however, many strategies to tackle poor housing, homelessness and neighbourhood problems have focused on enforcement (Jordan, 1996), rather than empowerment. For example, Edinburgh City council considered implementation of a by-law outlawing 'aggressive begging' (*Inside Housing*, 1998) and the Social Exclusion Unit's strategy for reducing street homelessness retained the option of forcing homeless people into hostels, if places were available (*Guardian,* 1998). These strategies mirrored the wider trend in housing policy towards tackling 'anti-social behaviour' in social housing through punitive mechanisms such as introductory tenancies and court injunctions (Scott and Parkey, 1998 and Chapter 13 in this volume).

The social exclusion agenda of the late 1990s has placed renewed emphasis on the *inclusion* of ordinary people in the policy process and in the delivery of initiatives such as the New Deal for Communities. However, until the very late 1990s, relatively little consideration had been given to the empowerment of homeless people and those in housing need (rather than tenants) in the processes by which housing policies are formulated and implemented. Moves towards empowering the most vulnerable can, however, be identified in Scotland, where the need to develop meaningful ways to involve homeless people in the policy process was acknowledged by the ministerial advisory group for the Scottish Rough Sleepers' Initiative (RSI Advisory Group, 1999).

The potential for conflict in an empowerment approach to tackling social exclusion also needs to be borne in mind. For example, community-based strategies can (and have) resulted in prejudice, discrimination and vigilante activities. Should principles of citizen empowerment override those of equal opportunities? This author does not believe so. Some safeguards against such outcomes may require to be built into strategies, to empower citizens in the policy process on an equal basis.

The New Labour government has also placed enormous emphasis on reintegration of excluded groups through the labour market and its Welfare to Work initiatives. The close association between social exclusion and unemployment reflected sustained, high, structural unemployment during the 1980s and early 1990s. In comparison, the mid-late 1990s witnessed a significant and continuing decline in Britain's unemployment count (*Labour Research*, 1998). The strength of the economy and the labour market situation could be expected to have a positive impact on the ability of the government to tackle social exclusion, although some time lag might be expected between falling unemployment and any quantifiable impact on 'social cohesion'. These favourable economic conditions preclude any 'test' of implementing integrative strategies in more adverse economic circumstances.

Policies to promote social inclusion advocated by the New Labour government, such as better service co-ordination and Welfare to Work, could have a beneficial impact on disadvantaged groups, including those who experience poor housing conditions or homelessness. Better employment prospects may help marginalised households to compete in the housing market and higher incomes will certainly facilitate fuller enjoyment of homes, through the ability to adequately furnish and maintain them. Service co-ordination could ease the process of gaining access to housing and support services, but, without additional resources, would be unlikely to offer a satisfactory solution to the fundamental inequalities which create exclusion.

Whether New Labour will be successful in tackling social exclusion will depend to a large extent on whether this becomes an aim which is adopted by the whole machinery of government. It is for this reason that the output of Social

Exclusion Unit, with its reporting line direct to the Prime Minister, is so important. Although its recommendations may change particular aspects of departmental policy, its wider aim is to shift the emphasis of the work of the whole range of Whitehall departments so that all see combating social exclusion as a key objective. One test of whether this is likely to happen may well be the response of Whitehall in general and the Treasury in particular to the forthcoming National Strategy for Neighbourhood Renewal (due for publication in 2000). This strategy will set out a proposed approach for dealing with England's most deprived neighbourhoods. It will aim to bridge the gap between the most deprived neighbourhoods and the rest; and to deliver on four key outcome targets in deprived neighbourhoods: more jobs, less crime and better health and educational achievement.

To be fully effective, the National Strategy for Neighbourhood Renewal will require commitment from a range of departments and services (such as police and health) which may traditionally have seen neighbourhood renewal as marginal to their concerns. If they are seen to be making substantial resource commitments to deprived neighbourhoods, and if they show themselves to be capable of changing their priorities at local level to meet new needs, these will be the indications that the comprehensive approach to tackling social exclusion is being taken seriously, and that the Social Exclusion Unit is having an effect.

The chapters in this volume have demonstrated the vast amount of research into poverty, poor housing, neighbourhood problems and homelessness. Increasingly, policy oriented research is commissioned, funded and undertaken by a wide range of agencies, including government and agents of government. The influence of policy makers on research, places constraints on the research agenda and the use of research findings. As argued by Lowe in Chapter 12, narrowly focused evaluations of specific policy initiatives are constrained by the contemporary direction of policy. That is to say, studies often focus on whether particular policies or initiatives are meeting their objectives, rather than whether they were an appropriate response to the problem they were supposed to address. Moreover, such studies reflect a short-term approach to developing 'quick fix solutions', which look for evidence of success within a very short time-scale (often 12-18 months), from initiatives which endeavour to tackle deeply rooted social issues. While such studies provide valuable data and insights, there remains a need for a longer-term dimension to policy development and the commissioning of policy relevant research.

Conclusion: on housing and social inclusion

The consideration of social exclusion and housing in this book has revealed a number of limitations to the term 'social exclusion', as well as its potential value to policy and practice. As indicated in Chapter 2, social exclusion remains a contested concept. 'Social exclusion' may not actually be the ideal term to describe the patterns of inequality and disadvantage in the housing system or other dimensions of welfare. Rather than debating a phenomenon termed 'social exclusion' it might be more helpful to talk in terms of the *social consequences* of exclusion from welfare, whether that be housing, education, employment, health or any combination of the many dimensions of welfare. Nevertheless, housing is a crucial component of well-being and of any conception of social exclusion/inclusion.

The social exclusion approach has highlighted the linkages across dimensions of welfare policy. Exclusion can be re-conceptualised as multidimensional, rather than comprehensive. Analysis needs to take account of the individual and combined effects of exclusive processes within and across policy areas. Issues such as street homelessness and 'anti-social behaviour' may not be solely housing problems, but they remain significant problems for housing providers.

Chapter 2 highlighted the lack of debate on the concepts of social inclusion, social integration or social cohesion. The incorporation of a 'vision' for an inclusive society and ideological principles into the policy process would embrace the notion of social inclusion more effectively. Nevertheless, the question remains as to whether any society would realistically expect to attain 'perfect' or 'total' social inclusion, and how that would be defined, identified, and measured. The notion of a continuum of welfare from an exclusive to an inclusive (or unequal to egalitarian) society would facilitate comparisons according to agreed indicators of inclusion/exclusion. Work on the design of such indicators has been taken forward both by central government (Gibb *et al*, 1998; DSS, 1999a) and by independent commentators (Howarth and Kenway, 1998). Given the limitations to the concept of social exclusion, however, a re-focus on the concept of inequality may offer greater potential for stimulating debate as to the degree of disadvantage which is tolerable or 'socially acceptable' in contemporary British society.

On a more practical level, there are clearly a number of ways in which housing can contribute to *social inclusion*. Social housing providers have been directly confronted with the consequences of social and economic exclusion in the 1990s. The development of multi-agency responses to exclusion and strategies for more cohesive communities seems to herald a changing role for the housing profession. They may have much to contribute to the development of wider strategies for tackling the social problems which are, all to often, manifested in social housing. However, housing policies and practices cannot yet be described as inclusive. Despite extensive debate as to the nature and scale of housing needs, there is still no overall goal that policy should ensure adequate housing provision for all citizens.

There has been significant progress towards recognition of the importance of the interaction of different policy areas with housing and homelessness. However, there remains a need for a more finely differentiated analysis of these interactions if co-ordinated policy approaches are to be effective. Housing policy and practice must take account of process and the dynamics of household formation and homelessness. More flexible mechanisms, which can react to social and economic change, are required in order to support households in times of crisis, and bring stability to local communities. There is also a need for improved exchange of practice and understanding across the relevant professions, most notably housing and social work. Most importantly, the experiences and views of excluded groups should be incorporated into mechanisms for policy development and service delivery. The emphasis should be on achieving housing and social cohesion, rather than merely ameliorating poor housing conditions and homelessness.

The notion of social exclusion is potentially useful but is also vulnerable to abuse. It is likely to remain a contested concept, possibly resulting in confusion, not to mention dismissal as simply a fashionable 'bandwagon', which loses any meaning if it is relentlessly reproduced in every social commentary. Despite the conceptual limitations, the high political profile of the debates on social exclusion could provide a valuable platform from which to raise more radical questions about housing, social policy and society. The notion of *inclusion* could, conceivably precipitate a reorientation of prevailing ideologies towards equality and collectivity, and away from 'free market' competition and individualism. The danger, however, is that unless there is more explicit recognition of the interdependency that creates the extremes of wealth and poverty, the rhetoric of social exclusion will again fail to challenge the worst excesses and inequalities of modern society.

BIBLIOGRAPHY

Alcock, P. (1997) *Understanding poverty.* London: Macmillan.

Aldbourne Associates (1993) *Managing neighbour complaints in social housing.* Aldbourne: Aldbourne Associates.

Allen, I. and Dowling, S. B. (1998) *Teenage mothers: decisions and outcomes.* London: Policy Studies Institute.

Anderson, I. (1994) *Access to housing for low income single people: a review of recent research and current policy issues.* York: Centre for Housing Policy, University of York.

Anderson, I. (1997) 'Homelessness and social exclusion: the situation of single homeless people in Great Britain', in Huth, M. and Wright, T. *International critical perspectives on homelessness.* Connecticut: Praeger, pp107-137.

Anderson, I. (1999) *Understanding single homelessness: the value of the concept of social exclusion,* D Phil Thesis. University of York.

Anderson, I. and Douglas, A. (1998) *The development of foyers in Scotland.* Edinburgh: Scottish Homes.

Anderson, I. and Morgan, J. (1997) *Social housing for single people? A study of local policy and practice.* Stirling: Housing Policy and Practice Unit, University of Stirling.

Anderson, I. and Quilgars, D. (1995) *Foyers for young people: evaluation of a pilot initiative.* York: Centre for Housing Policy, University of York.

Anderson, I., Kemp, P. and Quilgars, D. (1993). *Single homeless people.* London: Department of the Environment.

Anderson, K. (1998) *Unlocking the future: tackling social exclusion.* Edinburgh: Chartered Institute of Housing (Scotland).

Arblaster, L., Conway, J., Foreman, A. and Hawtin, M. (1996) *Asking the impossible?* Bristol: Policy Press.

Arnold, P., Bochel, H., Broadhurst, S. and Page, D. (1993) *Community care: the housing dimension.* York: Joseph Rowntree Foundation.

Arnstein, S. R. (1969) 'A ladder of citizen participation', *American Institute of Planners Journal,* July.

Association of District Councils (1994/5) *Winning communities* London: ADC

Association of Metropolitan Authorities (1988), *A strategy for racial equality in housing: 3 Allocations.* London: AMA.

Atkins, D., Champion, T., Coombes, M., Dorling, D. and Woodward, R. (1996) (1996) *Urban trends in England: latest evidence from the 1991 Census.* Department of the Environment Urban Research Report. London: HMSO.

Atkinson, A. B. (1998) 'Social exclusion, poverty and unemployment' in Atkinson, A. B. and Hills, J. (eds.), *Exclusion, employment and opportunity,* CASE paper No. 4. London: London School of Economics.

Atkinson, A. B., Gardiner, K., Lechene, V. and Sutherland, H. (1993) *Comparing poverty in France and the United Kingdom.* STICERD Welfare State Discussion Paper No. 84. London: London School of Economics.

Atkinson, R. and Kintrea, K. (1998) *Reconnecting excluded communities: the neighbourhood impacts of owner-occupation.* Edinburgh: Scottish Homes.

Atkinson, R. and Moon, G. (1994) *Urban policy in Britain. The city, the state and the market*. London: Macmillan.

Audit Commission (1986) *Managing the crisis in council housing*. London: HMSO.

Audit Commission (1989) *Urban regeneration and economic development: The local government dimension*. London: HMSO.

Babb, P. and Bethune, A. (1995) 'Trends in births outside marriage', *Population Trends*, 81, Autumn.

Bailey, N. (1996) 'Recent trends in the deregulated private rented sector', *Housing Research Review*, Summer: pp28-32.

Bakke, E. W. (1940) *Citizens without work: a study of the effects of unemployment upon the workers' social relations and practices*. New Haven: Yale University Press.

Balchin, P. (1995) *Housing policy: an introduction*. London: Routledge (Third edition).

Ballard, R. (1996) 'The Pakistanis: stability and introspection' in Peach, C. (ed.), *Ethnicity in the 1991 Census, Volume Two*. HMSO, London, pp121-149.

Bannister, J., Dell, M., Donnison, D., Fitzpatrick, S. and Taylor, R. (1993) *Homeless young people in Scotland: the role of the social work services*. Edinburgh: HMSO.

Baumgartner, M. (1988) *The moral order of the suburbs*. Oxford: Oxford University Press.

Beatson, M. (1995) *Labour market flexibility*. London: Department of Employment.

Beatty, C., Fothergill, S., Gore, T. and Henrington, A. (1997) *The real level of unemployment*. Sheffield: Centre for Regional Economic and Social Research, Sheffield Hallam University.

Becker, S. (1997) *Responding to poverty: the politics of cash and care*. London: Longman.

Bell, M. (1996) *The causes of abandonment and vacancy in private sector dwellings and some suggested solutions*. York: MA dissertation, University of York.

Berghman, J. (1995) 'Social exclusion in Europe: policy context and analytical framework', in Room, G. (ed.), *Beyond the threshold: the measurement and analysis of social exclusion*. Bristol: Policy Press, pp10-28.

Berthoud, R. and Ford, R. (1996) *Relative needs overview of an analysis of variations in the living standards of different types of households*. London: Policy Studies Institute.

Berthoud, R. and Kempson, E. (1992) *Credit and debt: the PSI report*. London: Policy Studies Institute.

Best, R. (1996) Successes, failures and prospects for public housing in the UK, *Housing Policy Debate,* 7.3, pp535-562.

Bevan, M. and Sanderling, L. (1996) *Private renting in rural areas*. York: Centre for Housing Policy, University of York.

Beveridge, W. H. (1950) New deal for housewives, *Town and Country Planning,* 18, pp6-10.

Bines, W. (1997) 'The health of homeless people' in Burrows, R., Pleace. N. and Quilgars, D. (eds.), *Homelessness and social policy*. London: Routledge.

Bines,W., Kemp, P., Pleace, N. and Radley, C. (1993) *Managing social housing*. London: HMSO.

Birchall, J. (1992) *Building communities the co-operative way*. London: Routledge and Kegan Paul.

Birchall, J. (ed.), (1992) *Housing policy in the 1990s*. London: Routledge.

Bivand, P. (1999) 'Tough-love on the dole', *Working Brief*, 107, August/September.

Blair, T. (1996) *New Britain: my vision of a young country*. London: Fourth Estate.

Blake, J. (1998) 'Litmus test for New Labour', *Roof*, January/February, pp18-20.

Blanc, L. (1998) 'Social integration and exclusion in France: some introductory remarks from a social transaction perspective', *Housing Studies,* 13.6, pp781-792.

Blundell, R. (1994) 'Work incentives and labour supply in the UK' in Bryson, A. and Mackay, S. *Is it worth working?* London: Policy Studies Institute.

Bonnerjea, L. and Lawton, J. (1988) 'No racial harassment this week': a study undertaken in the London Borough of Brent. London: Policy Studies Institute.

Botting, B., Rosato, M. and Wood, R. (1998) 'Teenage mothers and the health of their children', *Population Trends,* 93, Autumn.

Bottomley, D., McKay, S. and Walker, R. (1997) *Unemployment and job seeking.* Department of Social Security Research Report. London: The Stationery Office.

Bovaird, A., Harloe, M. and Whitehead, C. (1985) 'Private rented housing: its current role', *Journal of Social Policy*, 14. 1, pp1-23.

Bowes, A., Dar, N. and Sim, D. (1997) 'Tenure preference and housing strategy: an exploration of Pakistani experiences', *Housing Studies,* 12.1, pp63-84.

Bowes, A., Dar, N. and Sim, D. (1998) *'Too white, too rough and too many problems': a study of Pakistani housing in Britain.* Stirling: University of Stirling Housing Research Report 3.

Bowes, A., McCluskey, J. and Sim, D. (1990) 'Racism and harassment of Asians in Glasgow', *Ethnic and Racial Studies,* 13.1, pp71-91.

Bradshaw, J., Stimson, C., Skinner, C. and Williams, J. (1999) *'Absent fathers?': non-resident fathers in Britain.* London: Routledge.

Bradshaw, N., Bradshaw, J. and Burrows, R. (1996) 'Area variations in the prevalence of lone parent families in England and Wales: a research note', *Regional Studies*, 30.8.

Bramley, G. (1998) 'Housing surpluses and housing need' in Keenan, P. *et al* (eds.), *Housing abandonment – causes, consequences and solutions.* York: Centre for Housing Policy, University of York.

Brion, M. (1995) *Women in the housing service.* London: Routledge.

Broad, B. (1993) *Leaving care in the 1990s.* London: Aftercare Consortium.

Brown, M. and Madge, N. (1982) *Despite the welfare state.* London: Heinemann.

Brown, T. and Passmore, J. (1998) *Housing and anti-poverty strategies.* Coventry/York: CIH/JRF.

Burbidge, M., Curtis, A., Kirby, K. and Wilson, S. (1981) *An investigation into difficult-to-let housing.* London: HMSO.

Burrows, R. (1997) *Contemporary patterns of residential mobility in relation to social housing in England.* York: Centre for Housing Policy, University of York.

Burrows, R. (1998) 'Mortgage indebtedness in England: an epidemiology', *Housing Studies*, 13.1, pp5-21.

Burrows, R. and Rhodes, D. (1998) *Unpopular places? Area disadvantage and the geography of misery.* Bristol: Policy Press.

Burrows, R., Pleace, N. and Quilgars, D. (eds.), (1997) *Homelessness and social policy.* London: Routledge.

Cairncross, L., Clapham, D. and Goodlad, R. (1989) *Tenant participation in housing management.* London: IoH/TPAS.

Cairncross, L., Clapham, D. and Goodlad, R. (1997) *Housing management, consumers and citizens.* London: Routledge.

Callan, T., Nolan, B., Whelan, B.J., Whelan, C. T. and Williams, J. (1996) *Poverty in the 1990s.* Dublin: Oak Tree Press.

Capita (1996) *A review of six early Estate Action schemes.* London: Capita.

Carey, S. (1995) *Private renting in England 1993/94.* London: HMSO.

Carlisle, J. (1996) *The housing needs of ex-prisoners.* York: Centre for Housing Policy, University of York.

Cars, G., Madinopour, A. and Allen, J. (1998) (eds.), *Social exclusion in European cities.* London: Jessica Kingsley.

Caskie, K. (1993) *Some change – some chance! Scottish local authorities response to homelessness and housing need among young people. How this has changed since 1990.* Edinburgh: Shelter (Scotland).

Cebulla, A., Abbott, D., Ford, J., Middleton, S., Quilgars, D. and Walker, R. (1998) *A geography of insurance exclusion. Perceptions of unemployment risk and actuarial risk assessment.* Paper presented to Second European Urban and Regional Studies Conference, University of Durham, September 1998.

Centre for Housing Research (1989) *The nature and effectiveness of housing management in Wales,* London: HMSO

Centrepoint (1996), *The new picture of youth homelessness in Britain.* London: Centrepoint.

CHAC (1939) *The management of municipal housing estates.* London: HMSO.

CHAC (1969) *Council housing purposes, procedures and priorities.* London: HMSO.

Chartered Institute of Housing (1998) *Opening the door: housing's essential role in tackling social exclusion,* Coventry: CIH

Chartered Institute of Housing (1998b) *Low demand for housing. Discussion paper.* Coventry: CIH.

Chartered Institute of Housing (1999) *Housing management standards manual.* Coventry: CIH.

Chartered Institute of Housing (undated) *More than bricks and mortar.* Coventry: CIH.

Chartered Institute of Housing in Scotland (1997) *Private sector housing – in need of urgent repair?* Edinburgh: CIH(S).

Cherlin, A. (1976) *Social and economic determinants of marital separation.* PhD dissertation, Los Angeles, University of California (available on microfilm from the British Library).

Child Poverty Action Group (1996) *Poverty: the facts.* London: CPAG.

Clapham, D. and Evans, A. (1998) *From exclusion to inclusion: helping to create successful tenancies and communities.* Tedddington: Hastoe Housing Association.

Clapham, D., Kemp, P. and Smith, S. (1990) *Housing and social policy.* London: Macmillan.

Clapham, D., Kintrea, K., Malcolm, J., Parkey, H. and Scott, S. (1995) *A baseline study of housing management in Scotland.* Edinburgh: Scottish Office.

Clinton, A., Murie, A., Paice, D., Tolen, F. and Williams, P. (1989) *The relative effectiveness of different forms of housing management in Wales.* Cardiff: Welsh Office.

Cole, I. (1993) 'The decentralisation of housing services' in Malpass, P. and Means, R. (eds.), *Implementing housing policy.* Buckingham: Open University Press.

Cole, I. and Furbey, R. (1994) *The eclipse of council housing?* London: Routledge.

Cole, I. and Shayer, S. (1998) *Beyond housing investment.* Sheffield: CRESR/Housing Corporation.

Cole, I. and Smith, Y. (1996) *From Estate Action to Estate Agreement*. Bristol: Policy Press.

Cole, I., Dixon, L. and Reid, B. (1998) *Estate profiling and community balance*. Sheffield: RESR/Housing Corporation.

Cole, I., Gidley, G., Ritchie, C., Simpson, D. and Wishart, B. (1996) *Creating communities or welfare housing?* Coventry: Chartered Institute of Housing.

Coleman, A. (1985) *Utopia on trial: vision and reality in planned housing*. London: Hilary Shipman.

Coleman, A. (1990) *Utopia on trial: vision and reality in planned housing*. London: Hilary Shipman. (Second edition).

Coles, B. (1995) *Youth and social policy: youth citizenship and young carers*. London: UCL Press.

Commins, P. (ed.), (1993) *Combating exclusion in Ireland 1990-1994: a midway report*. Brussels: European Commission (Cited in Berghman, J. 1995).

Commission for Racial Equality (1984) *Race and council housing in Hackney*. London: CRE.

Commission for Racial Equality (1987) *Living in terror: a report on racial violence and harassment in housing*. London: CRE.

Commission for Racial Equality (1988) *Racial discrimination in a London estate agency: report of a formal investigation into Richard Barclay and Co*. London: CRE.

Commission for Racial Equality (1989) *Racial discrimination in Liverpool City Council*. London: CRE.

Commission for Racial Equality (1990) *Racial discrimination in an Oldham estate agency: report of a formal investigation into Norman Lester and Co*. London: CRE.

Commission for Racial Equality (1993) *Housing associations and racial equality*. London: CRE.

Commission on Social Justice (1994) *Social justice: strategies for national renewal*. London: Vintage.

Corbett, G. (1998) *The Children (Scotland) Act and homelessness: the first six months*. Edinburgh: Shelter (Scotland).

Council of the European Communities (1992) *Treaty on European Union*. Brussels: Council of the European Communities.

Cousins, C. (1998) 'Social exclusion in Europe: paradigms of social disadvantage in Germany, Spain, Sweden and the United Kingdom. *Policy and Politics*, 26.2, pp127-146.

Cowan, D. (1998) 'Reforming the homelessness legislation', *Critical Social Policy,* 18.4, pp435-464.

Craig, T., Hodson, S., Woodward, S. and Richardson, S. (1993) *Off to a bad start: a longitudinal study of homeless young people in London*. London: Mental Health Foundation.

Crook, A., and Kemp, P. (1996) *Private landlords in England*. London: HMSO.

Crook, A. D. H., Darke, R. A. and Dixon, J. D. (1996) *A new lease of life? Housing association investment in local authority estates*. Bristol: Policy Press.

Department of Social Security (1995) *Households below average income: a statistical analysis 1979-1992/93*. London: The Stationery Office.

Department of Social Security (1997a) *Households below average income: a statistical analysis 1979-1994/95*. London: The Stationery Office.

Department of Social Security (1997b) *Social security statistics 1997*. London: The Stationery Office.

Department of Social Security (1998a) *Children first: a new approach to child support.* July.

Department of Social Security (1998b) *New ambitions for our country: a new contract for welfare.* Cm 3805. London: The Stationery Office.

Department of Social Security (1999a) *A new contract for welfare: children's rights and parents' responsibilities*, Cm 4349, July.

Department of Social Security (1999b) *Opportunity for all: tackling poverty and social exclusion.* First Annual Report, 1999. Cm 4445, London: Department of Social Security.

Department of the Environment (1981) *An investigation of difficult-to-let housing: Volume 1: general findings,* London: DoE, HDD Occasional Paper 3/80.

Department of the Environment (1987) *Housing: the government's proposals.* London: HMSO.

Department of the Environment (1989a) *Living in temporary accommodation.* London: HMSO.

Department of the Environment (1989b) *The nature and effectiveness of housing management in England.* London: HMSO.

Department of the Environment (1992) *Competing for quality in housing.* London: HMSO.

Department of the Environment (1993a) *English house condition survey 1991.* London: HMSO.

Department of the Environment (1993b) *Housing consequences and relationship breakdown.* London: HMSO.

Department of the Environment (1994) *Access to local authority and housing association tenancies: a consultation paper.* London: DoE.

Department of the Environment (1995) *1991 Deprivation index: a review of approaches and a matrix of results.* London: HMSO.

Department of the Environment (1996) *Study of homeless applicants.* London: HMSO.

Department of the Environment (1997) *Mapping local authority estates using the 1991 index of local conditions.* London: HMSO.

Department of the Environment, Transport and the Regions (1997) *Regeneration programmes: the way ahead.* London: The Stationery Office.

Department of the Environment, Transport and the Regions (1998a) *Select committee tenth report: housing.* London: The Stationery Office.

Department of the Environment, Transport and the Regions (1998b) *Modern local government – in touch with the people.* London: The Stationery Office.

Department of the Environment, Transport and the Regions (1998c) *English house condition survey 1996.* London: The Stationery Office.

Department of the Environment, Transport and the Regions (1999) *Best Value in housing: framework.* Consultation Paper, London: DETR.

Dex, S. and McCullogh, A. (1997) *Flexible employment: the future of Britain's jobs.* London: Macmillan.

Dix, J. (1995) *Assessing the housing, health and support needs of single homeless people living in hostel accommodation in Cardiff.* Cardiff: City Housing Department.

Dorling, D. (1996) *Identifying disadvantaged areas: health, wealth and happiness.* York: Joseph Rowntree Foundation Area Regeneration Programme Position Paper.

Drewitt, R. and Heidemann, W. (1973) 'Migration and social polarization: a study in five areas of megalopolis' in Hall, P. (ed.), *The containment of urban England. Volume One*. London: Allen and Unwin.

Dunleavy, P. (1981) *The politics of mass housing 1945-75*. Oxford: Clarendon Press.

Dunmore, K., Strode, M., Cousins, L., Stewart, J. and Bramley, G. (1997) *A critical evaluation of the low cost home-ownership programme*. London: Housing Corporation.

Dwelly. T. (1997) 'Brief: minister without poverty', *Roof*, November/ December, pp20-22.

Dyer, D. (1993) *Local authority housing waiting-lists in Scotland*. Edinburgh: Scottish Office Central Research Unit.

Eardley, T. and Corden, A. (1996) *Self-employed earnings and income distribution*. York: Social Policy Research Unit, University of York.

Edin, K. and Lein, L. (1997) *Making ends meet: how single mothers survive welfare and low-wage work*. New York: Russell Sage Foundation.

Edwards, R. and Duncan, S. (1997) 'Supporting the family: lone mothers, paid work and the underclass debate', *Critical Social Policy*, 17.4, pp29-49.

Ermisch, J. (1990) *Fewer babies, longer lives: policy implications of current demographic trends*. York: Joseph Rowntree Foundation.

Ermisch, J., Di Salvo, P. and Joshi, M. (1995), *Household formation and the housing tenure decisions of young people*. Colchester: ESRC Research Centre on Micro-social Change, University of Essex.

Esping-Anderson, G. (1990) *The three worlds of welfare capitalism*. Cambridge: Polity Press.

European Commission (1989) 'Interim Report on the Second European Poverty Programme', *Social Europe*, Supplement 2/89.

European Commission (1993) 'Growth, competitiveness, employment – the challenges and ways forward into the 21st century'. Brussels: *Bulletin of the European Communities*, Supplement 6/93.

European Commission (1994) *European social policy – the way forward for the Union*, COM(94)333, Brussels.

Evans, A. (1996) *We don't choose to be homeless,* Report of the National Inquiry into Preventing Youth Homelessness. London: CHAR.

Evans, M. (1995) *Out for the count: the incomes of the non-household population and the effect of their exclusion from national income profiles*. STICERD Welfare State Discussion Paper No. 111. London: London School of Economics.

Evans R. (1998) *Housing Plus and urban regeneration: what works, how why, where?* London: Housing Corporation.

Farthing, S. and Lambert, C. (on behalf of the University of the West of England and Oldfield King Planning) (1996) *Land, planning and housing associations*. Source Report No. 10, London: Housing Corporation.

Featherstone, M. (1995) *Undoing culture: globalization, postmodernism and identity*. London: Sage.

Field, F. (1989) *Losing out: the emergence of Britain's underclass*. Oxford: Blackwell.

Field, F. (1997) *Reforming welfare*. London: Social Market Foundation, September.

Fielder, S. and Smith, R. (1996) *Vacant dwellings in the private sector*. London: Department of the Environment.

Fieldhouse, E. (1996) 'Putting unemployment in its place: using the samples of anonymised records to explore the risk of unemployment in Great Britain in 1991', *Regional Studies,* 30.2. pp119-133.

Finch, H., Lovell, A. and Ward, K. (1989) *Empty dwellings: a study of vacant private sector dwellings in five local authority areas.* London: Department of the Environment.

Fitzpatrick, S. (1997) *Pathways to independence: the experience of young homeless people.* Unpublished PhD thesis, University of Glasgow.

Fitzpatrick, S. and Clapham, D. (1999) 'Homelessness and young people' in Hutson, S. and Clapham, D. (eds.), *Homelessness: public policies and private troubles.* London: Cassell, pp173-190.

Fitzpatrick, S. and Stephens, M. (1999) 'Homelessness, need and desert in the allocation of council housing', *Housing Studies,* 14.4, pp413-431.

Ford, J. (1989) 'Casual work and owner occupation', *Work, Employment and Society,* 3.1.

Ford, J. (1998) *Risks, job insecurity and home-ownership.* London: Shelter.

Ford, J. (1999) *Housing and rent arrears: attitudes, beliefs and behaviour.* Coventry: Chartered Institute of Housing.

Ford, J. and Burrows, R. (1999) 'The costs of unsustainable home-ownership', *Journal of Social Policy,* Volume 28, Part 2, pp305-330.

Ford, J. and Seavers, J. (1998) *Housing associations and rent arrears: attitudes, beliefs and behaviour.* Coventry: Chartered Institute of Housing.

Ford, J. and Wilcox, S. (1994) *Affordable housing, low incomes and the flexible market.* London: National Federation of Housing Associations.

Ford, J., Burrows, R., Wilcox, S., Cole, I. and Beatty, C. (1998) *Social housing rent differentials and social exclusion.* York: Centre for Housing Policy, University of York.

Ford, J., Kempson, E. and England, J. (1996) *Into work? The impact of housing costs and the benefit system on people's decision to work.* York: Joseph Rowntree Foundation.

Ford, J., Quilgars, D., Pleace, N. and Burrows, R. (1997) *Young people and housing.* London: Rural Development Commission.

Ford, R., Marsh, A. and Finlayson, L. (1998) *What happens to lone parents: a cohort study 1991-1995. A report of research carried out on behalf of the Department of Social Security by the Policy Studies Institute*, DSS Research Report No.77. London, HMSO.

Ford, R., Marsh, A. and McKay, S. (1995) *Changes in lone parenthood 1989 to 1993. A study carried out on behalf of the Department of Social Security by the Policy Studies Institute.* DSS Research Report No.40, London, HMSO.

Fordham, G., Kemp, R. and Crowsley, P. (1997) *Going the extra mile: implementing 'Housing Plus' on five London housing estates.* York: Joseph Rowntree Foundation.

Forrest, R. and Kearns, A. (1999) *Joined-up places? Social cohesion and urban regeneration.* York: York Publishing Services.

Forrest, R. and Kennett, P. (1999a) *Constructed communities: tales from a New Town*, Paper presented to the 14th World Congress of Sociology, Montreal, July.

Forrest, R. and Kennett, P. (1999b) *Changed (e)states: from planned communities to deregulated spaces?* Paper presented to the 14th World Congress of Sociology, Montreal, July.

Forrest, R. and Murie, A. (1988) *Selling the welfare state: the privatisation of public housing.* London: Routledge.

Forrest, R., Gordon, D. and Murie, A. (1996) 'The position of former council homes in the housing market', *Urban Studies,* 33.1, pp125-136.

Forrest, R., Murie, A. and Williams, P. (1990) *Home ownership: differentiation and fragmentation.* London: Unwin Hyman.

Forrest, R., Murie, A., Hawes, D., Bridge, G. and Smart, G. (1995) *Leaseholders and service charges in former local authority flats.* London: HMSO.

Fothergill, S., Kitson, M. and Monk, S. (1985) *Urban industrial change: the causes of the urban-rural contrast in manufacturing employment trends,* Department of the Environment and Department of Trade and Industry Inner City Research Programme No.11. London: HMSO.

Fotheringham, D. (1993) 'Singles play a new tune', *Housing,* Dec.1993/Jan.1994.

Franklin, B. (1999), 'More than community care: supporting the transition from homelessness to home' in Hutson, S. and Clapham, D. (eds.), *Homelessness: public policies and private troubles.* London: Cassell, pp191-207.

Friedrichs, J. (1996) *Context effects of poverty neighbourhoods on residents,* Keynote address at ENHR/SBI Housing Research Conference on Housing and European Integration, Helsingor, Denmark, August 26-31.

Furlong, A. and Cartmel, F. (1997) *Young people and social change: individualisation and risk in late modernity.* Buckingham: Open University Press.

Gallie, D. (1994) 'Are the unemployed an underclass? Some evidence from the Social Change and Economic Life Initiative', *Sociology,* 28.3, pp755-56.

Gardiner, K., Hills, J., Falkingham, J., Lechene, V. and Sutherland, H. (1995) *The effects of differences in housing and health care systems on international comparisons of income distribution,* STICERD Welfare State Discussion Paper No. 110. London: London School of Economics.

Garfinkel, I., McLanahan, S., Meyer, D. and Seltzer, J. (1998) *Fathers under fire: the revolution in child support enforcement.* New York: Russell Sage Foundation.

Garside, P., Grimshaw, R. and Ward, F. (1990) *No place like home: the hostels experience.* London: Department of the Environment.

Gibb, K., Kearns, A., Keoghan, M., Mackay, D. and Turok, I. (1998) *Revising the Scottish Area Deprivation Index.* Edinburgh: The Stationery Office.

Gilchrist, R. and Jeffs, T. (1995) 'Foyers: housing solution or folly?', *Youth and Policy,* 49: pp1-12.

Goode, J., Callendar, C. and Lister, R. (1998) *The distribution of income within families receiving social security benefits.* London: Policy Studies Institute.

Goodman, A. and Webb, S. (1994) *For richer, for poorer: the changing distribution of income in the United Kingdom, 1961-1991.* London: Institute for Fiscal Studies.

Gordon, D. and Forrest, R. (1995) *People and places II: social and economic distinctions in England.* Bristol: SAUS.

Gordon, D. and Pantazis C. (eds.), (1997) *Breadline Britain in the 1990s.* Aldershot: Avebury.

Gordon, I. (1996) 'Family structure, educational achievement and the inner city', *Urban Studies,* 33.3, pp407-423.

Goss, A. (1961) 'Neighbourhood units in British New Towns', *Town Planning Review,* 32.1.

Gray, B., Finch, H., Prescott-Clarke, T., Cameron, S., Gilroy, R., Kirby, K. and Mountford, J. (1994) *Rent arrears in local authorities and housing associations in England.* London: Department of the Environment.

Green, A. (1994) *The geography of poverty and wealth: evidence on the changing spatial distribution and segregation of poverty and wealth from the Census of Population 1991 and 1981.* Coventry: Institute of Employment Research, University of Warwick.

Green, A. E. (1998) *Employment, unemployment and non-employment.* Coventry: Institute for Employment Research, University of Warwick.

Green, A. E. and Owen, D. (1997) *Where are the jobless? Changing unemployment and non-employment in cities and regions.* Bristol: The Policy Press.

Green, H., Thomas, M., Iles, N. and Down, D. (1996) *Housing in England 1994/5: a report of the 1994/5 Survey of English Housing.* London: HMSO.

Gregg, P. and Wadsworth, J. (1995) 'A short history of labour turnover, job tenure and job security, 1975-1993', *Oxford Review of Economic Policy,* 11.1.

Greve, J. (1991) *Homelessness in Britain.* York: Joseph Rowntree Foundation.

Griffiths, M., Parker, J., Smith, R., Stirling, T. and Trott, T. (1996) *Community lettings: local allocations policies in practice.* York: Joseph Rowntree Foundation.

Guardian (1998) Streets' tsar to have big budget, 8 July, p8.

Harding A. (1997) *Hulme City Challenge – did it work?* Liverpool: EUIA, Liverpool John Moores University.

Harrison, M., Karmani, A., Law, I., Phillips, D. and Ravetz, A. (1996) *Black and minority ethnic housing associations. An evaluation of the Housing Corporation's black and minority ethnic housing association strategies.* London: Housing Corporation.

Harrison, M. L. (1995) *Housing, 'race', social policy and empowerment.* Aldershot: Avebury.

Haskey, J. (1984) 'Social class and socio-economic differentials in divorce in England and Wales', *Population Studies,* 38.

Haskey, J. (1995) 'Trends in marriage and cohabitation: the decline in marriage and the changing pattern of living in partnerships', *Population Trends,* 80, Summer.

Haskey, J. (1998) 'One parent families and their dependent children in Great Britain', *Population Trends,* 91, Spring.

Hastings, A., McArthur, A. and McGregor, A. (1996) *Less than equal? Community organisations and estate regeneration partnerships.* Bristol: Policy Press.

Hedges, B. and Clemens, S. (1994) *Housing Attitudes Survey.* London: HMSO.

Henderson, J. and Karn, V. (1987) *Race, class and state housing: inequality and the allocation of public housing in Britain.* Aldershot: Gower.

Henning, C. and Lieberg, M. (1996) 'Strong ties or weak ties? Neighbourhood networks in a new perspective', *Scandinavian Housing and Planning Research,* 13, pp3-26.

Heraud, B. J. (1968) 'Social class and the New Towns', *Urban Studies,* 5.1 pp33-58.

Hickman, P. (1997) 'Is it working? The changing position of young people in the UK labour market', in Roche, J. and Tucker, S. (eds.), *Youth in society: contemporary theory, policy and practice.* London: Sage.

Hills, J. (1995) *Income and wealth, Volume 2: a summary of the evidence.* York: Joseph Rowntree Foundation.

Hills, J. (1998a) *Income and wealth: the latest evidence.* York: Joseph Rowntree Foundation.

Hills, J. (1998b) 'Does income mobility mean that we do not need to worry about poverty' in Atkinson, A. B. and Hills, J. (eds.), *Exclusion, employment and opportunity,* CASE paper No. 4. London: London School of Economics.

Hills, J. (1998c) 'Housing: a decent home within the reach of every family?' in Glennerster, H. and Hills, J. (eds.), *The state of welfare: the economics of social spending*. Oxford: Oxford University Press (second edition).

Hobsbawm, E. (1977) *The age of capital 1848-1875*. London: Abacus.

Hobsbawm, E. (1987) *The age of empire 1875-1914*. London: Weidenfeld and Nicolson.

Hobsbawm, E. (1994) *The age of extremes 1914-1991*. London: Michael Joseph.

Hogarth, T., Elias, P. and Ford, J. (1996) *Mortgages, families and jobs*. London: Institute for Employment Research.

Holmans, A. (1995) *Housing demand and need in England, 1991 to 2011*. York: Joseph Rowntree Foundation.

Holmans, A. (1996) 'A decline in young owner-occupiers in the 1990s', *Housing Finance,* February, pp13-20.

Holmans, A. and Simpson, M. (1999) *Low demand: separating fact from fiction*. Coventry: Chartered Institute of Housing.

Home Office (1992) *The national prison survey 1991: main findings*. London: HMSO.

Home Office (1997a) *Getting to grips with crime: a new framework for local action – a consultation document*. London: Home Office.

Home Office (1997b) *Community Safety Orders: a consultation paper*. London: Home Office.

Home Office (1997c) *Tackling youth crime*. London: Home Office.

Home Office (1998) *Supporting families: a consultation document*. London: Home Office.

Hooker, R. H. (1901) 'Correlation of the marriage rate with trade', *Journal of the Royal Statistical Society*, LXIV, September.

Hoover, E. M. and Vernon, R. (1962) *Anatomy of a metropolis*. Doubleday: New York.

Housing Corporation (1996) *Black and minority ethnic housing needs: an enabling framework*. Consultation Paper, London: Housing Corporation.

Housing Corporation (1997a) *Registered Social Landlords in 1996: performance indicators*. London: Housing Corporation.

Housing Corporation (1997b) *Managing voids and difficult-to-let property*. Source Research 21.

Housing Corporation (1998a) *Best value for Registered Social Landlords*. London: Housing Corporation.

Housing Corporation (1998b) *Building a better future: revitalising neighbourhoods*. London: Housing Corporation.

Housing Management Advisory Panel (1995) *Seen to be fair: a guide to allocating rented housing*. Cardiff: HMAP.

Housing Research Group (1981) *Could local authorities be better landlords?* London: City University.

Howarth, C. and Kenway, P. (1998): 'A multidimensional approach to social exclusion indicators' in Oppenheim, C. (ed.), *An inclusive society: strategies for tackling poverty*. London: IPPR.

Howes, E. and Mullins, D. (1997) 'Finding a place – the impact of locality on the housing experience of tenants from minority ethnic groups' in Karn, V. (ed.), *Ethnicity in the 1991 Census, Volume Four*. London: HMSO, pp189-220.

HSAG (1978) *Organising a comprehensive housing service*. London: Department of the Environment.

Hutson, S. (1999) 'The experience of "homeless" accommodation and support' in Hutson, S. and Clapham, D. (eds.), *Homelessness: public policies and private troubles.* London: Cassell, pp208-225.

Hutson, S. and Clapham, D. (1999) *Homelessness: public policies and private troubles.* London: Cassell.

Hutson, S. and Jones, S. (1997) *Rough sleeping and homelessness in Rhondda Cynon Taff.* Pontypridd: University of Glamorgan.

Ihlanfeldt, K. R. and Sjoquist, D. L. (1998) 'The spatial mismatch hypothesis: a review of recent studies and their implications for welfare reform', *Housing Policy Debate,* 9.4.

Immervoll, H., Mitton, L., O'Donoghue, C. and Sutherland, H. (1999) *Budgeting for fairness? The distributional effects of three Labour budgets.* University of Cambridge Department of Applied Economics Micro-Simulation Unit Research Note No.32, 12 March.

Independent (1997) 'Blair: why we must help those excluded from society', 8 December, p1.

Inland Revenue (1997) *Inland Revenue Statistics 1997.* London: The Stationery Office.

Inside Housing (1998) 'Beggar's victory on breach of peace charge', 29 May, p4.

Inside Housing (1997) 'Armstrong orders revival of ethnic initiative', 19 September, p3.

Institute for Women's Policy Research (IWPR) (1995) *Welfare that works: the working lives of AFDC recipients.* Washington DC.

Jargowsky, P. A. (1996) *Poverty and place: ghettos, barrios and the American city.* New York: Russell Sage Foundation.

Jarman, B. (1983) 'Identification of underprivileged areas', *British Medical Journal,* 286, 28 May, pp1705-1709.

Jarvis, S. and Jenkins, S. (1997) 'Low income dynamics in 1990s Britain', *Fiscal Studies*, 18.2, pp123-42.

Johnson, E. S., Levine, A. and Doolittle, F. (1999) *Fathers' fair share: helping poor fathers manage child support.* New York, Russell Sage Foundation.

Johnston, G. (1995) *The transformation of American families: employment dislocation and the growth of female-headed families.* Pennsylvania State University, Population Research Institute PAA Paper.

Jones, G. (1987) 'Leaving the parental home: an analysis of early housing careers', *Journal of Social Policy*, 16.1, pp49-74.

Jones, G. (1993) *On the margins of the housing market: housing and homelessness in youth.* Working Paper No.3, Young People in and out of the Housing Market Research Project. Edinburgh: Centre for Educational Sociology, University of Edinburgh and SCSH.

Jones, G. (1995a) *Leaving home.* Buckingham: Open University Press.

Jones, G. (1995b) *Family support for young people.* London: Family Policy Studies Centre.

Jordan, B. (1996) *A theory of poverty and social exclusion.* Cambridge: Polity Press.

Joseph Rowntree Foundation (1995) *Inquiry into income and wealth, Volume 1.* York: Joseph Rowntree Foundation.

Karn, V., Lickless, R., Hughes, D. and Crawley, J. (1993) *Neighbour disputes: responses by social landlords.* Coventry: Chartered Institute of Housing.

Karn, V. and Sheridan, L. (1994) *New homes in the 1990s. A study of design, space and amenity in housing association and private sector production,* Manchester/York: University of Manchester/Joseph Rowntree Foundation.

Kasarda, J. D. (1989) 'Urban industrial transition and the underclass', *Annals of the American Academy of Political and Social Science,* 501, January.

Katz, M. B. (1989) *The undeserving poor: from the war on poverty to the war on welfare.* New York: Pantheon.

Keenan, P. (1998) 'Residential mobility and low demand', in Keenan, P., Lowe, S. and Spencer, S. (eds.), (1998) *Housing abandonment – causes, consequences and solutions.* York: Centre for Housing Policy, University of York.

Keenan, P., Lowe, S. and Spencer, S. (eds.), (1998) *Housing abandonment – causes, consequences and solutions.* York: Centre for Housing Policy, University of York.

Keenan, P., Lowe, S. and Spencer, S. (1999) 'Housing abandonment in inner cities – the politics of low demand for housing', *Housing Studies,* 14.5, pp703-716.

Kelly, G. and McCormick, J. (1998) 'Private interests and public purposes: exclusion and the private sector' in Oppenheim, C. (ed.), *An inclusive society: strategies for tackling poverty.* London: IPPR.

Kemp, P. (1992) 'Housing', in Marsh, D. and Rhodes, R. *Implementing Thatcherite policies: audit of an era.* Buckingham: Open University Press, pp65-80.

Kemp, P. (1994) *Students and the private rented sector in Scotland.* A briefing note for Scottish Homes. (unpublished)

Kemp, P. (1998) *Housing Benefit: time for reform.* York: Joseph Rowntree Foundation

Kemp, P. and Rhodes, D. (1994) *Private landlords in Scotland.* Edinburgh: Scottish Homes.

Kempson, E. (1996) *Life on a low income.* York: Joseph Rowntree Foundation.

Kempson, E., White, M. and Forth, J. (1997) *Rents and work incentives.* London: Policy Studies Institute.

Kiernan, K. and Mueller, G. (1998) *Who are the divorced and who divorces?* London: London School of Economics, Centre for the Analysis of Social Exclusion CASE paper No.7.

Kiernan, K., Land, H. and Lewis, J. (1998) *Lone motherhood in twentieth-century Britain: from footnote to front page.* Oxford: Clarendon Press.

Komarovsky, M. (1940) *The unemployed man and his family: the effect of unemployment upon the status of the man in fifty-nine families.* New York: Dryden Press.

Labour Market Trends (1998) Department for Employment and Education, July.

Labour Research (1998) Unemployment, 87(6), p28.

Labour Party (1997) *New Labour: because Britain deserves better.* London: The Labour Party.

Lampard, R. (1994) 'An examination of the relationship between marital dissolution and unemployment' in Gallie, D., Marsh, C. and Vogler, C. (eds.), *Social change and the experience of unemployment,* Oxford: Oxford University Press.

Lansley, S. (1979) *Housing and public policy.* London: Croom Helm.

Le Grand, J. and Bartlett, W. (1992) *Quasi markets and social policy.* Basingstoke: Macmillan.

Lee, P. and Murie, A. (1997) *Poverty, housing tenure and social exclusion.* Bristol: Policy Press.

Lee, P., Murie, A. and Gordon, D. (1995) *Area measures of deprivation: a study of current methods and best practices in the identification of poor areas in Great Britain,* Birmingham: Centre for Urban and Regional Studies. University of Birmingham.

Lee, P. and Murie, A. (1999) 'Spatial and Social Divisions within British Cities: Beyond Residualisation', *Housing Studies,* 14.5, pp625-640.

Lee, P., Murie, A., Marsh, A. and Riseborough, M. (1995) *The price of social exclusion.* London: National Federation of Housing Associations.

Legg, C. (1981) *Could local authorities be better landlords?* London: City University.

Leisering, L. and Walker, R. (eds.), (1998) *The dynamics of modern society: poverty, politics and welfare.* Bristol: Policy Press.

Levitas, R. (1996) 'The concept of social exclusion and the new Durkheimian hegemony', *Critical Social Policy,* 16.1, pp5-20.

Li, P. L. (1992) 'Health needs of the Chinese population' in Ahmad, W.I.U. (ed.), *The politics of 'race' and health.* Bradford: University of Bradford Race Relations Research Unit.

Lichter, D., McLaughlin, D., Kephart, G. and Landry, D. (1992) 'Race and the retreat from marriage: a shortage of marriageable men?', *American Sociological Review,* 57.6, pp781-799.

Lichter, D., McLaughlin, D. and Ribar, D. (1997) 'Welfare and the rise in female-headed families', *American Journal of Sociology,* 103.1, pp112-143.

Lindblom, E. N. (1991) 'Towards a comprehensive homelessness-prevention strategy', *Housing Policy Debate,* 2.3.

Lindley, R. and Wilson, R. (1998) *Review of the economy and employment.* London: Institute for Employment Research.

Lister, R. (ed.) (1996) *Charles Murray and the underclass: the developing debate.* London: IEA Health and Welfare Unit.

Lloyd, D. (1997) 'A plan to abolish the underclass', *New Statesman,* 29 August, pp14-16.

London Planning Advisory Committee (1997) *Affordable housing, regeneration and sustainability in London: Working Party Report.* London: London Planning Advisory Committee and Association of London Government Members.

Loney, M. (1983) *Community against government. The British Community Development Project 1968-78: a study of government incompetence.* London: Heinemann.

Love, A. M. and Kirby, K. (1994) *Racial incidents in council housing: the local authority response.* London: HMSO.

Lowe, S. (1998) 'Such total abandon', *Inside Housing,* 3 July, pp10-11.

Lowe, S., Spencer, S. and Keenan, P. (eds.), (1999) *Housing abandonment in Britain: studies in the causes and effects of low demand housing.* York: Centre for Housing Policy, University of York.

Mack, J. and Lansley, S. (1985) *Poor Britain.* London: Allen and Unwin.

Mackintosh, S. and Leather, P. (1993) *Renovation file. A profile of housing conditions and housing renewal policies in the UK.* Oxford: Anchor Housing Trust.

Maclagan, I. (1992) *A broken promise: the failure of the youth training policy.* London: Youthaid and the Children's Society.

Maclennan, D. and Kay, H. (1994) *Moving on, crossing divides.* London: HMSO.

Maclennan, D. and Pryce, G. (1998) *Missing links: the economy, cities and housing.* London: National Housing Federation.

Malpass, P. and Means, R. (eds.), (1993) *Implementing housing policy.* Buckingham: Open University Press.

Malpass, P. and Murie. A. (1994) *Housing policy and practice,* (Fourth edition). London: Macmillan.

Mandelson, P. (1997) *Labour's next steps: tackling social exclusion.* Fabian Pamphlet 581. London: Fabian Society.

Marsh, A., Ford, R. and Finlayson, L. (1997) *Lone parents, work and benefits: the first effects of the Child Support Agency to 1994.* Department of Social Security Research Report No.61. London: HMSO.

Marsh, D. and Rhodes, R. (eds.), (1992) *Implementing Thatcherite policies: audit of an era.* Buckingham: Open University Press.

McCormick, J. (1996) *The European Union: politics and policies.* Oxford: Westview Press.

McCrone, G. and Stephens, M. (1995) *Housing policy in Britain and Europe.* London: UCL Press.

McGregor, A., Fitzpatrick, I., McConnachie, M. and Thom, G. (1995) *Building futures. Can local employment be created from housing expenditure?* Bristol: SAUS.

McKay, S. and Marsh, A. (1994) *Lone parents and work: the effects of benefits and maintenance,* Department of Social Security Research Report No.25. London: HMSO.

McKendrick, J. (1995) *Lone parenthood in Strathclyde Region: implications for housing policy.* School of Geography Working Paper 30, Manchester: University of Manchester.

McLanahan, S. and Garfinkel, I. (1989) 'Single mothers, the underclass and social policy', *Annals of the American Academy of Political and Social Science,* January.

McLaughlin, E. (1992) *Unemployment, labour supply and the meaning of money.* Belfast: Queen's University.

Mead, L. (1986) *Beyond entitlement: the social obligations of citizenship.* New York: Free Press.

Merrett, S. and Smith, R. (1986) 'Stock flow in the analysis of vacant residential property', *Town Planning Review,* 57.1.

Middleton, S., Ashworth, K. and Braithwaite, I. (1997) *Small fortunes: spending on children, childhood poverty and parental sacrifice.* York: Joseph Rowntree Foundation.

Millar, J. (1994) 'Understanding labour supply in context: households and income' in Bryson, A. and Mackay, S. (eds.), *Is it worth working?* London: Policy Studies Institute.

Morris, J. and Winn, M. (1990) *Housing and social inequality.* London: Hilary Shipman.

Morris, T. (1958) *The criminal area.* London: Routledge and Kegan Paul.

Moynihan, D. P. (1965) *The Negro family: the case for national action.* Office of Policy Planning and Research, US Department of Labor, March (reprinted in facsimile in Rainwater, L. and Yancey, W. L. (1967) *The Moynihan Report and the politics of controversy.* London: M.I.T. Press). Page references are to the original.

Moynihan, D. P. (1986) *Family and nation: the Godkin lectures.* London: Harcourt Brace Jovanovich.

Murie A. (1997) 'The social rented sector, housing and the welfare state in the UK' *Housing Studies,* 12.4, pp437-462.

Murie, A., Nevin, P. and Leather, P. (1998) *Changing demand and unpopular housing.* London: Housing Corporation.

Murray, C. (1984) *Losing ground: American social policy 1950-1980.* New York: Basic Books.

Murray, C. (1990) *The emerging British underclass.* London: IEA Health and Welfare Unit.

Murray, C. (1994) *Underclass: the crisis deepens.* London: IEA Health and Welfare Unit.

Murray, C. (1996a) 'The emerging British underclass' in Lister, R. (ed.), *Charles Murray and the underclass: the developing debate.* London: IEA Health and Welfare Unit, pp23-53.

Murray, C. (1996b) 'Rejoinder', in Lister, R. (ed.), *Ibid.,* pp81-94.

Murray, C. (1996c) 'Underclass: the crisis deepens' in Lister, R. (ed.), *Ibid.,* pp99-135.

NACRO (1996) *Crime, community and change: taking action on the Kingsmead Estate in Hackney.* London: NACRO.

National Federation of Housing Associations (1995) *The social housing product: a discussion and consultation paper.* London: NFHA.

Northern Housing Research Partnership (1997) *Housing in the north: current provision and demand.* Chester-le-Street: Northern Consortium of Housing Authorities.

Oatley, N. and Lambert, C. (1995), 'Evaluating competitive urban policy: the City Challenge initiative' in Hambleton, R. and Thomas, H., *Urban policy evaluation: challenge and change.* London: Paul Chapman Publishing, pp141-157.

Office for National Statistics (1998a) *Living in Britain: results from the 1996 General Household Survey.* Social Survey Division, London: The Stationery Office.

Office for National Statistics (1998b) *Social Trends 28.* London: The Stationery Office.

Office for National Statistics (1998c) 'The effects of taxes and benefits on household income, 1996/97', *Economic Trends,* April, pp33-67.

Osborne, S. and Shaftoe, H. (eds.), (1995) *Safer neighbourhoods? Success and failure in crime prevention.* London: SNU.

Owen, D. (1993) *Ethnic minorities in Great Britain: housing and family characteristics.* 1991 Census Statistical Paper No. 4, Coventry: University of Warwick Centre for Research in Ethnic Relations.

Page, D. (1993) *Building for communities: a study of new housing association estates.* York: Joseph Rowntree Foundation.

Page, D. (1994) *Developing communities.* London: Sutton Hastoe Housing Association.

Papps, P. (1998) 'Anti-social behaviour strategies – individualistic or holistic?' *Housing Studies,* 13.5, pp639-654.

Parker, H. (1999) 'Tackling poverty – an acceptable living standard', *Poverty,* 103, Summer.

Paugham, S. (1995) 'The spiral of precariousness: a multidimensional approach to the process of social disqualification in France', in Room, G. (ed.), *Beyond the threshold.* Bristol: Policy Press.

Pawson, H (1998a) 'Gravity defied: local authority lettings and stock turnover in the 1990s' in *Housing Finance Review 1998/9.* York: Joseph Rowntree Foundation.

Pawson, H. (1998b) 'Residential instability and tenancy turnover' in Keenan, P. *et al* (eds.), *Housing abandonment – causes, consequences and solutions.* York: Centre for Housing Policy, University of York.

Pawson, H. and Bramley, G. (forthcoming) 'Understanding recent trends in residential mobility in council housing in England', *Urban Studies.*

Pawson, H., Kearns, A., Keoghan, M., Malcolm, J.and Morgan, J. (1997) *Managing voids and difficult-to-let property.* London: Housing Corporation.

Pearl, M. (1998) *Social housing management: a critical appraisal of housing practice.* Basingstoke: Macmillan.

Pedreschi, T. (1991) *A survey of Scottish local authority and New Town housing for single people.* Edinburgh: Scottish Council for Single Homeless.

Perri 6 (1997) *Escaping poverty: from safety nets to networks of opportunity.* London: Demos.

Phillips D. (1986), *What price equality? A report on the allocation of GLC housing in Tower Hamlets.* GLC Housing Research and Policy Report No.9. London: GLC.

Philo, C. (ed.), (1995) *Off the map: the social geography of poverty in the UK.* London: CPAG.

Pinto, R. (1993) *The Estate Action initiative: council housing management and effectiveness.* Aldershot: Avebury.

Pinto, R. (ed.), (1995) *Developments in housing management and ownership.* Manchester: Manchester University Press.

Pleace, N., Ford, J., Wilcox, S., and Burrows, R., (1998) *Lettings and sales by Registered Social Landlords 1996/7.* London: National Housing Federation/Housing Corporation.

Pleace, N. (1995) *Housing vulnerable single homeless people.* York: Centre for Housing Policy, University of York.

Pleace, N. (1998) 'Single homelessness as social exclusion: the unique and the extreme', *Social Policy and Administration*, 32.1, pp46-59.

Pleace, N. and Quilgars, D. (1997), 'Health, homelessness and access to health care services in London' in Burrows, R., Pleace, N. and Quilgars, D. (eds.), *Homelessness and social policy.* London: Routledge.

Portes, A. and Landolt, P. (1996) The downside of social capital, *American Prospect,* Summer, pp18-21.

Power, A. (1984) *Local housing management.* London: Department of the Environment.

Power, A. (1987a) *The crisis in council housing: is public housing manageable?* London: London School of Economics Discussion Paper 21.

Power, A. (1987b) *Property before people: the management of twentieth century council housing.* London: Allen and Unwin.

Power A. (1991a) *Running fast to stand still.* London: Priority Estates Project.

Power, A. (1991b) *Housing management: a guide to quality and creativity.* Harlow: Longman.

Power, A. (1997) *Estates on the edge.* London: Macmillan.

Power, A. and Mumford, K. (1999) *The slow death of great cities?Urban abandonment or urban renaissance.* York: Joseph Rowntree Foundation/York Publishing Services.

Power, A. and Richardson, L. (1996) *Housing Plus: an agenda for social landlords?* London: LSE Housing.

Power, A. and Tunstall, R. (1995) *Swimming against the tide: polarisation and progress in twenty unpopular council estates 1980-95.* York: Joseph Rowntree Foundation.

Power, A. and Tunstall, R. (1997) *Dangerous disorder: riots and violent disturbances in 13 areas of Britain 1991-92.* York: York Publishing Services.

Prescott-Clarke, P., Clemens, S. and Park, A. (1994) *Routes into local authority housing: a study of local authority waiting lists and new tenancies.* London: HMSO.

Price Waterhouse (1995) *Tenants in control: an evaluation of tenant-led housing management organisations.* London: Department of the Environment.

Pugh, M. (1998) *Barriers to work: the spatial divide between jobs and welfare recipients in metropolitan areas.* Washington DC: The Brookings Institution Center on Urban and Metropolitan Policy.

Pullinger, J. and Summerfield, C. (1997) *Social focus on families.* London: Office for National Statistics.

Purcell, K. (1998) 'Flexibility in the labour market' in Lindley, R. and Wilson, R. *Review of economy and employment 1997/8: labour market assessment.* Coventry: University of Warwick Institute for Employment Research.

Puttnam, R. (1993) 'The prosperous community: social capital and economic growth', *American Prospect,* Spring, pp35-42

Puttnam, R. (1996) 'The strange disappearance of civic America', *American Prospect,* Winter, pp34-48.

Puttnam, R. (1998) 'Foreword' to *Housing Policy Debate,* 9.1.

Quilgars, D. and Anderson, I. (1997) 'Addressing the problem of youth homelessness and unemployment: the contribution of foyers', Chapter 15, pp216-228 in, Burrows, R., Pleace, N. and Quilgars, D. *Homelessness and social policy.* London: Routledge.

Rainwater, L. (1970) *Behind ghetto walls: black families in a federal slum.* Republ. Harmondsworth: Penguin Books, 1973.

Randall, G. and Brown, S. (1996) *From street to home: an evaluation of Phase 2 of the Rough Sleepers' Initiative.* London: Stationery Office.

Ratcliffe, P. (1996), *'Race' and housing in Bradford: addressing the needs of the South Asian, African and Caribbean communities,* Bradford: Bradford Housing Forum.

Ratcliffe, P. (1997) '"Race", ethnicity and housing differentials in Britain' in Karn, V. (ed.), *Ethnicity in the 1991 Census, Volume Four.* London: HMSO, pp130-146.

Reynolds, F. (1986) *The problem housing estate.* Aldershot: Gower.

Rhodes, D. and Kemp, P. (1997) *The Joseph Rowntree Foundation index of private rent and yields, first quarter 1997.* York: Centre for Housing Policy, University of York.

Roberts, K. (1997) 'Is there an emerging British "underclass": the evidence from youth research' in MacDonald, R. (ed.), *Youth, the underclass and social exclusion.* London: Routledge.

Robertson D. and Bailey N. (1996) *Review of the impact of Housing Action Areas.* Research Report 47, Edinburgh: Scottish Homes.

Robinson, F. (1997) *The City Challenge experience: a review of the development and implementation of Newcastle City Challenge.* Newcastle: Newcastle City Challenge West End Partnership Ltd.

Robson, B., Bradford, M., Deas, I., Hall, E., Harrison, E., Parkinson, M., Evans, R., Garside, P. and Harding, A. (1994) *Assessing the impact of urban policy.* London: Department of the Environment.

Robson, B., Bradford, M. and Tye, R. (1995) 'The development of the 1991 Local Deprivation Index' in Room, G. (ed.), *Beyond the threshold: the measurement and analysis of social exclusion.* Bristol: Policy Press.

Room, G. (ed.), (1995a) *Beyond the threshold: the measurement and analysis of social exclusion.* Bristol: Policy Press.

Room, G. (1995b) 'Poverty and social exclusion: the new European agenda for policy and research', in Room, G (ed.), *Beyond the threshold: the measurement and analysis of social exclusion.* Bristol: Policy Press, pp1-9.

Room, G. *et al.* (1990) *New poverty in the European Community,* London: Macmillan (cited in Room, G. 1995a).

Room, G. *et al.* (1992) *National policies to combat social exclusion.* First Annual Report of the European Observatory on Policies to Combat Social Exclusion. Brussels: European Commission (cited in Room, G. 1995a)

Rugg, J. (1996) *Closing doors.* York: Centre for Housing Policy, University of York.

RSI Advisory Group (1999) *The Scottish Rough Sleepers' Initiative: a review by the RSI Advisory Group.* Edinburgh: The Scottish Office.

Rutter, M. and Madge, N. (1976) *Cycles of disadvantage.* London: Heinemann.

Ryder, R. (1984) 'Council house building in County Durham, 1900-39: the local implementation of national policy' in Daunton, M. J. (ed.), *Councillors and tenants: local authority housing in English cities, 1919-1939.* Leicester: Leicester University Press.

Sarre, P., Phillips, D. and Skellington, R. (1989) *Ethnic minority housing: explanations and policies.* Aldershot: Avebury.

Schaffer, F. (1972) *The New Town story.* London: Paladin.

School for Policy Studies (1997) *Absolute and overall poverty in Britain.* University of Bristol.

Scott, S. and Parkey, H. (1996a) *Too close for comfort: neighbour problems.* Paper presented at CHRUS/ENHR Conference, Glasgow University, May 1996.

Scott, S. and Parkey, H. (1996b) *An introduction to social rented housing in Scotland.* Edinburgh: Chartered Institute of Housing.

Scott, S. and Parkey, H. (1998) 'Myths and reality: anti-social behaviour in Scotland', *Housing Studies,* 13.3, pp325-345.

Scottish Executive (1999) *Scottish Household Survey Bulletin 1.* Edinburgh: The Stationery Office.

Scottish Homes (1997) *Scottish House Condition Survey: Main Report.* Edinburgh: Scottish Homes.

Scottish Office (1995) *Statistical Bulletin, Housing Series* (1995/3).

Scottish Office (1998a) *Statistical Bulletin, Housing Series* (1998/2).

Scottish Office (1998b) *Statistical Bulletin, Housing Series* (1998/1).

Scottish Office (1998c) *Social exclusion in Scotland: a consultation paper.* Edinburgh: The Stationery Office.

Scottish Office (1999a) *Social inclusion: opening the door to a better Scotland.* Edinburgh: The Scottish Office.

Scottish Office (1999b) *Social inclusion: opening the door to a better Scotland. Strategy.* Edinburgh: The Scottish Office.

Scottish Office Development Department (1999a) *Gossip: the newsletter for social inclusion partnerships,* March, p1. Edinburgh: Scottish Office Development Department.

Scottish Office Development Department (1999b) *Gossip: the newsletter for social inclusion partnerships,* June, p1. Edinburgh: Scottish Office Development Department.

Seed, P. and Lloyd, G. (1997) *Quality of Life.* London: Jessica Kingsley.

Sefton, T. (1997) *The changing distribution of the social wage.* STICERD Occasional Paper 21. London: London School of Economics.

Shaw, A. (1988) *A Pakistani community in Britain.* Oxford: Blackwell.

Shelter (1998) *Ethnicity and housing.* London: Shelter.

Shouls, S., Whitehead, M., Burstrom, B. and Diderichsen, F. 'The health and socio-economic circumstances of British lone mothers over the last two decades', *Population Trends,* 95, Spring.

Silver, H. (1994) 'Social exclusion and social solidarity: three paradigms', *International Labour Review,* 133.5/6, pp531-578.

Simpson, A. (1981) *Stacking the decks: a study of race, inequality and council housing in Nottingham.* Nottingham: Nottingham Community Relations Council.

Smith, D. (ed.), (1992) *Understanding the underclass.* London: Policy Studies Institute.

Smith, R. and Merrett, S. (1987) 'Empty dwellings: the use of the rating records in identifying and monitoring vacant private housing in Britain', *Environment and Planning A,* 19.6, pp783-791.

Smith, R. and Merrett, S. (1988) 'Empty dwellings and tenure switching: a British case study' *Housing Studies,* 3.2, pp105-111.

Snape, V. B. (1992) *'Foyers': what young people think.* London: Young Homelessness Group and Centrepoint Soho.

Social Exclusion Unit (1998a) *Rough sleeping,* Cm 4008, London: The Stationery Office (Also on Internet at http:l/www.open.gov.uklcolseu/seu home.htm).

Social Exclusion Unit (1998b) *Bringing Britain together: a national strategy for neighbourhood renewal,* Cm 4045. London: The Stationery Office.

Social Exclusion Unit (1998c) *What is social exclusion?* Social Exclusion Home Page: http:/lwww.open.gov.uklco/seu.

Social Exclusion Unit (1999a) *Teenage pregnancy,* Cm 4342. London: The Stationery Office.

Social Exclusion Unit (1999b) *Information from web site, http://www.cabinet-office.gov.uk/seu/*

Solow, R. M. (1998) *Work and welfare* (ed.), Amy Gutmann. Princeton: Princeton University Press.

Somerville, P. (1998) 'Explanations of social exclusion: where does housing fit in?' *Housing Studies,* 13.6, pp761-780.

South, S. J. (1985) 'Economic conditions and the divorce rate: a time-series analysis of the postwar United States', *Journal of Marriage and the Family,* 47.1, pp31-41.

Southall, H. and Gilbert, D. (1996) 'A good time to wed?: marriage and economic distress in England and Wales, 1839-1914', *Economic History Review,* XLIX.

Spencer, P. (1996) 'Reactions to a flexible labour market', *British Social Attitudes Survey,* Report no. 13. London: Social and Community Planning Research.

Spicker, P. (1987) 'Poverty and depressed estates: a critique of Utopia on trial', *Housing Studies,* 2.4, pp283-292.

Spicker, P. (1998) *Housing and social exclusion.* Edinburgh: Shelter Scotland.

Spiers, F. (1999) *Housing and social exclusion.* London: Jessica Kingsley.

Stearn, J. (1993) 'Single parents in firing line', *Inside Housing,* 10.38, 1 October, p1.

Sternlieb, G. and Burchell, R. (1974) 'Housing abandonment in the urban core', *Journal of the American Institute of Planners,* 4, pp321-332.

Stewart, I. (1991) 'Estimates of the distribution of personal wealth II: marketable wealth and pension rights of individuals 1976 to 1989', *Economic Trends*, November, pp99-110.

Stewart, M. and Taylor, M. (1995) *Empowerment and estate regeneration: a critical review*. Bristol: Policy Press.

Stockley, D., Canter, D. and Bishopp, D. (1993) *Young people on the move*. Guildford: University of Surrey Department of Psychology.

Stoker, G. (1991) *The politics of local government*. London: Macmillan.

Suttles, G. (1972) *The social construction of communities*. Chicago: University of Chicago Press.

Synthèses (1996) No 5, *Revenues et patrimoines des ménages*. Paris: INSEE.

Taylor, M. (1995) *Unleashing the potential: bringing residents to the centre of regeneration*. York: Joseph Rowntree Foundation.

Taylor-Gooby, P. (1991) *Social change, social welfare and social science*. Hemel Hempstead: Harvester Wheatsheaf.

Temkin, K. and Rohe, W. (1998) 'Social capital and neighbourhood stability: an empirical investigation', *Housing Policy Debate*, 9.1, pp61-88.

Testa, M., Astone, N., Krogh, M. and Neckerman, K. (1993) 'Employment and marriage among inner city fathers', in W.J.Wilson (ed.), *The ghetto underclass*. London: Sage.

Thatcher, M. (1993) *The Downing Street years*. London: HarperCollins.

Thomas, D. M. (1927) *Social aspects of the business cycle*. Alfred A. Knopf, republ. New York: Gordon and Breach 1967.

Thorns, D. (1976) *The quest for community: social aspects of residential growth*. London: Allen and Unwin.

Thornton, R. (1990) *The new homeless: the crisis of youth homelessness and the response of local authorities*. London: SHAC.

Turner, B. (1996) 'Sweden', Chapter Seven, pp99-112, in Balchin, P. *Housing policy in Europe*. London: Routledge.

Times (1998) 'Brown splashes out £40bn', p1 and various pages, 15 July.

Torbier, E. (1974) *Aspects of the New York housing market*. Unpublished paper.

Townsend, P. (1979) *Poverty in the United Kingdom*. Harmondsworth: Penguin.

Townsend, P. (1987) *Life and labour in London*. London: CPAG.

Townsend, P. (1993) *The international analysis of poverty*. London: Harvester Wheatsheaf.

Townsend, P., Phillimore, P. and Beattie, A. (1988) *Health and deprivation: inequality in the north*. London: Croom Helm.

Tunstall, R (1996) 'Participation, self-help and social exclusion: the impact of tenant management organisations', *Paper presented to Housing Studies Association conference*, September, Birmingham.

Turner, J. (1976) *Housing by people: towards autonomy in building environments*. London: Marion Boyars.

Turok, I. and Edge, N. (1999) *The jobs gap in Britain's cities: employment loss and labour market consequences*. Bristol, The Policy Press.

Turok, I. and Webster, D. (1998) 'The New Deal: jeopardised by the geography of unemployment? *Local Economy*, 12.4, pp309-328.

Urban Task Force (1998) *Urban Task Force Prospectus 07.98*. London: DETR.

Urry, J. (1995) *Consuming places*. London: Routledge.

Van Allberg, M. (1974) 'Property abandonment in Detroit', *Wayne Law Review*, 20, pp25-37.

Wadhams, C. (1998) *Reinvestment plus – creating thriving neighbourhoods*. Birmingham: Harding Housing Association.

Walentowicz, P. (1992) *Housing standards after the Act. A survey of space and design standards on housing association projects in 1989/90,* Research Report 15. London: NFHA.

Walker, A. (1996) 'Blaming the victims' in Lister, R. (ed.), *Charles Murray and the underclass: the developing debate.* London: IEA Health and Welfare Unit, pp61-74.

Walker, A. (1997) 'Introduction: the strategy of inequality' in Walker, A. and Walker, C. (eds.), *Britain divided: the growth of social exclusion in the 1980s and 1990s.* London: CPAG.

Walker, J., McCarthy, P. and Simpson, R. (1991) *The housing consequences of divorce,* Housing Research Findings No. 25. York: Joseph Rowntree Foundation.

Walker, R. (1995) 'The dynamics of poverty and social exclusion', Chapter Six, pp102-128, in Room, G. (ed.), *Beyond the threshold: the measurement and analysis of social exclusion.* Bristol: Policy Press.

Wallace, M. and Denham, C. (1996) *The ONS classification of local and health authorities of Great Britain.* London: HMSO.

Watson, S. and Austerberry, H. (1986) *Housing and homelessness: a feminist perspective.* London: Routledge.

Watson, S. and Gibson, K. (ed.), (1995) *Postmodern cities and spaces.* Oxford: Blackwell.

Webster, D. (1997) 'Promoting jobs could reduce lone parenthood', *Working Brief,* 88, October.

Webster, D. (1998a) *The cross-section relationship between unemployment and lone parenthood: a multiple regression analysis of 1991 Census data for local authorities in Great Britain,* revised, March.

Webster, D. (1998b) 'What housing professionals should be telling economists – the spatial component of economic development', *Paper to Planning Exchange Conference*, Glasgow, 22 January.

Welsh Office (1995) *Anti-social behaviour on council estates: a consultation paper on probationary tenancies for council tenants in Wales.* Cardiff: Welsh Office.

Westwood, S. and Williams, J. (eds.), (1997) *Imagining cities: scripts, signs, memory.* London: Routledge.

Whelan, B. and Whelan, C. (1995) 'In what sense is poverty multi-dimensional?' pp29-48, in Room, G. (ed.), *Beyond the threshold: the measurement and analysis of social exclusion.* Bristol: Policy Press.

White, M. and Forth, J. (1998) *Pathways through unemployment: the effects of a flexible labour market.* York: York Publishing Services.

Wilcox, S. (1993) *Housing finance review.* York: Joseph Rowntree Foundation.

Wilcox, S. (1994) *Housing finance review.* York: Joseph Rowntree Foundation.

Wilcox, S. (1996) *Housing review 1996/97.* York: Joseph Rowntree Foundation.

Wilcox, S. (1997) *Housing finance review 1997/98.* York: Joseph Rowntree Foundation.

Wilkinson, R. (1996) *Unhealthy societies.* London: Routledge.

Williams, F. (1997) *New approaches to thinking about poverty and social exclusion.* Paper presented at 'On the Margins: Social Exclusion and Social Work' Conference, Social Work Research Centre, University of Stirling. 7-10 September.

Williams, F. with Pillinger, J. (1996) 'New thinking on social policy research into inequality, social exclusion and poverty', pp1-32 in Miller, J. and Bradshaw, J. (eds.), *Social welfare systems: towards a research agenda.* Bath Social Policy Papers, No 24, University of Bath.

Willmott, P. (ed.), (1994) *Urban Trends 2: a decade in Britain's deprived urban areas.* London: Policy Studies Institute.

Wilson, D. *et al* (1994) 'Spatial aspects of housing abandonment in the 1990s: the Cleveland experience' *Housing Studies,* 9.4, pp493-510.

Wilson, W. (1994) *Lone parents and housing.* House of Commons Library Research Paper 94/11, London.

Wilson, W. J. (1987) *The truly disadvantaged: the inner city, the underclass, and public policy.* Chicago: Chicago University Press.

Winchester, R. (1999) 'Teen angst', *Inside Housing,* 25 June.

Wood, M. and Bryan, J. (1997) *Housing in the north: a study of empty homes.* Northern Consortium of Housing Associations (NCHA).

Wood, M. and Vamplew, C. (1999) *Neighbourhood images in Teesside: regeneration or decline?* York: York Publishing Services.

Working Party of Housing Directors (1976) *Housing in multi-racial areas.* London: Community Relations Commission.

Wrench, J., Qureshi, T. and Owen, D. (1996) *Higher horizons: a qualitative study of young men of Bangladeshi origin,* Department for Education and Employment Research Study RS80. London: The Stationery Office.

Yanetta, A., Third, H. and Pawson, H. (1997) *Nomination arrangements in Scotland.* Edinburgh: Scottish Office.

Young, G. (1996) *Private rented tenants in Scotland: analysis of the Scottish House Condition Survey 1991,* Social Report 7. Edinburgh: Scottish Homes.

Young, M. and Lemos, G. (1997) *The communities we have lost and can regain.* London: Lemos and Crane.

Zipfel, T. (1994a) *On target: extending partnership to tackle problems on estates.* London: PEP.

Zipfel, T. (1994b) *Estate Management Boards.* London: PEP.

INDEX

affordability, 168-170
allocations, 195, 197-198
American experiences of exclusion, 114-115, 179-180, 215
anti-social behaviour, 198-201
Armstrong, Hilary, 104

'Best Value', 155, 161, 176, 205
Bevan, Aneurin, 171
Birmingham, 95, 183
Bradford, 104, 106, 183

Cardiff, 90, 105
Child Support Agency, 113, 127-129
City Challenge, 106, 148, 177-178, 182-183, 185
Commission on Social Justice, 14, 119
Community Development Programme, 208
community lettings, 105, 172, 197-198
community safety, 200
Compulsory Competitive Tendering, 154-155, 204
Conservative government, 8, 89, 204

decentralisation, 155
Department of Environment, Transport and Regions, 152
deprivation indices, 58, 79-80

Edinburgh, 225
employment/unemployment, 35, 42-57, 115-119
English regions, 174
    and area satisfaction, 69-78
Enterprise Zones, 147
Estate Action, 147-149, 152-153, 154, 156, 158-160, 204
estate regeneration, 147-162, 174, 215
Estates Renewal Challenge Fund, 204, 224
European Union, 7, 10, 27
ex-prisoners, 84, 86

Field, Frank, 9, 121
foyers, 90-91, 144-145
France, 172-173
origins of social exclusion concept, 6, 7

Garden Cities movement, 171, 210

Germany, 7
Glasgow, 87, 89, 95, 98, 113, 119, 124, 168

Hackney, 95
Hill, Octavia, 166, 192
homelessness, 37, 81-92, 100-102, 140-142, 222
    (see also single homeless)
hostels, 89-90, 144
housing abandonment, 177-190
Housing Action Trusts, 148, 154
housing associations, 19, 95-97, 101, 143-144, 163-176, 194
    black and minority ethnic associations, 103-104
Housing Benefit, 24, 54-56, 126, 133, 142, 145-146, 170, 178
Housing Corporation, 96, 103, 122, 164-165, 175-176
housing management, 154-156, 191-206
'Housing Plus', 106, 174-176, 205, 215
housing renewal policies, 105-107, 147-162, 227
housing standards, 96
housing tenure, 211-214
    and area satisfaction, 64-73
and employment, 47-52
and income, 35-36
and minority ethnic groups, 94-96
and polarisation, 150
and young people, 137-144

income, 22-41, 123-124
Inland Revenue, 32

Job Seekers Allowance, 45, 53, 54, 133

Knowsley, 119,124

Lambeth, 119
Leeds, 178, 181, 186
Liverpool, 95,124
London, 69-75, 77, 80, 83, 84, 99, 119, 165, 196, 210
lone parents, 38-39, 83, 108-130
low demand housing, 184-186, 196
Luton, 106

Manchester, 174, 178, 181, 185-186
Mandelson, Peter, 15
Marxist approach, 7
Middlesbrough, 73, 78
minority ethnic groups, 37-38, 56, 82-83, 85, 93-107, 114-115, 116
Murray, Charles and the 'underclass' debate, 8-10, 15, 120-121, 132

National Minimum Wage, 46
neighbour disputes, 198-201
neighbourhood satisfaction, 59ff., 214-217
Newcastle, 174, 178, 181-183, 186
'New Deal' initiatives, 15, 53, 124, 129, 134, 161, 175, 225-226
New Labour government, 6, 8, 14-17, 104, 122-124, 125, 174-175, 190, 223-226
'New Right' philosophy, 8, 121, 225
New Towns, 171, 209-210, 213, 217-218
Nottingham, 95
Northern Ireland, 83

Oldham, 98
owner-occupation, 69-70, 72-73, 100-101, 139-140, 188

Policy Action Teams, 17
private rented sector, 69-70, 72, 142-143, 178, 188

racial harassment, 99-102
relationship breakdown: see lone parents
Right to Buy, 52, 96, 140, 159, 165, 170, 194, 202, 211-213
Rough Sleepers Initiative, 16, 92, 113, 224-226

Scottish Homes, 94, 96, 136
Scottish Office, 17, 106
Scottish Parliament, 17, 111
Sheffield, 168
Shelter, 83, 141
single homeless people, 20, 83, 87-88, 91, 140-142
Single Regeneration Budget, 106, 148, 161, 177-178, 185, 204
social exclusion, concepts of, 6-21
Social Exclusion Unit, 15-17, 81, 84, 150, 161, 181, 190, 225
Social Fund, 142
social rented sector, 70-73, 140-142, 147-162, 191-206
stock transfer, 204
Sunderland, 78
Sweden, 7

taxation, 34
Tenant Management Organisations, 149, 156-157, 160
Tenants' Choice, 154, 204
Thatcher, Margaret, 121-122, 127
Tower Hamlets, 95

'Underclass' debate: see Murray
Urban Development Corporations, 147-148
Urban Programme, 148

Wales, 112-113
welfare benefits, 53-56, 123ff., 133-134
'Welfare to Work', 15, 17, 53, 124-125, 226
Welsh Office, 96
Working Families Tax Credit, 126, 129

young single people, 39-40, 87, 131-146
    leaving care, 83-84, 85